TO THE WHITE CLOUDS

TO THE WHITE CLOUDS

Idaho's Conservation Saga, 1900-1970

J. M. NEIL

Washington State University Press
Pullman, Washington

Washington State University Press
PO Box 645910
Pullman, Washington 99164-5910
Phone: 800-354-7360
Fax: 509-335-8568
E-mail: wsupress@wsu.edu
Web site: wsupress.wsu.edu

Library of Congress Cataloging-in-Publication Data

Neil, J. Meredith, 1937-
    To the white clouds : Idaho's conservation saga, 1900-1970 / by J.M. Neil.
        p. cm.
    Includes bibliographical references (p.   ).
    ISBN 0-87422-276-1 (alk. paper)
    1. Wilderness areas--Idaho--History--20th century. 2. Nature conservation--
Idaho--History--20th century. I. Title.
QH76.5.I2N45 2004
333.72'09796--dc22   2004020796

Cover: "The White Clouds"—photograph by Andrew H. Sewell.

Fine Quality Books from the Pacific Northwest

For Ian and Emily

Table of Contents

Preface

BOOKS CAN HAVE A WAY of developing lives of their own, becoming dramatically different from what authors originally intended. It certainly is true of this one. I started out with a seemingly simple question: why did Idaho become one of the first states to establish very large, federally designated wilderness areas? Considering the vigorous objections of many Idahoans to wilderness preservation since the 1960s, why were three Primitive Areas—encompassing more than three million acres—set aside between 1930 and 1937 with only the slightest protest?

There is a substantial and ever growing literature on wilderness preservation in the United States, beginning, of course, with Roderick Nash's seminal *Wilderness and the American Mind* (released in 1967; now in a third edition). But most of that literature is written from a national perspective. There is far less focusing on particular states, including the Idaho scene. Consequently, I thought it might be useful to take a look at the wilderness preservation movement in Idaho.

Lacking scholarly treatments on most aspects of my chosen subject, I began investigating newspapers published during the 1920s in towns, particularly Salmon and Challis, located near what became the Idaho Primitive Area in 1930 (now part of the Frank Church River of No Return Wilderness). Although I found some editorial worry evinced over "tin-can tourists" (i.e., early-day auto excursionists) and what they were doing to Idaho's backcountry, of much more significance to me was Idahoans' expressed concern for game preservation. It quickly became clear that federally mandated wilderness areas were welcomed by a great majority of Idaho sportsmen during the 1930s as bigger and better game preserves. By 1930, Idaho already had over three million acres in game preserves set aside by state statute. However, there was no way to keep those preserves road-less, whereas federally designated Primitive Areas would prevent the intrusion of new roads. And, as prevailing opinion then had it, the devastation of Idaho's big game populations could only be prevented by sharply limiting access by automobiles.

The history of game preservation in Idaho is inextricably connected to the national forests, which encompass the great bulk of the state's big game habitat. To pursue that story, I found it necessary to look at a larger number of newspapers published throughout the state. Before I knew it, I was exploring topics far afield from wilderness preservation. In fact, I finally realized that an overall history of conservation in Idaho was needed—only then could we have an adequate context for understanding wilderness preservation in Idaho.

There were fairly obvious markers for the beginning and conclusion of this book. No substantial conservation efforts occurred until the arrival of the U.S. Forest Service in the early twentieth century, so this marks our starting point. The 1970 gubernatorial campaign—where the fight over proposed large-scale mining in the White Clouds played a major role in the election's outcome—provides a climax.

For reasons I expand on in "A Note on Sources," the documentation for this study is derived primarily from newspapers. Some scholars caution that newspapers can be unreliable for being biased and incomplete. I agree, but I also would observe that all types of sources that scholars use can have comparable limitations. Consequently, since there is no recourse to having completely disinterested and comprehensive sources at hand, a historian must work with those available, while striving for balance and thoroughness when conveying any conclusions. Furthermore, for many topics dealt with in this book, there really are no plausible alternative sources. Even if the state's archival holdings were far more complete than they are now, I believe newspapers still would remain the best way to learn, for instance, how early-day forest rangers were perceived by local people, or how Idahoans dealt with wildlife and scenic attractions.

Though a historian's work is inescapably a solitary one, it also is heavily reliant on librarians and archivists to provide materials for study. I was blessed with the ever-cheerful helpfulness of staff members at the Idaho State Historical Society Library, Idaho State Library, Boise Public Library, and Special Collections at Boise State University's Albertsons Library.

Research and writing have their own pleasures, but they are greatly enhanced by the prospects for publication. Therefore, I am most grateful for the enthusiastic support of Glen Lindeman, Editor-in-Chief, and his colleagues at Washington State University Press.

J. M. Neil
Boise, Idaho

Prologue

Conservation Wins an Election

I N 1970 IDAHOANS SURPRISED the nation by choosing Cecil Andrus—"the first Western governor to be elected on an environmental program," as Andrus would proudly note in his autobiography.[1] How did this happen? Even with the widespread popularity of environmental concerns in that year when the first Earth Day was celebrated in Idaho and the nation, why did such a traditionally conservative state as Idaho seemingly change its spots? Never before had Idahoans elected anyone to statewide office on an environmental program. Why now?

Almost everyone agreed that it had to do with "Saving the White Clouds." Governor Don Samuelson's autobiography completely ignored the subject when he discussed his loss to Andrus, but both "Big Don's" supporters and his critics agreed that the White Clouds did him in. The Twin Falls *Times-News*, the only major Idaho paper to endorse Samuelson, conceded that this issue probably contributed the most to Samuelson's defeat. On the other side, the Lewiston *Morning Tribune* celebrated the victory of what it had called, two days before the election, "The View from a Snowy Peak"—"In the White Clouds for the first time in the long chop-and-dig history of this state, we have not taken it for granted that a payroll outranked other considerations."[2]

The payroll in question would be from a molybdenum mine proposed by ™the American Smelting and Refining Company (commonly known as ASARCO) in the White Cloud Peaks, located east of the Sawtooth Range, northwest of Sun Valley, and south of Challis. The "other considerations" were the scenic appeal of a relatively pristine wilderness termed "magnificent" by the New York *Times* and "superb" by the Twin Falls *Times-News*; and its Castle Peak was, "the mother of all Idaho landmarks," according to Andrus.[3]

By the end of 1970, Castle Peak had, indeed, become a landmark. But only a few years before, almost no one had the slightest notion of where it or any of the other White Clouds might be, let alone what they might look like. No roads led into the forty square miles jammed with scores of alpine peaks and lakes, and less than five hundred hikers a year ventured into the range. The area was so obscure that even the residents of Challis and Custer

County knew little about it. "I've lived here 62 years," said county commissioner Bob Hammond, "and didn't know where the White Clouds were until this controversy blew up."[4]

So why the controversy? Miners originally settled Idaho, and mining had continued to be a major source of jobs for the following century. The mines were commonly in out-of-the-way mountainous locations. "I can't see why it's such a big deal," Boise's *Idaho Statesman* quoted Willis Buxton, mayor of Challis. "Heck, we've had mining in the White Clouds for years." Besides, "there are lots of places just as pretty as the White Clouds."[5]

Fewer and fewer every year, a growing number of Idahoans would have responded. "There is a critical balance," Andrus later told Susan Stacy, "that we have to reach for in the tug between jobs, development and preserving."[6] And many Idahoans (a voting majority in 1970, as it turned out) feared that the state was in danger of losing those places most important for it to keep. The Idaho Falls *Post-Register* spoke for many when it repeatedly urged the "vital importance of preserving these fast disappearing wilderness-type areas," which are "uniquely endowed for preservation."[7]

Thus, the White Clouds in general and Castle Peak in particular became symbols for a bundle of interrelated public policy questions that Idahoans felt compelled to confront. "The White Clouds—Rich or Happy?" was the way Bill Hall phrased the issue in a Lewiston *Morning Tribune* editorial: "the peaks are symbolic of Idaho's turning a corner—or trying to—in the question of conservation."[8] On the one hand, Governor Don Samuelson spoke for the traditional option of increased payrolls and tax base. As he told a Coeur d'Alene news conference in May 1969, and reiterated throughout the state for the next fifteen months, the proposed mine would impact only 3,000 acres, a minute portion of the millions of acres of public lands in Idaho, and only one lake out of fifty-four in the White Clouds area. On the other hand, it would generate 350 jobs, with a $40 million investment, and more millions in taxes for a county that desperately needed economic development. "From such a tiny region," he concluded, "the contribution would be king-sized in benefits."[9]

A terrible choice, responded Lewis Hower in an editorial originally published in the May 15, 1969, issue of the Emmett *Messenger-Index* and widely reprinted throughout the state. The White Clouds are "far more rare than diamonds, more rewarding than the greatest factory." "A hallmark of civilization," Hower concluded, "is sensitivity to beauty, beauty that is not held accountable to earn a profit or to fill any other need, beauty that is revered for its own sake."[10]

Rank undemocratic elitism, charged those favoring the ASARCO proposal. Their most articulate spokesman was R.J. Bruning, editor of the Wallace *North Idaho Times*, whose "Stream of Thought" column regularly appeared in several other Idaho papers. Bruning dismissed Hower's appeal as speaking only for the "few people who have the time and the money for lengthy and expensive wilderness trips. Somehow our hearts can't bleed for these people."[11] So ASARCO wanted to put in a road to its mine? "What's wrong with roads?" Bruning asked. "Let's have more roads for the average recreationist—not fewer so that only the wealthy leisure class can enjoy the outdoors."[12] After all, recreational use of mining roads would be just another example of the multiple-use doctrine that had been the U.S. Forest Service's basic philosophy for many years.

Keith Whiting, regional manager for ASARCO, urged support for this example of multiple use. Mining, recreation, and tourism can be compatible, he assured his audience at the University of Idaho College of Mines; "all contribute to the betterment of our way of life."[13]

"Multiple Use Is Fishing for Carp," snorted the Lewiston *Morning Tribune.* "The issue today is really recreation, not conservation," it editorialized. People are in flight from the artificiality of Disneyland, and they want unsullied surroundings for their recreation. Compromise be damned! "Multiple use is fly-fishing downstream from a dredging operation. It is damming a river and calling it recreation when you visit the viewpoint overlooking the dam. It is casting for fish and catching potato peelings."[14]

As the reference to Disneyland hinted, the White Clouds issue reached far beyond Idaho's borders. It received nationwide attention, not only from specialized publications such as the Sierra Club *Bulletin* and the Wilderness Society's *Living Wilderness*, but from such mainstream newspapers as the *Christian Science Monitor* and the New York *Times*, and magazines like *Life* and *Smithsonian*. The White Clouds issue provoked the National Wildlife Federation to engage in litigation for the first time in its thirty years' existence.

The issue was not simply wilderness preservation versus industrial development. The fact was that neither Samuelson nor Andrus nor any other Idaho official had any authority to decide the issue. Nor could the Forest Service act decisively, even though the proposed mine was deep within the Challis National Forest. Federal law—specifically, the Mining Act of 1872—gave the widest possible leeway to prospectors and miners on public land. If ASARCO filed claims, no one had the power to deny them. If ASARCO requested approval to build a road into its mine, neither the Forest Service nor anyone else could say no.

Environmental groups were infuriated by what they saw as an outrageously anachronistic federal law. It denied them the opportunity to persuade the public that it did not need a molybdenum mine in the White Clouds nearly as much as it needed to preserve the area's wilderness character. And the record of the mining industry did nothing to calm fears. "Once the public knows your granddad was a horse thief," as ASARCO supporter R.J. Bruning ruefully put it, "they keep the car locked up when you're around."[15]

With no realistic chance of repealing or even significantly revising the 1872 mining law, environmentalists turned their attention to the Forest Service, and found it woefully wanting. Having summarized the White Clouds face-off, *Life* lashed out at the men in green: "the trouble with this fight is that there is no referee. The Forest Service, logical candidate for the job, is hiding under the ring with its Smokey-the-Bear hat over its face."[16]

Gratuitous and even unfair as this criticism might have been in the case at hand, there was a long history that gave it a certain persuasiveness. As we will see, the Forest Service had labored since its first arrival in Idaho, back at the beginning of the twentieth century, to overcome local objections to its management of nearly one-quarter of the state's area by convincing Idahoans that conservation and economic development were compatible. "No industry will or can be injured by the forest reserve administration," Major Frank Fenn, the first forest superintendent in Idaho, had repeatedly assured those nervous about the implications of federal controls.[17] He would have included tourism and recreation as industries as well among those most discussed at the time: logging, mining, and grazing.

This had become so widely believed by the 1960s that the effort to create a Sawtooth National Park, championed by Senator Frank Church, was rejected as a needless innovation. To quote an editorial broadcast by KSRA radio in Salmon, Idaho, in September 1960:

> anything more which would be done beyond the present recreational and in-formational services accomplished and planned by the Forest Service would be lilly gilding of the first degree—entirely detrimental to the natural beauty of an area which is one of the most spectacular in the entire country.[18]

Now, however, the chickens were coming home to roost. Neither those interested in scenic preservation nor the proponents of industrial development were satisfied that the Forest Service could be counted on to produce satisfactory results.

The White Clouds controversy provoked Governor Samuelson to launch an attack on the agency unparalleled in Idaho since the death of Senator Weldon Heyburn in 1912. He blamed the Forest Service for the controversy having even occurred. At the Western Governors Conference in Seattle in July 1969, he stated that, had the Forest Service not publicized ASARCO's application for a road, there "would have been no controversy and people would not be stirred up all over the nation."[19] As he toured the state, he repeatedly condemned the agency for its evident reluctance to "fulfill their obligation to enforce the provisions of the [mining] statutes."[20] In fact, Samuelson told an audience in Idaho Falls, the Forest Service was guilty of "changing rules to suit their own purposes."[21] Ranging far beyond the White Clouds issue, the governor accused the Ogden region, responsible for the national forests in Idaho south of the Salmon River, of disobeying national directives for maximizing timber production, packaging timber sales in such large blocks that it drove small operators out of business, and being so "completely recreation minded"[22] that grazers and loggers never got a fair shake. In short, as he put it in a speech to a Lions Club in Idaho Falls, "the administration of the Forest Service in this district stinks to high heaven."[23]

There were plenty of critics ready to take issue with Samuelson on specific charges. Many editorials pointed out, for example, that the Forest Service could not legally keep quiet about ASARCO's application for a road to the proposed molybdenum mine. But there was a notable silence when it came to defending the Forest Service itself. Nothing like the KSRA editorial pertaining to the proposed Sawtooth National Park could be heard or read in the mass of words broadcast and printed in Idaho on the White Clouds issue.

Take, for example, Senator Frank Church. A leading proponent of the Wilderness Bill of 1964 and greatly concerned about protecting the White Clouds, didn't he speak up on behalf of the agency? Not at all. Never mind that it had been the Forest Service which set aside over three million acres of protected wilderness in Idaho during the 1930s. Church adamantly opposed the way the Forest Service acted by administrative fiat, when the senator believed such action should be taken by way of public hearings and by legislating in Congress. Thus, when the Forest Service announced in 1962, after several years of meetings and consultations with local interests, plans for a Hells Canyon Scenic Area, Church bitterly denounced the scheme. Rather than an example of multiple use, it "might better be cited as an example of unbridled bureaucratic license." In his opinion, the way the agency developed its plan "illustrates the need to restore to the Congress, as the Wilderness Bill would do, authority over proposals for special use priorities."[24]

The *Morning Tribune*, usually a supporter of Church, protested his "unnecessarily harsh swipe." It denied that anything "underhanded" had been going on and concluded that there was no reason to abuse "anybody who has worked as hard to protect the forests and primitive areas of the land as have the men of the Forest Service."[25] In the debate over the White Clouds, Church kept a discreet silence about his distrust of the Forest Service, but neither Lewiston's *Morning Tribune* nor any other major Idaho paper came to the defense of the agency when Samuelson mounted his attack.

The sportsmen were no more supportive. Regardless of the fact that the Forest Service had, from the first years of the century, strongly supported game preservation and management, wildlife groups criticized what they saw as the agency's ineffectuality when it came to protecting the White Clouds. Announcing its support for a national park, the Idaho Wildlife Federation declared, "it is evident the Forest Service either lacks the administrative muscle or it considers mining in the White Clouds to be more important than the public trust to protect from destruction the high quality surface rights."[26]

Finally, the new environmental groups, which played such an important role in raising the public outcry against ASARCO's presence at the base of Castle Peak, found the Forest Service altogether too cautious in the way it responded to the challenge. The Idaho Alpine Club, based in Idaho Falls, was one of the very first groups to raise the cry of alarm. Learning in mid-September 1968 that a small exploratory team from ASARCO had been in the White Clouds since May, Edward Anderson, the club's president, condemned the Forest Service's failure to raise an alarm sooner: "this secrecy is inexcusable."[27]

The White Clouds, in short, marked an end as well as a beginning. While the debate over the mine at Castle Peak signaled the time when environmentalism became a regular player in Idaho politics, it also represented the end of the Forest Service's hegemony as the protector of the state's wild places and wild things.

The aim of this book is to see how Idaho arrived at this confrontation over the White Clouds in 1970—to see how a state particularly jealous of its rights and suspicious of anything that smacked of federal control came to have millions of acres of federally protected wilderness. The story entails far more than the evolution of federal policies; it also involves a surprising range of other topics, including the history of game preserves in Idaho, and a review of local attitudes toward scenic preservation, various wild animals, and environmental pollution. To get to the White Clouds, in short, requires a seventy-year tour of Idaho's environmental history in the twentieth century.

ENDNOTES

1. Cecil Andrus and Joel Connelly, *Cecil Andrus: Politics Western Style* (Seattle: Sasquatch, 1998): p. 19.
2. B.H. [Bill Hall], "The View from a Snowy Peak," editorial in Lewiston *Morning Tribune* (November 1, 1970): p. 4.
3. "The Environmental Issue," New York *Times* (November 6, 1970): p. 40; "White Cloud Mountains Are Hidden, Towering Range of Sawtooth Region," Twin Falls *Times-News* (May 31, 1964): p. 21; *Cecil Andrus*, p. 82.
4. Bob Leeright, "Challis Residents Take Dissenting Views on Drive to Block White Clouds Mining," Boise *Idaho Statesman* (July 26, 1970): p. C11.
5. *Ibid.*, "Challis Mayor Cites Mining in White Clouds Since 1877," Boise *Statesman* (July 23, 1970): p. B3.
6. Susan M. Stacy (ed.), *Conversations: A Companion Book to Idaho Public Television's "Proceeding On Through a Beautiful Country," A History of Idaho* (Boise: Idaho Educational Public Broadcasting Foundation, 1990): p. 128.
7. "Why Castle Peak Should Not Be Mined," editorial in Idaho Falls *Post-Register* (May 5, 1969): p. 4.
8. B.H., "The White Clouds—Rich or Happy?" editorial in Lewiston *Morning Tribune* (July 4, 1969): p. 4.
9. "White Clouds Mining: Nothing to Lose, Claims Samuelson," Coeur d'Alene *Press* (May 14, 1969): p. 12.
10. Untitled editorial reprinted in Boise *Statesman* (May 20, 1969): p. 4.

11. R.J. Bruning, "Stream of Thought," Boise *Statesman* (September 14, 1969): p. 4.

12. R.J. Bruning, "Another View on Castle Peak," Boise *Statesman* (April 7, 1969): p. 4.

13. "Mining Plan for 'Clouds' Defended," Boise *Statesman* (December 4, 1969): p. C5.

14. B.H., "Multiple Use Is Fishing for Carp," editorial in Lewiston *Morning Tribune* (September 3, 1969): p. 4.

15. R.J. Bruning, "Stream of Thought," Boise *Statesman* (May 25, 1969): p. 4.

16. Donald Jackson, "Whose Wilderness?" *Life* (January 9, 1970): p. 112.

17. "Forest Reserves," Boise *Statesman* (September 2, 1905): p. 3.

18. Text of editorial on station KSRA (September 18, 1960) in Frank Church Papers (Boise State University Library Special Collections), Box 93, Folder 3. The history of the effort to create a Sawtooth National Park is covered in Douglas W. Dodd, "Preserving Multiple-Use Management: The U.S. Forest Service, the National Park Service, and the Struggle for Idaho's Sawtooth Mountain Country, 1911–1972" (Ann Arbor, Mich.: UMI Dissertation Services, 2002).

19. John Corlett, "Samuelson Scores Forest Service for Publicizing Road Application by Mining Firm," Boise *Statesman* (July 31, 1969): p. B9.

20. "Governor Says Law Orders Road Permit," Boise *Statesman* (October 1, 1969): p. 17.

21. "Samuelson Upholds Mine Stand," Boise *Statesman* (September 11, 1969): p. A10.

22. "Samuelson Reiterates Mine Stand," Boise *Statesman* (September 17, 1969): p. D1.

23. Alice Dieter, "Silent Mountain Peak Presided over Idaho's Biggest Battle in 1969," Boise *Intermountain Observer* (December 27, 1969): pp. 6, 7.

24. "Church Statement Critical of 'Bureaucratic License' in Scenic Area's Creation," Boise *Statesman* (June 14, 1962): p. 22.

25. "A 'Stroke of the Pen' Decision?" editorial in Lewiston *Morning Tribune* (June 15, 1962): p. 4.

26. "Wildlife Federation Raps Reticence of Forest Service on White Clouds," Boise *Statesman* (April 11, 1970): p. 16.

27. "Club Sees Threat to Scenic Area," Idaho Falls *Post-Register* (September 26, 1968): p. 17.

I

The Forest Service Arrives

T CAME WITH BREATHTAKING SPEED and scope. In 1899, the two forest reserves in Idaho amounted to only 650,000 acres, just a bit more than 1 percent of the state's total area. By 1907, a mere eight years later, Idaho's seventeen "National Forests" (as they were renamed that same year) had ballooned to 20,336,427 acres, enclosing well over one-third of the state.[1] Put another way, national forests in Idaho then covered more ground than the total areas of Massachusetts, Rhode Island, Connecticut, New Jersey, Delaware, and Maryland combined.

The timing was wonderful or terrible, depending on one's point of view, which tended to reflect one's geographical location within the state. In the predominantly semiarid south, where growth over the next several decades would come through large-scale irrigation projects, protection of watersheds was absolutely vital; therefore, national forests were welcomed. Furthermore, the rapidly escalating sheep industry, numbering more than three million head by the turn of the century, had already raised the specter of overgrazing and violent confrontations between stockmen pushing and shoving for space on the public domain for their flocks. Consequently, the forest rangers' impositions of grazing controls in the national forests were soon welcomed as necessary peacemaking by a disinterested third party.

North of the Salmon River, on the other hand, the thousands of square miles of readily merchantable timber had just begun, in the first years of the twentieth century, to attract the attention of major lumbermen, and the arrival of the U.S. Forest Service was no more welcome to many northern Idaho residents than cops at a teenage beer bust. In both cases, the tantalizing prospects for untrammeled pleasure were cut short by the arrival of infuriatingly sensible authorities.

The national forests were created for what now seem the very best of motives. They reflected a growing national concern for the rapidity with which the forests of Maine, Michigan, Minnesota, and Wisconsin had been exhausted, as well as the evidence seen in many sections of the country that rapid deforestation could result in major erosion and flood control problems.

As conceived by Gifford Pinchot, the nation's Chief Forester (1898–1910), and President Theodore Roosevelt, national forests were intended to apply the principles of conservation to the vast forestlands of the West, avoiding disastrous plunder and abandonment by the timber barons in favor of "the greatest good for the greatest number over the long haul," Pinchot's favorite statement of his goal. The mission was to save the forests for the people. To quote the *Use Book* (the Forest Service's basic policy manual):

> Forest reserves are for the purpose of preserving a perpetual supply of timber for home industries, preventing destruction of the forest cover which regulates the flow of streams, and protecting local residents from unfair competition in the use of forest and range. They are patrolled, at Government expense, for the benefit of the Community and home builder.[2]

Northern Idaho vociferously begged to differ. The intrusion of the Forest Service threatened to regulate and restrain the development of a vigorous lumbering industry exploiting timber on federal lands just as it got started. Without adequate development capital or transportation links to national markets, the lumbermen of northern Idaho had only been able to serve local needs for mining-timbers and settlers' building needs. "Prior to two years ago," as the Coeur d'Alene *Independent* editorialized in August 1902, " we had nothing but a home market for our timber."[3] Only nine hundred men found employment in the Idaho timber industry in 1900. Then, all at once—and during the same few years that national forests were being created with such abandon, or so it seemed to northern Idahoans—major infusions of "eastern capital" brought the construction of large new sawmills throughout northern Idaho, from Grangeville to Sandpoint, with what promised to be the nation's largest being planned by the Weyerhaeuser interests in Lewiston.

"Timber's Day Is Coming" the Lewiston *Morning Tribune* jubilantly proclaimed.[4] And the St. Maries *Gazette* saw the "Dawning of a New Era" when the Howard Land, Lumber and Logging Company announced in the spring of 1903 that it was hiring three hundred men to harvest timber along the St. Maries River. "It will be the starting point when logging in this section commences in good earnest, and will mock into insignificance the logging that has been done in this section in the past."[5]

But now that bright new day was in danger of being snuffed out; the forest reserves "will make of northern Idaho a howling wilderness." The forest conservation policy "may look good on paper at Washington," the editor of the Sandpoint *Pend d'Oreille Review* concluded, "but to us who are here and must stand the result of its enforcement it is a blow, severe and unwarranted."[6] Far from conserving the forests for ordinary people, the editorial claimed, the reserves cruelly and arbitrarily set aside huge blocks of timber until "the big companies can get to them." Then the timber would be sold off in large lots for the big mills, and the little guy would have no chance of getting his share.

Without the reserves, the whole country would be settled in small parcels with "a little money for all of us; not big money for a few of us." Despite repeated assurances by the Forest Service of its benign intentions, most people in northern Idaho believed that the Sandpoint editor had it right, that "the moneyed powers" were behind it all.[7]

Senator Weldon Heyburn stepped forth as the most adamant and persistent spokesman for those opposing the creation of national forests. An attorney and mine owner from Wallace, Heyburn opposed the forest conservation program from the beginning. As early as September 1899 (five years before he was elected to the U.S. Senate) he was arguing that "the wealth of such a state as ours is estimated in a large measure by the amount of land available for settlement. Why," he asked an interviewer for the Boise *Statesman*, "should we acquiesce to a policy that thus reduces our available assets?"[8]

Heyburn welcomed the opportunity to cross swords with the Forest Service whenever it presented itself, supremely confident that he was defending fundamental American freedoms. In September 1906, he went to Boise to attend the National Irrigation Congress, which had invited him as well as Gifford Pinchot to speak. "In the Midst of Hisses and Cheers," as the *Statesman* reported it, he spoke more than an hour, lambasting Pinchot and his bureaucrats. "You have been told," he reminded his audience, "of the 'policy' of the administration! The administration has no right to have any policy unless it is expressed in Statute law! Government by policy belongs to kingdoms and empires, not to republics!" As for the alleged need to protect western forests, protect them "from what? Their owners? From the American citizens who own them?"[9] As he had told the Senate earlier in the year, "It is men we want, not trees."[10]

Most Idahoans admired Heyburn's spunk, and many believed he was fighting for a vital cause. The *Morning Tribune* reported that he was "highly esteemed in Lewiston" for "his great and fearless fight" against the national forests.[11] Demonstrating that Heyburn had supporters elsewhere in the state, the Idaho Falls *Register* reprinted an editorial from the *Morning Tribune* lauding his "masterful and irresistible arraignment of the forest reserve looters and blackguards."[12] Although it "was not in accord" with his views on the national forests, the Twin Falls *News* admired "the fight he made on the question." He "is earnest, tenacious, talented, and fearless."[13]

The critical issue, for Heyburn and those who adopted his stance toward national forests, was land use. They scoffed at the notion of forests providing essential flood control protection. The Bitterroot forest reserve "will not save a spoonful of water for any purpose," snorted the editor of the *Idaho County Free Press* in Grangeville.[14] Few stockmen used the national forests of northern Idaho for grazing. And, in fact, even if timber in the national forests could not be exploited, plenty was available on private lands to nourish a rapidly growing lumber industry, which saw employment increase from 900 in 1900 to 2,500 in 1910 and more than 5,500 in 1920. But they did not want national forests because, ultimately, they did not want to see the area remain primarily a timberland. Their vision of how Idaho should grow and develop was summarized in Heyburn's catchphrase—"we want men, not trees." They saw nothing wrong with the clearing of the forests in Michigan, Wisconsin, and Minnesota and admired the farms and towns that replaced them. They hoped that a similar process would come to Idaho. Heyburn was quoted as saying that he would rather have one man on the land than ten thousand trees, and he preferred one cow to "whole herds of spotted fawns."[15]

Lamenting the addition of "Another Forest Reserve," the Sandpoint *Northern Idaho News* complained that Pinchot and his department "seem to be determined that Northern Idaho shall be killed as a business and home-building community if possible and instead be converted into one huge forest and game preserve."[16] According to the Coeur d'Alene *Press*, "the people do not object to forest reserves on the mountainous watersheds, but they have first cause to protest against a policy that includes the cream of the timber and farm lands."[17] (In actuality, the forest reservations were required by law to exclude land primarily suited for agriculture.)

Nor were they placated when the Forest Service slowly and reluctantly released some relatively small and scattered parcels of land for settlement. Even if those lands were taken up, the settlers had no hope "of further settlement and growth, without which," the Lewiston *Morning Tribune* concluded, "their own holdings cease to have value or inducements."[18] In other words, the settlers were not looking for a way to escape into the woods, but yearned to see the land "settled up," thereby enhancing the value of their own property. In any case, the real issue remained the highest and best use for major portions of each county in northern Idaho. Responding to the Forest Service's suspicions that settlers were timber hogs in disguise, the Sandpoint *Pend d'Oreille Review* claimed, "there is no denying the fact that much wooded land in Bonner County will make the best kind of farms. This country is not unlike the terribly 'ravaged' sections of Michigan and Wisconsin," where the forests were cut and farms replaced them; "we want to see in this locality a dairy and agricultural country."[19]

No one had any way of proving the point one way or the other. Much of northern Idaho might, indeed, be potentially rich farmland, or, quite to the contrary, it might be, like New England's hardwood forests, best left in timberland. Despite Forest Service assertions that it analyzed the areas carefully before designating which should be included within national forests, most of Idaho remained unsurveyed for several decades after their establishment. Consequently the *Morning Tribune* was not far off the mark when it claimed that, lacking any topographical maps for most of the state, "the bureau merely marks off huge territories known to contain timber and lets it go at that."[20] If this approach to forest conservation had been followed in the early years of American history, the *Pend d'Oreille Review* argued, the country would remain nothing more than "a fringe upon the Atlantic seaboard."[21]

This may seem to be a rather extreme conclusion, but the fact remains that northern Idaho's proportional share of the state's population steadily declined after 1900, from 36.15 percent to 32.67 percent in 1910, 26.05 percent in 1920, and 21.51 percent in 1990. A plausible argument could be posited that the decline derived from the area's inability to settle the great swatches of national forest. (It is also noteworthy, however, that the passage of the 1902 Newlands Reclamation Act, subsidizing irrigated farms in southern Idaho, started a massive land rush and population shift to the Snake River plain.)

Faced with the absence of any data that would conclusively prove the best use of the land, many Idahoans felt that farmers ought to be able to move into the forested regions and make their own tests. As Senator William Borah put it, "I say that it is not within the power of the [forest] bureau to determine whether a man can make a farm out of a particular piece of land."[22] In fact, he denied any possibility of an objective judgment of the matter beyond trial and error. He asserted that no one was competent to judge whether land in the national forests was primarily suited for timber, mining, or agriculture, "until the farmer has been given a chance to go upon the reserve and in good faith and with honest purpose to make a living and build a home."[23]

Infuriated by the Forest Service's refusal to allow piecemeal settlement within the national forests, Heyburn and his supporters attacked the character of service personnel. Gifford Pinchot was guilty of "a brazen effrontery," which the *Morning Tribune* concluded "can only come from a diseased mind."[24] And the young Easterners he sent out to manage the forests were nothing more than effete layabouts. "I have seen them," Heyburn claimed, "lolling around the hotels of the watering places dressed in green, with cocked hats, emulating the forest[er]s of...Germany."[25] These "Cigarette Willies," as a Sandpoint editor dubbed them, had no idea how to judge local conditions. "If one of these so-called expert foresters could...tell the difference between a sagebrush and a tall tamarack, we miss our guess of his ability."[26] Even worse, the Boise *Capital News* quoted statements on the floor of the state legislature to the effect that many of the rangers were "half-breed Indians" and "poachers," who were "ignorant, vicious, and unapproachable by reason of common sense."[27] Nor were these critics willing to back off when they were accused of intemperance. Responding to such an editorial in the Boise *Statesman*, the Lewiston *Morning Tribune* shot back: "the only other fit way we know of discussing" what it called the "infamy" of national forests in Idaho "is with a club to beat over the heads of the enemies of the country."[28]

In point of fact, however, the early-day rangers were not "enemies of the country." They were neither dandified Eastern tenderfeet nor local reprobates. The Forest Service aimed to hire men knowledgeable of the area in which they would work, and, at least in Idaho, it did an outstanding recruiting job. They were men like R.H. Rutledge, the first supervisor for the Coeur d'Alene National Forest, who had grown up on a ranch in Round Valley, south of Cascade. If they spent their early years elsewhere, they had proved themselves in Idaho prior to joining the Forest Service. Emile Grandjean, for example, the first supervisor for the Boise National Forest, emigrated from Denmark as a young man and spent several years in the Sawtooths as a professional hunter, providing meat for the tables of Wood River miners, before becoming a ranger.

Frank A. Fenn, perhaps the best of the lot, certainly played a key role in gaining acceptance of the Forest Service and its mission in Idaho. His adventurous background surely helped. Born in California, he came with his family to the Florence gold mines in 1862, where he attended the first school in the territory. In 1869 he went to Annapolis, the first Idahoan appointed to the U.S. Naval Academy. After two years, he dropped out to tour the world. Three years later, Fenn returned to Idaho County, ranching and teaching school. During the 1877 Nez Perce War, he joined the Idaho militia and won a battlefield promotion to major, a title that he used thereafter. Clearly a man of political talents, Major Fenn moved in 1891 with his wife and three children to Boise, having received appointment as chief clerk of the state Land Board. Five years later, he was elected to the state legislature from Boise. The next year, he read law and was admitted to the bar. After a brief service in the Spanish American War, he practiced law in Boise. Appointed chairman of the Republican State Central Committee in 1900, Fenn gained appointment in 1901 as the first superintendent of all forest reserves in Idaho. He served in various Forest Service positions until he retired in 1921 and returned to Idaho County, spending his last years as publisher of the Kooskia *Mountaineer*.[29]

Major Fenn proved to be an indefatigable publicist for the Forest Service in Idaho. He traveled throughout the state, and spoke with newspaper editors whenever possible. "The policy of the government," he assured the Lewiston *Teller*, "is to preserve the forests in the highest continued production for the benefit of the people of Idaho."[30] He insisted that management of the national forests was based on a common-sense approach: "Uncle Sam…is doing no more than any private holder of similar property would do."[31] Fenn told the Wallace *Press* that far from protecting the interests of the large lumber syndicates, "the forest service is constantly opposing them" in order to give the small operator a decent chance to thrive.[32] And the miners need not fear interference with their business. National forests were aiming to assure them of an adequate supply of timber and to void the machinations of "kid glove miners" trying to trick honest miners out of their claims. Ignoring Heyburn's argument that potential farmlands were being unwisely retained as forests, Fenn reiterated his position that the Forest Service respected the rights and prerogatives of homesteaders. Although those trying to "hold down" claims under the Timber and Stone Act "are all wrong" and "their schemes will be balked," Fenn repeatedly insisted that the Forest Service placed no barrier to agricultural use of appropriate lands within the boundaries of the national forests.[33]

He believed that once the local residents got used to the Forest Service, most opposition would disappear. After all, no legitimate activity in the forests would be injured. "Every interest is subserved."[34] Reporting to the *Statesman* that timber was being sold rapidly in the Sawtooth National Forest, he proudly noted that revenues were jumping up. "Yes, sir, the reserves are working out like a charm."[35]

Although prematurely optimistic about the acceptance of national forests in Idaho, Fenn did seem to have a charmed touch in dealing with potentially difficult confrontations with forest users. Meeting in Boise with sheepmen in the spring of 1906 regarding grazing regulations, he invited their participation. "I do not dream to be an authority on the subject and…decided to let the whole matter be adjusted by the various sheep owners themselves." The result? "Sure. We can't expect everybody to be satisfied; but there have been no injustices done."[36] Similarly, the next spring in Salmon, meeting with stockmen, "Mr. Fenn came here to aid in making the most of the condition as it exists." According to the Salmon *Idaho Recorder*, "he asked the citizens to assist in working out the best results under the laws and regulations as we find them." Typically, Fenn captured the local editor's attention by regaling him with accounts of the Nez Perce War.[37] Concluding its report on the major's visit, Salmon's other paper assured its readers that "the users of the range will always get fair play at his hands."[38]

Given the nearly unanimously negative comments from Idaho leaders, one might assume that Frank Fenn's conduct was a rare exception to the generally obnoxious behavior of Forest Service personnel in Idaho. While Senator Heyburn was the most adamantly hostile member of the Idaho congressional delegation, Senator Fred Dubois was the only one to speak on the Forest Service's behalf, and once Borah had replaced him in March 1907, it would be many years before the agency would hear another kind word from any member of the Idaho delegation.

State legislators were also prone to belittle the rangers. At several sessions, the legislature passed memorials damning both the theory and practices of national forests. Thus, in 1907, Representative W.L. Gleason of St. Maries introduced a memorial asking Congress to pass laws so the people's rights could not be suspended "at the will and pleasure of a department agent."[39]

Accompanying arguments asserted that the national forests were "the work of rainbow-dressing faddists."[40] Although James Fogg spoke up, saying national forests were good for Fremont County, and James Surridge said he had decided they were also good for Idaho County, the memorial easily passed. The core of the complaint, as an editorial in the Boise *Capital News* put it, was that forest users found it humiliating and un-American when they had to go to the "forest autocrat" with "proper humility and make humble petitions for their rights."[41]

Nevertheless, newspapers of the time almost never reported anything controversial regarding the conduct of rangers and their supervisors. In 1909 Grandjean publicly criticized the enforcement procedures of the game warden, angering Governor James Brady, who fired off a protesting letter to Gifford Pinchot. But that incident was virtually the only one of its kind. Most of the time the reports indicated that Fenn's management style was fairly typical. Take, for example, the issue of treeless areas within national forests. Sawtooth National Forest Supervisor Woods asked the Hailey Commercial Club in May 1909 for an expression of opinion, since a congressional committee was expected to visit and study the question. After an extended discussion, the *Wood River Times* reported, "it was made plain that only a few of the wealthy sheepmen still opposed the reserve system." "The prevailing opinion," the paper concluded, "was evidently that instead of decreasing the reserve area it should be increased."[42]

Idaho received much attention from top Forest Service officials in the first decade of the century. Gifford Pinchot visited every year between 1904 and 1907, and again in 1909. His boss, Secretary of Agriculture Wilson, also came in 1909. Although this may have been in recognition of the sheer size of the national forests in Idaho, it was, for Wilson, explicitly in response to Senator Heyburn's continued attacks on the Forest Service, and we may assume that it also had much to do with Pinchot's travel schedule. The assumption gains plausibility from the fact that, after Heyburn's death in 1912, the visits from Washington, D.C., immediately dropped off.

The visits to his constituency had only limited success in countering Heyburn. According to the Coeur d'Alene *Morning Journal*, Pinchot's appearances in northern Idaho in the summer of 1907 were intended "to stifle the opposition" and "discredit" Senator Heyburn and Congressman French. Pinchot found an attentive audience wherever he visited, but, the *Morning Journal* concluded, the people continued to support Heyburn and agreed with him "that it was men and not trees that the state of Idaho wanted."[43] The St. Maries *Gazette* conceded that Pinchot's conservation policy "is correct," but repeated the charge that it was unfair to Idaho, "taking away the assets of the locality for the advancement and benefit of others."[44] In Lewiston, the *Evening Teller* reported that Pinchot "presented in a most pleasing manner" his ideas to an audience of one thousand. However, "the practical applications of the reserve policy were aggressively attacked by Congressman French."[45]

Agriculture Secretary Wilson, returning to Washington, D.C., after his visit to Pocatello and Mackay in 1909, claimed that Heyburn "is clear out of tune with public support in Idaho." Wilson found the people of Idaho "overwhelmingly in favor of what we have done and are doing."[46] But Idahoans knew, even if Wilson did not, that he only visited southern Idaho, while Heyburn's strength was concentrated in the north. In any case, Senator Borah found it easy to dismiss the significance of Wilson's brief visit. Borah doubted whether Wilson ever got off the train. "He went there and met a few of the people whom he could meet on a very rainy, bad day, and went away."[47]

No such criticism could apply to Pinchot's visits. In 1905 he came to Boise, met with Governor Frank Gooding, and hammered out a settlement of several issues. The most important had to do with the "school sections," the lands set aside in each township of the public domain for endowing public schools. Gooding and Pinchot agreed that they should be consolidated, and, where possible, exchanged to remove them from within national forests. Although Heyburn continued to hector federal authorities about school lands, the Gooding-Pinchot conference marked the beginning of amicable state-federal relations concerning the administration of Idaho's national forests. And those depended on another product of their conference, the agreement to leave administrative decisions, so far as possible, "in the hands of men on the ground."[48] Despite the angry condemnations of Heyburn and his supporters, the interests of peaceful relations between forest users and managers were best served by relying on such men as Fenn to minimize conflicts.

In 1906 Pinchot returned to Boise to attend the national irrigation convention. After debating with Heyburn at Riverside Park, he left with Major Fenn for a tour of the national forests, passing through Idaho City, Stanley Basin, and on to Hailey. Pinchot frequently gained admiration for his social talents. As the Coeur d'Alene *Press* put it the next year, he "is a man of pleasing address, a good mixer, and not the autocrat many had been led to believe" him to be.[49] Those social graces helped bring many to express trust in his programs. Thus, the Idaho City *World* reported that a large group of local citizens met with Pinchot and Fenn and seemed to be "strongly in favor of having all of this country placed in the forest reserve."[50] Similarly, the *Wood River Times* expected, following the meeting in Hailey with a group of stockmen, "Good Results to Follow," specifically "the adoption of a comprehensive plan to get the greatest possible wealth out of the reserves."[51]

The following year, after speaking in Pocatello and Boise, Pinchot went with Fenn to tour northern Idaho, with public meetings in Coeur d'Alene and Lewiston. He must have noticed how much less receptive audiences were in the north. Pinchot made every effort to reassure them. In Coeur d'Alene, he denied that "we are taking away any of your country." Rather, "we are simply conducting a supervision that will prevent waste and monopoly."[52]

Nevertheless, his definition of waste did not fit local concerns. While Pinchot claimed that he wanted to allow as many homestead plots as possible in the national forests, he remained unyielding about what he perceived as the stripping of woodlands: "I will not help any man to get timber, skin the land and move on."[53] This proved, to the *Morning Journal*'s editor and very possibly many of his readers, that the only result of the Chief Forester's visit was to "let the people know the unalterable determination of the Forestry department to construe and enforce the law…in the most arbitrary manner possible."[54]

Pinchot's sharply differing receptions in southern and northern Idaho dramatized not only the distinct opinions in the two sections, but also the physical conditions characterizing the two parts of the state. As William L. Rich, state senator from Bear Lake County (in the southeast corner of the state), summed up the problem during debate in the Idaho Senate in February 1907, the conditions "in the northern and southern parts of the state were so different that the same rules could not very well apply in both sections."[55] In fact, the Forest Service already had acknowledged this by placing northern Idaho in the district (later region) administered from Missoula, Montana, while southern Idaho national forests were managed from Ogden, Utah. This arrangement has continued to the present. While the two sections of Idaho have now become accustomed to working together on many issues, it was not until the early 1950s with the anti-dredging initiative that a statewide consensus on conservation concerns finally began to emerge.

Northern Idaho did, eventually and grudgingly, make its peace with the Forest Service. "It is an old rule," conceded the editor of the Salmon *Lemhi Herald* in 1907, that "what can't be cured must be endured." Consequently, there was no relief from grazing rules imposed by the Forest Service except "to make the regulations as bearable as possible."[56] The following year, the Grangeville *Standard-News* told its readers that "the forest reserves are here to stay."[57] The Lewiston *Morning Tribune* never made such a concession statement and, as late as 1937, refused to report Pinchot's speech when he returned to Lewiston for a gala occasion sponsored by the timber industry. However, most other papers north of the Salmon River had followed the lead of the Grangeville editor within a couple of years of Heyburn's death in 1912.

In southern Idaho, on the other hand, the arrival of the national forests was commonly welcomed. In at least two cases, they were created in direst response to petitions from local residents. The Pocatello Forest Reserve was promulgated in 1903 to protect the water supply for the city of Pocatello, and local support for it never wavered. "The forest service may have made mistakes in the past," the Pocatello *Tribune* editorialized in May 1910, "but the Pocatello reserve is not one of them."[58] In 1905 the Cassia National Forest, encompassing 326,000 acres in the mountains of southern Twin Falls County, came into being to "preserve a perpetual timber supply for the settlers on the Twin Falls tract," who feared that without this protection, "every stick of timber" would have been soon taken.[59]

Newspapers of the time frequently reported requests of stockmen, miners, and farmers to have the boundaries of neighboring national forests expanded to include them, for the sake of equity in the use of resources. Thus, in January 1906 farmers in Council petitioned Major Fenn to be included in the Weiser National Forest to protect them from the sheepmen, who monopolized the grazing lands. At the same time, the sheepmen of Mountain Home asked Fenn to include them in the Sawtooth National Forest so that grazing rights could be fairly apportioned. That same spring of 1906, people of Washington County asked for inclusion of the Seven Devils area in a national forest to assure that miners had a dependable supply of mining timbers. Meanwhile, miners in Bear Valley (northwest of the Sawtooth Mountains) wanted inclusion to protect them from the encroachments of sheepmen. Consequently, the *Statesman* found Heyburn's opposition "most regrettable," affirming that Forest Service "policy is in the interest of the public in such a manner that all opposition to it will disappear in a very short time."[60] When, three months later, the 1907 legislature passed a resolution criticizing the national forest system, the *Statesman* insisted that it "is with us to stay, because it is right."[61]

Although the Boise *Statesman* would change its tune within a few years, taking on much of the same tone as the Lewiston *Morning Tribune*, most southern Idahoans quickly got over any initial objections they had about Forest Service policies, for several reasons. In the first place, there was a process of give and take, with both users and the Forest service striving to develop a workable system. On the one hand, agency personnel worked hard to adjust rules and regulations wherever possible, so that they would fit local needs and conditions. Thus, when stockmen argued that requiring grazing rights to be renewed annually did not give them adequate motive to make necessary improvements, such as fence upkeep, the Forest Service soon responded by awarding grazing rights for longer periods, initially for three years, then eventually ten years. On the other hand, stockmen sometimes had to make adjustments. The Forest Service remained adamant that it would not tolerate monopoly and, therefore, limited each sheepman to no more than ten thousand head in the national forests. Although the large operators, including Governor Gooding, argued that such restrictions would "virtually destroy the sheep industry in Idaho,"[62] they learned to live with the limitation.

Idahoans, particularly in the south, increasingly recognized the necessity for the Forest Service's conservationist policies. "The way we were ruining the country," Blaine County pioneer sheepman Ben Darrah admitted, "some sort of regulation was necessary... If the [Sawtooth] National Forest had not been created, the area it now embraces would soon have been a dust bed."[63] In August 1909 the Pocatello *Tribune* lauded the plans for a conservation congress at the Alaska-Yukon-Pacific Exposition in Seattle: "conservation in the west should be encouraged and practiced while there are gifts of nature to conserve."[64] Three months later, Governor James Brady returned from a tour of state timberlands in northern Idaho convinced that they should not be sold, but conserved "for the whole people"[65] (a statement worthy of Pinchot himself). To gain a sense of how far Idahoans had come in accepting the concept of forest conservation, we need only recall the opinion of Governor Frank Steunenberg (1897–1901): "the pretext that our lands and forests are the just inheritance of posterity is not only hackneyed, but illegal and overdrawn."[66]

North Idaho was, by the second decade of the twentieth century, showing an increasing willingness to accept the Forest Service's presence. For example, the Coeur d'Alene *Press* in early 1913 published an article on "Selling National Forest Timber" by the new Chief Forester, Henry Graves, which took a position diametrically opposed to that of recently deceased Senator Heyburn. Graves saw "the crucial test" of national forest management as "the power to resist" the demand to sell timber cheap on the specious grounds that such actions would enable the public to buy lumber cheap. In effect, the extensive selling of cheap lumber would deplete timber resources.[67] The next year in Grangeville, A.F. Parker of the *Globe* concluded his assessment of "The Wealth of Our Forestry," by stating: "Personally, the only fault I have found with the forest conservation system is that it was not inaugurated 200 years ago."[68]

For Parker and many other Idahoans, the Forest Service also gained popularity because of its work to "open up" forested lands with trails, roads, and telephone lines. The *Statesman* reported in June 1907 that the Forest Service helped build a wagon road in Idaho County with an investment of $2,000, twice as much as that provided by the county. This "shows the service intends to make good" on its promises to "assist improvements in those sections embraced in reserves."[69] That same year, the Forest Service's W.E. Herring visited Boise, encouraging local boosters with the news that the agency would spend $10,000 in the area for 225 miles of roads and 35 miles of telephone lines.

Similar news came to nearly all areas of the state. To note a few examples, another 138 miles of trails were also started in 1907 in the Priest River National Forest at a cost of $5,200. In 1908 Frank Fenn asked for $35,000 for trails, telephone lines, bridges, and buildings in his Bitterroot National Forest, a request that more than doubled the 1907 budget of $17,000. The Twin Falls *News* reported in January 1909 that during the previous fiscal year, the Forest Service had built in Idaho 582 miles of trails, 118 miles of roads, and 187 miles of telephone lines. By 1913, $30,000 had been spent in the Salmon National

Forest. "By means of trails and telephones," the Salmon *Lemhi Herald* observed the following year, "the forestry bureau is opening up the wilderness to the westwards so that habitation in that country is not half lonesome."[70] At the end of the 1915 fire season, the Nez Perce National Forest, with headquarters in Grangeville, looked back with pride on what had been accomplished: 700 miles of trail, 264 miles of wagon road, and 240 miles of telephone lines.

Much of this work, of course, was done with the aim of assisting in fire protection and suppression, but it was welcomed by the public for the recreational possibilities. Thus, a 1913 headline in the *Statesman*—"Wonderland of the Payette to Be Opened to Boise Vacationists"—welcomed the construction of a road along the South Fork of the Payette River, from Banks east through Garden Valley and, eventually, on to Lowman. This provided a scenic route for motorists and, the *Statesman* reported, opened up fine grouse hunting and fishing for those wanting to get away from it all.[71]

Recreational use of the national forests was certainly not an afterthought. As early as February 1904, R.H. Charlton, a federal forest inspector, assured Pocatellans that hunting and camping would be allowed in the newly created Pocatello Forest Reserve. In fact, the whole reserve would "be managed in a manner so as to make it a great park or pleasure resort."[72] Campers were encouraged in all Idaho national forests, even when they came in such numbers that rangers found it hard to provide enough pasturage for horses. At Priest Lake, not only did the Forest Service issue a booklet with suggestions to make campers' visits easier, but also by 1912, it had set aside six hundred lots along the lake for "special use," that is, for vacation cottages. However, it would not be until the 1920s that the agency got into the vacation cottage business in a big way.

Forest Service personnel actively encouraged recreational use of the national forests. According to the Idaho Falls *Post*, "everything feasible" was "being done" to make visitors comfortable.[73] M.E. Benedict, supervisor of the Sawtooth National Forest, assured Boiseans that the Sawtooths were a "Big State Asset" with "several thousand tourists" visiting in 1916, perhaps doubling the number of the year before. The Forest Service had installed telephones every ten miles and put up good directional signage.[74] Large, colored maps were released for the Sawtooth National Forest in 1916 and the Boise National Forest in 1917. In short, as the *Wood River Times* expressed in May 1916, "the national forests are not 'reserved' with the idea of hoarding them up as a miser might," but were held "apart for use, not disuse."[75]

Quite clearly, the national forests were no longer seen as the creation of outside intruders. The Forest Service had succeeded in its efforts to gain acceptance in Idaho, but in the process, an idea had been planted that would come back to haunt it. Assuring local people that no "legitimate" interest need be sacrificed in conserving the forests was plausible enough in the first years of the century, when Idaho was barely beyond the frontier stage. But what would happen when more extensive development started forcing Forest Service planners to decide which uses should be enhanced at the expense of others?

Take, for example, the Selway National Forest. When split off from the Clearwater National Forest in 1911, it encompassed 1.8 million acres, twice the area of Rhode Island. It constituted, in the words of the Kooskia *Mountaineer*, "one of the most undeveloped regions in the whole United States," without a single town or village, and only one post office at Lowell. Without an accurate map or even a thorough field inspection of the whole area, it stood as "a storehouse of timber wealth, but at present" with "treasures…inaccessible."[76]

Under the circumstances, people might have entertained a wide variety of alternative scenarios for the fate of the Selway National Forest. It was not obvious at the time that some future uses would preclude others. But in less than a generation, choices would have to be made. When most of the Selway forest became a vast game preserve, and in 1936, a formally designated Primitive Area, it lost its possibilities as a "storehouse of timber wealth," to say nothing of a pastoral settlement as favored by Senator Heyburn. Conservation and wilderness preservation, in short, entailed far more challenging choices than Fenn and his colleagues realized when the national forests were first established in Idaho.

ENDNOTES

1. "Forest Reserves Information," Boise *Statesman* (August 7, 1907): p. 6.
2. 1905 *Use Book*, quoted in Harold K. Steen, *The U.S. Forest Service: A History* (Seattle: University of Washington Press, 1976): p. 79.
3. "Growth of the Lumber Business," editorial in Coeur d'Alene *Independent* (August 29, 1902): p. 4.
4. "Timber's Day Is Coming," editorial in Lewiston *Morning Tribune* (January 10, 1900): p. 4.
5. "Dawning of a New Era," St. Maries *Gazette* (May 12, 1903): p. 1.
6. "The Impending Reserve," editorial in Sandpoint *Pend d'Oreille Review* (January 25, 1906): p. 4.
7. "Not Right," editorial in Sandpoint *Pend d'Oreille Review* (February 1, 1906): p. 4.
8. "Forest Reserves," Boise *Statesman* (September 15, 1899): p. 3.
9. "In the Midst of Hisses and Cheers," Boise *Statesman* (September 5, 1906): pp. 1, 2.
10. "Forest Reserves in Senate," Lewiston *Morning Tribune* (January 30, 1906): pp. 1, 4.
11. "He Terms It Dead Country," Lewiston *Morning Tribune* (October 24, 1906): p. 6.
12. "The Waste of Timber," Idaho Falls *Idaho Register* (February 16, 1906): p. 4.
13. "Senator Heyburn," Twin Falls *News* (July 13, 1906): p. 4.
14. "Worse and Worse," editorial in Grangeville *Idaho County Free Press* (December 11, 1902): p. 2.
15. "Forest Service Is Criticized by Heyburn," Boise *Statesman* (March 8, 1910): p. 1.
16. "Another Forest Reserve," Sandpoint *Northern Idaho News* (January 26, 1906): p. 1.
17. "Want Reserve Lands," editorial in Coeur d'Alene *Press* (January 3, 1907): p. 2.
18. "Forest Reserve Methods," Lewiston *Morning Tribune* (May 16, 1904): p. 2.
19. "The Settlers Not the Timber Hog," editorial in Sandpoint *Pend d'Oreille Review* (July 11, 1907): p. 4.
20. "Extremity of Forest Bureaucrats," editorial in Lewiston *Morning Tribune* (January 20, 1906): p. 4.

21. "Forester Graves' Article," editorial in Sandpoint *Pend d'Oreille Review* (August 23, 1912): p. 2.
22. "Administration of Reserves Criticized," Boise *Statesman* (March 15, 1910): pp. 1, 4.
23. "Senator Wilson Confers with Sheepmen of Idaho," Pocatello *Tribune* (September 1, 1909): pp. 1, 6.
24. "Conserve, Not Reserve, the Natural Resources," editorial in Lewiston *Morning Tribune* (January 15, 1910): p. 4.
25. "Heyburn Attacks Forestry Service," Coeur d'Alene *Morning Journal* (May 7, 1908): p. 1.
26. "Cigarette Willies," Sandpoint *Pend d'Oreille Review* (March 8, 1906): p. 1.
27. "Forest Reserve Detriment," editorial reprinted in Coeur d'Alene *Morning Journal* (February 28, 1909): p. 2.
28. "Idaho Forest Reserve Infamy," editorial in Lewiston *Morning Tribune* (December 4, 1906): p. 4.
29. There is no full-scale biography of Frank Fenn. The best summary of the highlights of his life is by Neal Parsell, *Major Fenn's Country* (Kooskia, Idaho: Upper Clearwater-Lochsa-Selway Chamber of Commerce, n.d.).
30. "Forest Reserve Policy," Lewiston *Teller* (December 30, 1902): p. 1.
31. "Forest Reserve Policy," Lewiston *Teller* (December 30, 1902): p. 1.
32. "Some Points on Forest Reserves," quoted in Boise *Statesman* (February 10, 1907): p. 4.
33. "A Defense of the Reserves," Lewiston *Morning Tribune* (April 4, 1905): p. 3.
34. Long interview with Frank Fenn in "Forest Reserve," Boise *Statesman* (September 2, 1905): p. 3, reprinted in "Idaho Forest Reserves," Coeur d'Alene *Press* (September 9, 1905): p. 1.
35. "Major Fenn on Forest Reserves," Boise *Statesman* (August 1, 1906): p. 3, reprinted in Lewiston *Teller* (August 7, 1906): p. 3.
36. "Sheep Owners Are Called In," Boise *Statesman* (April 11, 1906): p. 6.
37. "The Stockmen Hear Major Fenn Talk!" Salmon *Idaho Recorder* (March 7, 1907): p. 1.
38. "Major Fenn," Salmon *Lemhi Herald* (March 7, 1907): p. 1.
39. James H. Hawley, *History of Idaho: The Gem of the Mountains* (Chicago: S.J. Clarke, 1920) I: p. 277.
40. "Resolution Disapproving Forest Reserve Administration," Boise *Statesman* (February 19, 1907): p. 2.
41. "Forest Reserves," editorial in Boise *Capital News* (February 19, 1907): p. 4.
42. "Commercial Club," Hailey *Wood River Times* (May 19, 1909): p. 1.
43. "Pinchot vs. Heyburn," editorial in Coeur d'Alene *Morning Journal* (July 11, 1907): p. 2.
44. Untitled editorial in St. Maries *Gazette* (June 28, 1907): p. 4.
45. "Interesting Debate on Forestry Problems," Lewiston *Evening Teller* (July 10, 1907): pp. 1, 5.
46. "Idaho Reserves Are Food for Thought," Boise *Statesman* (September 28, 1909): pp. 1, 3.
47. "Administration of Reserves Criticized," Boise *Statesman* (March 15, 1910): pp. 1, 4.
48. "Official Idaho and the National Government Bury Forestry Hatchet," Boise *Statesman* (September 6, 1905): p. 3.
49. "Pinchot's Policy," editorial in Coeur d'Alene *Press* (July 1, 1907): p. 2.
50. Quoted in "Want a Reserve," Boise *Statesman* (September 14, 1906): p. 4.
51. "Good Results to Follow Gifford Pinchot's Visit to Hailey," Hailey *Wood River Times* (September 20, 1906): p. 1.
52. "Pinchot Explains Policy," Boise *Statesman* (July 3, 1907): p. 3.
53. "Pinchot on Reserves," Coeur d'Alene *Press* (June 29, 1907): pp. 1, 6.
54. "Pinchot and Forest Reserves," editorial in Coeur d'Alene *Morning Journal* (June 30, 1907): p. 4.
55. "Debate on Forest Reserves Held in the Senate," Boise *Statesman* (February 28, 1907): p. 3.
56. "Talks on Forest Reserve Rules," Salmon *Lemhi Herald* (March 7, 1907): p. 1.
57. "Forest Reserves," editorial in Grangeville *Standard-News* (August 13, 1908): p. 2.
58. "Pure Water Supply," editorial in Pocatello *Tribune* (May 28, 1910): p. 4.
59. Untitled story in Twin Falls *News* (September 1, 1905): p. 1.
60. "Forest Reserves," editorial in Boise *Statesman* (November 23, 1906): p. 4.
61. "Forest Reserves," editorial in Boise *Statesman* (February 19, 1907): p. 4.
62. Gooding quoted in "Sheep in the Sawtooth Forest," Hailey *Wood River Times* (November 17, 1908): p. 1.

63. Darrah quoted in Victor O. Goodwin and John A. Hussey, *Sawtooth Mountain Area Study, Idaho: History* (N.p.: U.S. Forest Service and National Park Service, 1965): pp. 68–69.
64. "Conservation in the West," editorial in Pocatello *Tribune* (August 14, 1909): p. 2.
65. "Timber Lands Great Asset of State," Boise *Statesman* (October 27, 1909): pp. 5, 6.
66. Quoted in William L. Graf, *Wilderness Preservation and the Sagebrush Rebellion* (Savage, Md.: Rowman and Littlefield, 1996): p. 69.
67. Coeur d'Alene *Press* (February 11, 1913): p. 2.
68. Grangeville *Globe* (May 21, 1914): p. 1.
69. "Forest Service Assists," editorial in Boise *Statesman* (June 16, 1907): p. 12.
70. "Improvements in the Forest," Salmon *Lemhi Herald* (September 18, 1914): p. 1.
71. Boise *Statesman* (August 17, 1913): p. 5.
72. "The Pocatello Forest Reserve a Great Park," Pocatello *Tribune* (February 23, 1904): p. 1.
73. "Recreation in the Forests," Idaho Falls *Post* (June 12, 1916): p. 8.
74. Boise *Statesman* (October 22, 1916): Section 2, pp. 1, 4.
75. "Summer Homes for Everyone," Hailey *Wood River Times* (May 4, 1916): p. 1.
76. "Trip of Inspection through Selway Forest," Kooskia *Mountaineer* (August 25, 1911): p. 1.

II

The Dawn of Wildlife Conservation

THE FATE OF WILDERNESS AREAS in Idaho would be shaped primarily by two forces, the policies of the U.S. Forest Service and the concerns of sportsmen throughout the state. The national forests encompassed large sections of Idaho that eventually would become wilderness areas. And sportsmen, the only organized, vocal force for conservation in Idaho until the late 1960s (the Idaho Conservation League dates back only to 1974), assured local acceptance of those wilderness areas when they received formal designation.

All of this came about after the turn of the twentieth century. In 1900 little more local concern was shown for wildlife conservation than for forest conservation. The Idaho legislature created the position of State Game Warden in the spring of 1899, but initially there was little effective enforcement. Prior to taking office as the first warden, Charles Arbuckle reported, "public sentiment seemed largely against the punishment of offenders, and convictions were almost impossible even for the most flagrant violations."[1] The fact that Arbuckle's first annual budget amounted to only $300 suggested that serious doubts remained about the importance or effectiveness of his office.

On the other hand, indiscriminate slaughter of deer, elk, and other game animals already had raised fears that they would be wiped out. Reporting on widespread complaints about the lack of game law enforcement, the Boise *Statesman* concluded in August 1901 that unless this changed, "fishing and hunting will sooner or later be a thing of the past."[2] Two years later, in his annual message to the legislature, Governor Frank Hunt declared the game warden system a "failure," and recommended game law enforcement be left to the county sheriffs, so sportsmen would know who was in charge.[3]

Forest rangers took an active interest in helping Idaho to conserve wildlife as well as its timber and rangeland. In January 1903, Major Fenn wrote to the *Statesman* from Kooskia, heartily seconding its editorial favoring the creation of game licenses. Fenn lamented the presence of out-of-state hunters "ruthlessly and wantonly" slaughtering elk in the Bitterroot Forest Reserve to support a thriving national market for elk teeth. He believed that requiring hunting licenses, along with designating rangers as deputy game wardens, could put a stop to these "vandals."[4]

State officials did deputize forest rangers to help enforce the game laws, and the legislature passed a hunting license law, but for the moment they did not respond to another suggestion from Fenn: "the Bitter Root forest reserve, naturally the home of the largest game extant, may easily become a magnificent game preserve where legitimate sport may be indulged indefinitely."[5] At the time, game preserves did not exist in Idaho and nearby states, and they initially raised local fears about federal controls comparable to those about the creation of national forests.

Not surprisingly, there was a strongly negative public reaction to a report at the end of 1905 that the game wardens of Idaho and Montana were planning to meet in Butte and discuss the possibility of designating the entire Bitterroot National Forest as a game preserve. Fenn thought it a great idea, of course, but the Grangeville *News* probably spoke for most Idahoans in denouncing the whole idea as "thoroughly at variance with the principles of equality among men," and "aping the methods of aristocratic England."[6] The Lewiston *Morning Tribune* believed "the whole suggestion is so contemptible that it cannot be discussed with patience."[7] In any case, Idaho's game warden quickly denied having any such talks with his Montana counterpart. He admitted that the Bitterroots would make "an ideal game refuge," but noted, "there is a prevalent opinion that there are enough reserves in this state."[8] Chalk one up for Senator Heyburn and his cohorts.

Interestingly, barely three years later the legislature passed HB 242, setting aside 220,000 acres in the Boise National Forest—covering the headwaters of the South Fork of the Payette River on the Sawtooths' western slope—as Idaho's first game preserve. Admittedly, it encompassed far less land than the four million acres of the Bitterroot National Forest, and it was in the southern rather than the northern part of the state. Nevertheless, it passed with virtually no press coverage and brought no public protest.

How did this happen? Emile Grandjean, then supervisor of the Boise National Forest, claimed that he just went and did it. "Realizing the necessity of the further protection of our game animals throughout the Forest, and since the State Game Warden did not enforce the laws, [I] drew up and caused to be introduced" the bill and then lobbied it through both legislative houses.[9]

Actually, the reasons for this success were far more complicated than simply attributing it to the pluck and luck of one forest ranger. The state's whole temper had changed since 1905, and there emerged, by March 1909 when HB 242 became law, a widespread and growing concern for game preservation. Specifically, the fate of elk awakened Idahoans to the overall need for wildlife conservation, and not just for some recognition of the charms of wild animals in general, or even a desire to maintain huntable herds of major game species.

In the first decade of the 1900s, there were growing reports that the remaining elk herds, particularly those centered in Yellowstone National Park, were suffering on inadequate rangelands and dying in terrible numbers each winter. In the fall of 1907, Governor Frank Gooding suggested that Idaho might create a "game park" near St. Anthony (an easy migratory distance from Yellowstone). It would be, in the opinion of Chief Deputy Game Warden Livingston, "a natural range for the elk,"[10] and the idea received favorable coverage from newspapers in Pocatello, Boise, and Lewiston.

Nothing ultimately came of Gooding's idea, but it inspired Pocatello to push ahead with something similar. "What's the matter," asked Forest Supervisor Peter Wrenstead, "with our trying to get something of the kind in the Pocatello national forest?"[11] It might be located, he suggested, within a half-mile of the city's limits and become a tourist attraction. Such was not to be the case. It took Pocatello over a decade to obtain shipments of elk to stock what, in 1919, the Idaho legislature declared to be a game preserve, and, despite early assurances by local observers to the contrary, the elk never really thrived in the Pocatello National Forest. Nor did their presence generate any substantial tourist visitation.

Nevertheless, Pocatello played a major role in alerting sportsmen throughout the state to the need for additional elk habitat. The Pocatello Elks Lodge (BPOE) started pressing for public acquisition of ranch lands near Jackson, Wyoming, for elk range. The Pocatello *Tribune* repeatedly sounded the alarm that "Elk Starve in the Park," citing in April 1911, "evidence of frightful mortality," with 500 carcasses reportedly in the Gardner River.[12] Such stories contributed to the formation that same spring of the National Association for Preservation of the Elk, headquartered in Washington, D.C., which urged BPOE lodges throughout the country to aid in the cause. Lodges in southern Idaho promptly did so at a joint meeting in Pocatello in mid-May. Typical of many such game preservation issues that arose later, those fearing for the welfare of elk refused to listen to any official reports gainsaying the alarm. Thus, the Pocatello *Tribune* only dutifully noted a July 1911 USDA Biological Survey report that elk conditions in Yellowstone were fairly decent, but clearly relished passing along two weeks later the observations of T. Nick McCoy, a rancher in Jackson, that there was "Fearful Mortality among Wyoming Elk."[13]

Whatever the objective facts might have been regarding Yellowstone elk, Idahoans' fears mobilized sportsmen to help the game warden secure trainloads of elk for transplanting in national forests throughout the southern half of the state. For example, in 1915 a train carload went to Black Lake near Council, and in 1918 another carload was freed near Arrowrock Dam. The government had no funds to pay for transportation costs or the necessary staff to oversee the program. Consequently, local sportsmen had to band together, raise money to get the elk to their area, and then oversee care and feeding until the animals could be released into the local wilds. The Pocatello *Tribune* announced in March 1916 the arrival of seventeen "perfectly good and active young elk," which would be fed for several weeks in a local stockyard.[14] The next year's batch of elk was too large to be transported into the forests, so the animals were directed through "a cordon of machines and men" from the stockyard and uphill to find their own way into the wilds.[15]

The tasks related to elk preservation stimulated a whole new interest in local sportsmen's organizations in Idaho. In December 1920, some twenty-five sportsmen met at the Pocatello Chamber of Commerce to organize a permanent group. At least some of those present probably had been in the "cordon" that directed the elk out of town in 1916.

Sportsmen's organizations in Idaho prior to about 1920 generally focused on their own pleasure outing goals, rather than on any serious concern for game preservation. Ephemeral exceptions might be found here and there, however, such as the Hailey Sportsmen's Club, which was organized in June 1902 to hire a private game warden. More typical was the Idaho Sportsmen's Association, formed in Boise in 1906 to promote trapshooting and "good fellow-ship."[16] It gave some thought in 1912 to a project to develop habitat for game birds, but as late as May 1920, according to Game Warden Otto Jones, the association "has merely been a figurehead…interested…in trap shooting" and meeting only annually.[17] An example of a somewhat more ambitious undertaking came with a club announced in September 1908 in Idaho Falls. This group, limited to one-hundred individuals, bought 480 acres near Sand Hole Lake at Hamer, forty miles northwest of Idaho Falls, "for exclusive hunting privilege," with a clubhouse and houseboats.[18]

In sharp contrast, sportsmen in the following decade organized to assure the existence of, and continued access to, wild game rather than to form exclusive clubs. In 1915 the Twin Falls *Times* called for "some drastic legislation" to prevent "every bit of ground along beautiful streams and lakes of the state" from being "gobbled up by people living outside the state."[19] In 1919 the Idaho Falls *Post* urged "every possible means of preservation," including local sportsmen's organizations, to prevent the rapid extermination of wild game.[20] The Wood River Fish and Game Club formed in December 1919, "to propagate, preserve, and protect fish and game."[21] A month later, the club voted to wire the state game warden that it would take responsibility for receiving twenty elk for the Hailey area.

By 1920 sportsmen strongly supported creating game preserves to assist in game preservation. Thus, the Pend d'Oreille Fish and Game Protective Association held its organizational meeting in Sandpoint on August 25, 1919, with the aim of helping to enforce game laws and having "this section placed

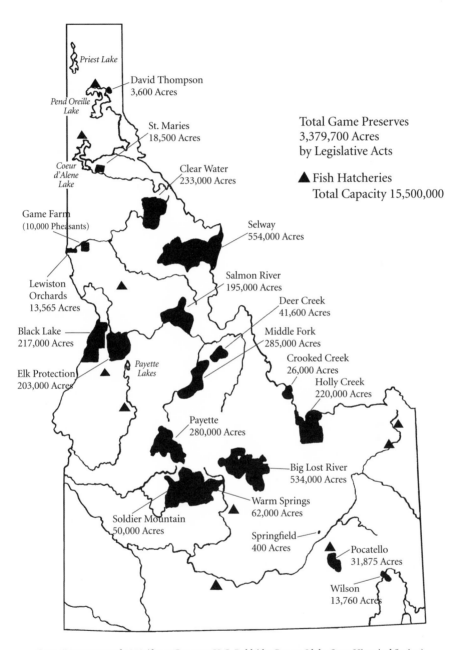

Game Preserves as of 1930 (from *Governor H.C. Baldridge Papers, Idaho State Historical Society*)

within the bounds of state, and afterward, of federal game preserves."[22] Long gone was the time when a game preserve seemed to be an "aristocratic" aberration. In 1917 alone, the legislature enacted laws protecting wild game in the Big Creek area northeast of McCall, along the Big Lost River near Mackay, and in the Selway area of Idaho County. At the same time, Lemhi County legislators and state game officials pressed for preserves in the Chamberlain Basin and along the Middle Fork of the Salmon River (major parts of what became, in 1930, the Idaho Primitive Area). By 1923, according to a report published in the Idaho Falls *Times-Register*, Idaho had 776,650 acres of national forest lands in game preserves. Although less than its neighbors—Wyoming had 929,983 acres and Utah 4,539,131 acres—it marked a major change in the thinking of Idahoans.

It is important to note, however, that these "wild game" measures encompassed only a few species of wild animals. In just a few cases, such as the Lewiston Orchards Game Preserve, enacted in 1915, were efforts focused primarily on preserving pheasants, ducks, geese, quail, and other birds popular with hunters. In most cases, therefore, sportsmen's talk about "wild game" meant big game—elk, deer, antelope, moose, mountain goats, and mountain sheep. These species were included in the big game censuses that began to be kept about 1915. A handful of other species, such as bear and beaver, were protected by game laws, but excluded from the censuses and from most sportsmen's concerns for wildlife protection.

Consequently a majority of the animals making up the wild kingdom were left out. In other words, support for game preservation went only a short way along the road toward an environmentally informed interest in a full range of wildlife conservation. Sportsmen did, at least prior to about 1920, limit the season and bag limits for a few species, with the explicit intention of assuring the continued existence of those same species. They did not, however, seriously focus on the preservation (or for that matter, the elimination) of many other, mainly smaller, species.

Thus, Frank Kendall asserted in the Game Warden Report for 1911–12 that "in every human being exists to a greater or lesser extent, the instinct to hunt and kill," and "just a few years ago in Idaho, men killed without discrimination and manifested [an] innate desire for conquest." But now, "the true sportsman" has a "horror of killing wantonly."[23] Clearly this applied only to elk, deer, and other large game. As for rabbits, coyotes, and other "varmints" (i.e., animals commonly seen as undesirable), no such restraints applied. Farmers and ranchers killed them as frequently as they could, and sportsmen occasionally indulged their taste for a mass killing. In November 1903, for example, the *Statesman* announced the formation of the Cross Country Hunt Club. Intending "To Exterminate Wild 'Varmints,'" the members would assemble on a ranch near Boise without firearms, drive coyotes, wildcats, foxes, jackrabbits, and other unwanted wild animals into a small space and club them to death.[24]

However, only rarely and spasmodically, at least prior to 1920, did sportsmen declare war on predators. In early 1916, the Lapwai Gun Club, along with Lewiston area farmers, announced the intention to exterminate magpies, along with hawks, coyotes, crows, and "other birds and animals that prey upon the game birds and the farmers' poultry."[25] But this was an exception. Although the 1907 legislature authorized the extermination of wolves, coyotes, wildcats, and cougars, Fish and Game officials had neither the budget nor, one suspects, the popular mandate to make any serious effort to follow through on that authorization.

But a new era was about to begin. In 1915, in response to pressures from agricultural interests, Congress began appropriations for systematic hunting and killing of all varieties of predators that preyed upon domestic livestock. The Department of Agriculture's Bureau of Biological Survey (the forerunner of what later became the Fish and Wildlife Service) took charge of this assignment. Idaho initially received $15,000. Luther J. Goldman, based in Pocatello, began hiring government hunters.

The government would not encourage killing of bears, the Kooskia *Mountaineer* reported, "unless they get to killing stock," but Goldman asked hunters to report any depredations of "coyotes, cougars, lynx, etc."[26] By the end of 1918, Goldman had thirty hunters on his payroll, who had shot and trapped a total of 3,502 predators: 2,807 coyotes, 8 wolves, 1 mountain lion, 344 bobcats, and 2 bears. Many others were presumed to have died from poisons placed in the wilds to kill predators.

The 1920s would see significant changes in attitudes about wildlife in Idaho, which, in turn, would lead to different policies. The resulting story of game preservation efforts will be addressed in Chapter IV, while the war on "varmints" will be recounted in Chapter V.

ENDNOTES

1. "First Biennial Report of the State Fish and Game Warden" (1900), unpaged.
2. "The Game Law," editorial in Boise *Statesman* (August 24, 1901): p. 4.
3. "Message of the Governor," Boise *Statesman* (January 7, 1903): p. 6.
4. "For Protection of the Game," Boise *Statesman* (January 30, 1903): p. 6.
5. *Ibid.*
6. "Proposed Game Preserves," editorial in Grangeville *News* (January 20, 1906): p. 4.
7. "The Idaho Game Preserve," editorial in Lewiston *Morning Tribune* (November 29, 1905): p. 4.
8. "Game Refuge Story a Myth," Boise *Statesman* (January 1, 1906): p. 5.
9. Grandjean quoted in Gordon S. Bowen, *Grandjean: Man of the Forests* (Boise: privately printed, 1987), pp. 33–35.
10. "Protection of Elk Proposed," Boise *Statesman* (October 21, 1907): p. 8.
11. "Game Park near Town," Pocatello *Tribune* (January 15, 1908): p. 1.
12. "Elk Starve in the Park," Pocatello *Tribune* (April 27, 1911): p. 1.
13. "Fearful Mortality among Wyoming Elk," Pocatello *Tribune* (July 27, 1911): p. 2.

14. "Young Elk Arrived in Good Shape," Pocatello *Tribune* (March 3, 1916): p. 1.
15. "Young Elk Turned Loose for the Hills Sunday Afternoon," Pocatello *Tribune* (March 31, 1917): p. 2.
16. W.C. Tatro, "The Idaho State Sportsmen's Association—Its Objects and Aims," *Idaho Fish and Game* (June 1914): pp. 4–5.
17. "Idaho Sportsmen May Reorganize," Boise *Statesman* (May 29, 1920): p. 6.
18. "Fishing and Hunting Club," Idaho Falls *Idaho Register* (September 29, 1908): p. 1.
19. "Pre-empting the State's Scenic Spots," editorial in Twin Falls *Times* (August 6, 1915): p. 2.
20. "Game in Vast Region of West Rapidly Being Exterminated," Idaho Falls *Post* (December 16, 1919): p. 3.
21. "Fish and Game Club Formed," Hailey *Wood River-News-Miner* (December 8, 1919): p. 1.
22. "Sportsmen of Bonner County to Organize for Protection," Sandpoint *Pend d'Oreille Review* (August 15, 1919): p. 7.
23. "Fourth Biennial Report of the Fish and Game Warden of the State Of Idaho, 1911–1912," pp. 5, 12–13.
24. "To Exterminate Wild 'Varmints,'" Boise *Statesman* (November 11, 1903): p. 6.
25. "War on Magpies," Lewiston *Morning Tribune* (March 1, 1916): p. 5.
26. "Government Will Take Part," Kooskia *Mountaineer* (December 9, 1915): p. 1.

III

The Early Years of Scenic Preservation

T
HE IRONIES AND CONTRADICTIONS of Idahoans' attitudes toward the most scenic areas of their state, and their initial efforts at conserving some portion of that heritage, might be symbolized in the fact that they aborted the first (and for many years the only) national park proposal in Idaho in favor of a major irrigation project. Even more telling, they commonly refused even to admit that they were sacrificing scenic preservation for economic development.

Few people at the time found anything wrong with Governor Frank Steunenberg's rationale for requesting the abandonment of the proposed Shoshone Falls National Park. Writing to the secretary of the interior in October 1900, Steunenberg claimed that the public, in supporting the proposal for a national park, was unaware of the Twin Falls Land and Water Company's plans for irrigating a great swath of land along the Snake River. "The proposed park," according to the governor, "would take some 50,000 acres right out of the heart of the tract" and thereby "defeat" the whole project. Given this turn of events, "everybody is agreed that the park should not be established." After all:

> It is inconceivable that the grandeur of the scenery immediately along the river could be materially improved or perpetuated by any thing the government might do in connection with a national park… On the other hand, under a system of irrigation, the arid plain can be converted into homes for thousands of our citizens, and alfalfa fields and orchards can be made to flourish to the very rim of the great canyon, forming a contrast between the quiet beauty of highly cultivated farms and the rugged grandeur of the canyon that can be rarely seen.[1]

In short, Idahoans could have their cake and eat it, too. Only slowly and reluctantly did they concede that the irrigation development reduced the flow of water to a mere trickle over Shoshone Falls except for a few weeks each year.

Now only a few miles northeast of the city of Twin Falls, Shoshone Falls was a major scenic attraction even in the days when pioneers struggled along the Oregon Trail.[2] Particularly before irrigation enabled the conversion of much of south central Idaho from a sagebrush desert into farmlands, observers were struck by the contrast between this huge waterfall and its barren surroundings. As one reporter phrased it in 1889, "never anywhere else was so beautiful a picture hung in so rude a frame; never anywhere else on a background so forbidding and weird, were so many glories clustered."[3]

It took no great imagination for enterprising entrepreneurs to see Shoshone Falls—this "Niagara of the West" that was actually higher than its namesake—as a place where a resort might be developed. As early as 1883, the Boise *Statesman* reported that plans were afoot for a "grand hotel" to be built on the edge of the falls.[4] By 1890 a syndicate based in Butte, Montana, and Omaha, Nebraska, had acquired title to the land around the falls and planned to spend substantial sums enhancing its tourist appeal.

At the same time, and rather surprisingly in view of the prevailing belief that private capital ought to exploit undeveloped resources as soon as possible, a movement was already surfacing to save Shoshone Falls by designating it a park. In March 1891, the *Statesman* raised the question, "Does the State Own the Falls?" If so, it could take control and "convert it into a grand State park."[5] Responding to the obvious question of costs, the editor denied any immediate need for great expenditures. "Preserving the surroundings in as near a state of nature as possible" was the first and most important task.[6]

Briefly it seemed like the park might actually be created and the falls preserved in all its original splendor. But the brand-new state was in no position to act. Having just been created in July 1890, Idaho had far more basic concerns, such as the complete lack of any year-round road connecting the northern and southern parts of the state. But its congressional delegation found a receptive audience in the national capital. Without any local opposition (Idahoans in the 1890s apparently seeing no competing uses for the land around the falls), plans for a park moved along quietly and smoothly. In August 1900, the General Land Office announced that it was withdrawing four townships (92,160 acres) around Shoshone Falls for a national park. "This is only a beginning," Hailey's *Wood River Times* jubilantly predicted; eventually the park would expand to reach up the Wood River and over Galena Summit to encompass Redfish Lake. In other words, what started at Shoshone Falls would end up in the Sawtooths.[7]

Only two months later it was all over when, as already noted above, the governor stepped in, requesting federal authorities to leave it alone. In February 1901, the Land Office's M.A. Meyerhoff visited the site and recommended in favor of reclamation rather than park designation, and the withdrawal order was revoked.

The free flowing days of the Snake River and Shoshone Falls soon ceased. In late 1903, wealthy entrepreneur W.A. Clark (also a U.S. senator from Montana) announced plans for a $1.5 million dam and power plant at the falls. He declared that "the beauty of Shoshone Falls which has excited the admiration of countless numbers of people will not be disturbed."[8] Amazingly enough, his assurances bore out; the dam does not significantly interfere with the fall's visual impact. However, when the gates of the new Milner Dam (located a few miles upriver) closed in 1905, the river went completely dry for twelve hours and flowed thereafter at full force only during the spring runoff. Milner Dam made possible irrigation of such a large area, and so dramatically changed the appearance of south central Idaho, that the area soon became known as the Magic Valley (a sobriquet it has carried ever since). But it also spelled the end of Shoshone Falls as an untrammeled natural wonder.

Nevertheless, hopes for some kind of park lingered on. In 1909 the legislature appropriated $2,000 for a park at the falls, provided Twin Falls County contributed a matching sum. The county met that requirement, but improvements at the park crept along for the next decade. Some lawn and trees were planted, and a small herd of deer was established. But in 1915, fire destroyed the Shoshone Falls Hotel with its dancing pavilion, and no replacement was planned. At the end of World War I, the people of Twin Falls decided to renovate the park as a war memorial. The idea was to raise $200,000, including a state grant of $50,000, but the 1919 legislature appropriated only $10,000, and fund-raising efforts proved equally disappointing, so the whole project was cancelled in December 1920.

The final effort to achieve a large-scale Shoshone Falls park came in 1924 when F.J. Adams (who had married Senator Clark's daughter and, therefore, was the major landowner around the falls) sent Arthur Carhart to study the possibilities. Carhart, at the time a landscape architect in Denver, is now recognized as one of the intellectual founders of the wilderness movement in America. In the late 1910s while with the Forest Service, he had campaigned for the first Primitive Areas in the United States. Alas, Carhart apparently saw little to work with at Shoshone Falls, although he admitted that the falls still had impact, "even now with the waters pouring over them only a fraction of the flow which formerly went over."[9] Nothing further was heard about a Carhart plan, and the park became what it remains today, a pleasant, local picnic grounds with, a few weeks a year, a huge waterfall.

Local boosters thought they might yet retrieve Shoshone Falls as a major tourist attraction by following the lead of Niagara Falls and installing dramatic night-lighting. In cooperation with F.J. Adams and the Idaho Power Company, local enthusiasts in late spring 1928 spent a sizeable sum, reported to be $12,000, to install floodlights (producing twenty-five million candlepower). On May 24, the switches were thrown, and a crowd numbering 5,000 oohed and ahhed. "It is a sight to stir the soul of the dullest man," the *Statesman* assured its readers; "It is awe-inspiring, impelling, frightening, stirring."[10] Boosters predicted that it would become "a drawing card for every town in the Snake river valley," because, just as surely as at Niagara Falls, it would at-tract hundreds of thousands of visitors.[11] They sent out promotional photos far and wide; newspapers throughout Idaho, at least, published them, from Pocatello and Idaho Falls to Lewiston and Coeur d'Alene.

But it was unsuccessful. For some reason, the floodlighted falls did not bring the projected crowds of sightseers. Perhaps the editor of the Twin Falls *News* put his finger on the problem when he reflected a few years earlier on the unusually heavy flow over the Falls: "take a good look and then a second, because Shoshone Falls will very shortly disappear for good and all… And that fact begets an uneasy, unhappy sort of feeling as though development somehow has stolen a march upon Twin Falls County and there isn't much of anybody to blame."[12]

As we have seen in the case of Shoshone Falls, Idahoans had highly con-flicting ideas about scenic preservation. On the one hand, they hated to lose any opportunity to profit from development of the state's natural resources, but on the other hand, they had a nagging sense that they really ought to preserve some of the best of the state's scenery and, just maybe, could make a profit at the same time.

Two editorials appearing in the *Statesman* in 1911 clearly expressed these differing motives. The first, published on February 15, expostulated: "And Now It's 'Conservation' of Scenery—What Next?" "Of course we love our scenery," the writer conceded while reflecting on a Colorado court decision, "but there are millions of square miles of scenery in the northwest." While we enjoy scenery "at rare intervals…we must have every moment of the day" electric power (or water for irrigation, he might have added, as in the case of Shoshone Falls).[13] On June 23, the editor returned to the subject with the thought that "there should be some common ground upon which the in-dustrial and the beautiful could meet." In his opinion, "Idaho cannot afford to convert her scenery into coin, nor can she afford to have progressiveness stifled by the hand of an immoderate asceticism."[14]

Presumably, an example of "immoderate asceticism" would have been to ban Milner Dam and thwart the irrigation of Magic Valley to save the full splendor of Shoshone Falls. Fortunately for Idahoans of the early twentieth century, the choices were not always so Manichean. In 1909 the legislature passed three bills aimed at scenic preservation—by creating parks, the only means that legislators at the time could think of to save choice bits of Idaho terrain. In addition to the appropriation of $2,000 for Shoshone Falls Park, legislators earmarked $15,000 for Heyburn Park on the same day. Those bills were preceded three days earlier by an authorization for the State Land Board to set aside acreage for a state park on Payette Lake in McCall. Together, the legislative acts set Idaho on the road toward scenic preservation, although in ways quite different from what legislators might have expected.

Heyburn Park, encompassing 7,825 acres along Lake Chatcolet at the southern end of Lake Coeur d'Alene, was not only Idaho's, but the Northwest's, first state park. In 1907, Senator Weldon Heyburn originally had proposed setting aside as a national park a popular camping and boating area on the northern edge of the Coeur d'Alene Indian Reservation. Summer recreationists feared that, with the opening of the reservation to settlement, the area would be lost for public use. As State Senator Jerome Day from Moscow put it when urging state funding in 1911, the danger was that unless a park held "the shoreline open to Idaho residents," it would be lined by summer cottages and the timber all logged off.[15]

Although Heyburn finally succeeded in gaining federal authorization to withdraw the land for park use, there seemed no likelihood that Congress would appropriate any money for its development. Consequently, he turned to the state, which agreed in 1909 to commit $15,000 from the Fish and Game Fund—$12,000 to purchase the land, and the remainder for improvements. Since the Fish and Game Fund did not have sufficient balances to pay this commitment, the 1911 legislature then appropriated $12,000 from the General Fund, to be repaid at $3,000 per year from the Fish and Game account. Regarding funds for development, there were "several hundred millions of feet" of mature timber, Governor Hawley reported after visiting the new park in the summer of 1911, ready to "be cut without working any injury to the park as a pleasure resort."[16]

Over the next several years, the Heyburn Park Commission built roads to and through the park, expanded camping and docking facilities, and provided for a growing number of houseboats, funded by selectively logging portions of the parkland. Although legislators from northern Idaho expressed fears that this would "strip the park entirely of timber," the state game warden (who had administrative charge of the park) dismissed these concerns as groundless.[17]

Finally, in mid-1920, the state asked a group of foresters from the University of Idaho to evaluate the timber, develop a plan for the management of Heyburn Park's recreational facilities and forests, and recommend sources of income to maintain the park. The public was assured that "every effort will be made to preserve the scenic value of the lake front."[18] Nothing was said about the park's scenic integrity as a whole.

Today, Heyburn State Park remains as an attractive natural setting for boaters, hikers, and campers, and it preserves public access to an extensive shoreline. However, as a monument to scenic preservation, it is almost as compromised as Shoshone Falls Park. The land was not completely logged off, as some local supporters had feared, but, to quote a guidebook published in 1989, "the woods that once boasted stands of western white pine, now contain but a few specimens" of that tree so attractive to loggers.[19] Neither local or state parks, it turns out, have been particularly important as ways to preserve the most notable aspects of Idaho's scenery. A few exceptions exist, to be sure, such as Coeur d'Alene's Tubbs Hill (1968) at the local level, and Bruneau Dunes (1967) and Harriman Ranch (1977) among the state parks. But, as the case of Payette Lakes makes clear, successful expressions of public concern for scenic preservation usually found other forms than the establishment and maintenance of parks.

Payette Lake (5,000 acres) and nearby Little Payette Lake (1,450 acres), some one-hundred miles north of Boise, have been a favorite recreation area for people in the Boise Valley throughout the twentieth century. The *Statesman* in May 1900 described this location as "one of the most beautiful spots in Idaho, with magnificent scenery, trout fishing and game of every description—an ideal outing place."[20] This assessment (which could be republished a century later without any significant change) introduced the announcement that Thomas McCall had opened a three-story, twenty-room hotel, a development that eventually led to the surrounding town being redesignated McCall (Lardo was the original name). The beauties of the Payette Lakes derived both from the area's surrounding forests and its relatively high elevation. Most large bodies of water in southern Idaho are reservoirs with few trees, while the lakes of northern Idaho (with three being far larger than the Payette Lakes) have elevations of about 2,000 to 2,500 feet, contrasted to McCall's 5,000 feet elevation. On the other hand, the hundreds of alpine lakes in central and southern Idaho are far smaller than Big Payette Lake. Summer outings to McCall, in short, offered both beautiful surroundings and cooler temperatures.

The importance of the Payette Lakes here, is the fact that preserving their scenic attractions became a persistent political issue. The legislature passed a law on February 25, 1925, declaring as a matter of public policy, "preservation of said lake in its present condition as a health resort and recreation place…to be a more necessary use than…as a storage reservoir for irrigation or power purposes."[21] To insure protection, the legislature vested in the governor the authority to hold in trust for the people of Idaho all unappropriated waters of Big Payette Lake. In other words, for the first time in Idaho history, the state officially declared scenic preservation a higher value than economic development. Thus, the Payette Lakes were saved from the fate analogous of Shoshone Falls, and, on a broader front, scenic preservation was determined to be, as a matter of public policy, the highest and best use for at least some parts of Idaho.

This did not come easily. Only after twenty years of public controversy did the legislature enact the 1925 law. Initially, some thought the Payette Lakes, or at least the adjacent lands owned by the state, should be declared a state park. The local *Long Valley Advocate* first made the pitch in January 1905. The expectation of railroad service by way of New Meadows raised fears of logging off the tall timber surrounding the lake. "With the threatened destruction of our immense bodies of timber, and the rapid settlement of the state," the editor urged "a strong and early effort…to preserve at least one of our most beautiful spots while it is possible to do so."[22]

The Boise *Statesman* reprinted the *Advocate*'s editorial and added one of its own in support: "Such a park would be of inestimable value to the state." With the arrival of rail service to McCall, "it will become one of the famed resorts of the continent."[23] In terrible contrast, according to the *Advocate*, allowing the area to be logged "would be like converting an Eden into a Kalahari desert." Why, "the very thought of such ruthless destruction makes one feel depressed."[24]

However, state legislators and respected attorneys, such as the young William Borah, responded with the strictest interpretation of the law. The state lands around the lakes were dedicated to the support of schools and could not, they believed, be used for parks or any other purpose. On the other hand, some compromise was possible. Instead of selling off the land to logging companies, it could be subdivided and leased for recreational cottages. The *Statesman* in November 1906 expressed the hope that cottage lot rental fees might be used to maintain a park, but state officials showed no inclination to pursue that option. In March 1907, Albert Freehafer of Council and George Barry of Sweet introduced into the senate a resolution directing the State Land Board "not to sell or otherwise dispose of any part of" the lands "within two miles of said Payette Lakes," but nothing came of this effort at this time.[25] Two years later, however, the legislature *did* pass, along with funding for the Shoshone Falls and Heyburn parks, authorization for the Land Board to withdraw property for park purposes, but the board took no immediate action on what, some fifty years later, finally became Ponderosa State Park.

In any case, the cottage lot-leasing scheme served as something of a holding action. On May 25, 1908, the same day that plans were announced to plat the first one hundred lots, Boiseans learned that they could get to McCall in one day, leaving at 7 A.M. on "the Pony" (a shuttle train to Weiser), transferring to the P.I.N. for a scenic rail journey to New Meadows, and then motoring on to McCall, arriving at 8 P.M. Scarcely an inviting itinerary, now that today it takes only a couple of hours to drive, but this "Through Service to the Lakes," as the *Statesman* billed it,[26] augured the beginning of the Payette Lakes as a readily accessible summer resort area. The following January, the Boise *Capital News* reported that plans were well advanced for bus service from Weiser to New Meadows and McCall. Thus, by the time railroad service came close enough to McCall to make logging economically feasible, recreational development already was a viable financial alternative.

Lot development, however, immediately brought another threat to the area's scenic preservation. In the summer of 1908, the Land Board came up with the idea of constructing a boulevard connecting the lots and circling the lakes. Possibly because it would be the least expensive route, state officials proposed running the boulevard along the beach. The cottage dwellers thought that a terrible idea and pressed F.A. Tollman, Boise's city engineer, to take a look. He concluded that the road should run to the rear of the beachfront lots, since it would be used by ranchers moving their cattle and produce a great deal of dust.

This issue was preempted by another, far graver threat to the lake's scenic integrity when a virtual bombshell landed in July 1908 in the form of a telegram from the Interior secretary, declaring that the Reclamation Service planned to use the lakes for a "conservation reservoir." A dam would be built that would raise the water level by fifteen feet. Not only would that require resurveying the lots for the beachfront cottages, but it would also wipe out most of the existing beaches and drown the shoreline trees. No further news was forthcoming about converting the Payette Lakes into an irrigation reservoir for two years, however, until the *Capital News* reported that the Black Canyon Irrigation District had voted an assessment of $38,500 on its users for ditches and a dam at Payette Lakes.

Initial skirmishing began the following year when the district approached the State Land Board in May 1911 with a formal proposal to use Payette Lakes as a reservoir, raising the water level by twenty feet to irrigate ninety thousand acres near Emmett. In reporting the proposal, the Boise *Statesman* asserted that this would destroy the lakes' beauty, and "all thought of a pleasure resort there would have to be abandoned."[27]

James Newport, president of the irrigation district, shot back that the *Statesman* "is entirely wrong in concept and unfair and unjust in statement." While admitting that seven hundred acres of land would be submerged, he insisted "no harm will be done the beauty, scenery, trees or shrubs of the lakes."[28]

Boise's *Capital News*, meanwhile, initially dismissed the whole debate as a big joke. In a letter in its columns, it asked with a sneer how could one worry over drowning a lake? McCall "ought to be proud to help the poor homesteaders."[29] A month later, it denied that there was "a word of truth in the assertion that the scenic beauty of the lakes would be greatly injured, for they would not be injured at all."[30]

The Land Board went up to have a look in mid-July. "It is plain to be seen," according to the Lewiston *Morning Tribune*'s correspondent at Lardo, "that they do not favor the plan."[31] State Auditor S.D. Taylor vowed that "under no circumstances would I favor the entire destruction of Payette Lakes as a resort."[32] However, he thought some compromise solution might be found. Similarly, Governor Hawley issued a long statement that explored various options without clearly backing any one of them. At its meeting on August

12, the board temporized by instructing State Engineer Robinson to report on possible damage and how much water could be stored. Nothing came of the engineer's report, while the Black Canyon Irrigation District appeared to drop all thought of a dam at McCall.

No further controversy cropped up for the next half-dozen years. Railroad tracks finally arrived and the McCall train depot was dedicated in August 1915. Resort use gradually increased, but at such a slow pace that the *Statesman* blamed the state for retarding development by holding its lands off the market "for speculative purposes." Apparently unaware that once rail service became available, it was only a matter of time before loggers proposed cutting timber around the lakes, the editor argued that the state should go ahead and sell the land in small lots, using some of the proceeds for building a driveway around the lakes and for "installing some landscape system."[33]

The battle to protect the scenic attractions of McCall was resurrected in earnest when the Land Board advertised a sale of timber along the lakes to be held on December 17, 1918. Boise's redoubtable Columbian Club jumped into the fray. With a membership including the wives of many of Boise's most influential leaders, it was, the editor of the McCall *Payette Lakes Star* moaned, "the greatest little dictator in the west... What the Columbian Club doesn't know about forestry and other matters, it makes up in enthusiastic protest."[34] The Land Board received protesting petitions from many Boise businessmen as well as from 188 club members.

The Land Board delayed responding until the legislature had a chance to consider the Columbian Club's request for some action prohibiting the board from selling timber around the lakes. "We must," argued the Columbian Club president, Mrs. Frank Johnesse, "recognize the importance of preserving our scenic area for park use and in so doing safeguard the spiritual forces" of the state.[35]

The legislature, however, did not accept this argument, and the Land Board moved ahead in late February 1919 by selecting Frank G. Miller to assist the state timber cruiser in marking trees that could be cut without detracting from the area's scenic values. In the fall of 1917, Miller had assumed the deanship of the School of Forestry at the University of Idaho. His credentials included not only experience in the timber industry, but also a master's degree from Yale, where he studied under Henry Graves (a friend of Gifford Pinchot, the former head of the U.S. Forest Service). In June the board spent three days at the lakes and concluded that Miller's initial recommendations ought to be followed, restricting the cut near the shores to that "absolutely necessary for the propagation of the forest."[36]

Dean Miller, however, got no further than the Columbian Club when it came to the idea of a state park at McCall. After studying the fifteen thousand acres of state-owned land on and near Payette Lakes, he reported to the Land

Board in January 1920. The area had, he believed, everything necessary to destine it to become, as the *Capital News* put it, "the Greatest Playground" in the Northwest. While the state might agree to "manage the timber to preserve the scenic beauty of the lake front," it dodged the proposal to establish a park.[37] Claiming that it had no funds to manage a park, the Land Board in March approved a plan to turn lands over to the federal government, if it would create and maintain a national park.

Meanwhile, the possibility of Payette Lakes becoming an irrigation reservoir reappeared. On August 15, 1919, without the approval of any state agency, men began digging a trench to lower the lake outlet and increase the flow into the Payette River. It turned out that the men worked for the Payette Water Users Association, which had appeared before the Land Board. The board, however, had referred the association to the reclamation commissioner, who, after consulting with the attorney general, concluded that he lacked jurisdiction. Clearly, this was a political hot potato. Nevertheless, it was, according to M.A. Bates, the editor of the *Payette Lakes Star*, a matter "too vital to allow the work to be controlled by corporations actuated only by financial self-interest." In his opinion, only the state or federal governments ought to build any dam affecting the lakes, and then only after the most careful study.[38]

After a hiatus of four years the dam proposal returned yet again, and the *Payette Lakes Star*'s opposition found sympathetic audiences far beyond its regular readership. The Kooskia *Mountaineer* reprinted Bates's plea: "These gifts of Nature should be too highly prized to permit of their defacement or destruction for the aggrandizement of any individual or any particular community."[39] The Hailey *Times-News-Miner* saw the move to convert the lakes into a reservoir "but a repetition of the old, old story of sacrificing everything on the alter of commercialism" that had sealed the fate of Shoshone Falls.[40]

The Friends of Payette Lakes took form on March 10, 1924, at a mass meeting in Boise, with branches elsewhere in the Boise Valley, dedicated to opposing Reclamation Service plans "to drain and ruin Big Payette Lake."[41] Its board included not only M.A. Bates, the vociferous editor, but also Carl Brown, McCall's leading sawmill owner, as well as Eugene Sherman, Boise's mayor. Faced with such political strength, W.G. Swendsen, the state reclamation commissioner, not surprisingly pledged his support. The controversy gained national attention, with the *Saturday Evening Post* and *Outdoor Life* dispatching reporters to cover the story. In September the Boise Chamber of Commerce concluded that irrigation needs were not urgent enough to justify the proposed dam. Earlier assurances from the irrigation district's president, James Newport, that the dam would not harm the lakes' scenic beauty sounded hollow, indeed.

The irrigationists bowed to the overwhelming pressure. In November 1924, the Lake Reservoir Company agreed with the Friends of Payette Lakes to limit water storage to that which fit within the lakes' normal high and low water marks. To eliminate the possibility of the battle recurring in the future, the legislature passed the 1925 law permanently assuring the primacy of recreation over irrigation interests at the Payette Lakes.

Idahoans could, in short, work effectively on a scenic preservation cause, but success was by no means guaranteed every time. No better proof of this can be offered than the sharply differing results of the national park movements for the Sawtooth Range and the Craters of the Moon.

The Sawtooths, with their dramatically pointed mountains backing the west side of Stanley Basin's alpine valley and a large scattering of lakes, including Redfish, Alturas, and Stanley, have always impressed visitors with their scenic attractions. While Shoshone Falls was often called the Niagara of the West, promoters were fond of referring to the Sawtooths as the Alps of America. As early as 1907, when roads were barely passable, the Challis *Silver Messenger* already reported hundreds of tourists enjoying Redfish Lake. The same year, it termed Stanley Lake "without doubt, one of the most beautiful lakes in the world,"[42] a judgment that many latter-day visitors would sustain.

The Sawtooths surely offered scenic values great enough, in the opinion of many Idahoans, to justify being nominated for national park status. Thus, in February 1916, the Sandpoint *Pend Oreille Review* cited the Pocatello *Tribune*'s editorial opinion that a national park would be "an important step toward preserving the game, the fish, and the timber,"[43] particularly since it bordered the large game preserve on the Payette headwaters. Furthermore, as Mrs. Jean Conly Smith put it in a *Statesman* feature story, "as a forest reserve it does not pay, and that use of it is skimming the land of the cream... This is not farming country."[44] Mrs. Smith had garnered the support of the federated women's clubs at their annual meeting in Mountain Home in the fall of 1911. They agreed that a national park would "prove a wonderful advertisement for the state, an asset both artistically and commercially."[45] Even the Lewiston *Morning Tribune*, usually a harsh critic of such proposals, tacitly agreed that the proposed park area "has very little value for anything but scenic, hunting, and scientific purposes."[46] In early 1913, a Sawtooth National Park proposal was first introduced for congressional consideration by Idaho's Representative Addison Smith and Senator James Brady.

So what was the problem? Why didn't the national park proposal get anywhere?

Both local and national organizations opposed it! On the local level, the woolgrowers strenuously objected to the loss of range for some twenty thousand sheep. It would also, they claimed, be a safe haven for predatory animals. Hugh Sproat, president of the Idaho Woolgrowers Association, told a women's group in Boise that if the area was under National Park Service management, they would say "no trespass," whereas the Forest Service welcomed grazers with the admonition, "come and use, but don't destroy."[47]

This brought a heated rebuttal from Irwin E. Rockwell, the state senator from Blaine County who in 1915 had sponsored Senate Joint Memorial #8, urging Congress to create the park: "the sordid ruthlessness of the 'master of the flocks' was never better illustrated than in this appeal to close all opportunity for a great national playground and art gallery within our state."[48] The *Statesman* expressed the belief that "it ought to be easy to get on common ground,"[49] and a compromise could be found meshing the interests of stockgrowers with those of recreationists.

It was quite a different story nationally. The problem was not one of congressional interest. Representative Addison Smith and Senator William Borah enthusiastically supported the park proposal. "The stupendous scenic grandeur" of the area struck Borah as "like the world turned upside down."[50] A month later, he wrote a feature story for the *Statesman* asserting a profoundly elemental appeal of the Sawtooths: "force seems to sit incarnate here, and one feels somehow or other that he is not far from the breeding ground of hurricane and storm."[51] But the Department of Agriculture brushed such rhetoric aside. Secretary Houston claimed that the scenic spots in the proposed park were inaccessible, and in any case, the scenery was not all that outstanding. "It would seem both unwise and unnecessary," he argued, "to lock up as a park a big mountain area, the primary use of which now and always must necessarily largely be as a producer of public wealth."[52] This was in striking opposition to the support heard from Secretary of the Interior Lane, whose only caveat was that the park area ought to be doubled to about 330,000 acres.

The point at issue here, as it would continue to be for the next half-century, was not the aesthetic merit or the best use of the area, but which federal agency would be responsible for managing it. Much of it lay within the Sawtooth National Forest, administered by Agriculture, while a national park would move administrative control to Interior's National Park Service (NPS).

Though national parks had been around since 1872, the NPS itself was only organized in 1916, and it quickly had become a new challenger to the Forest Service in regard to controlling significant tracts of the public domain. It was understandable that Idahoans might miss the bureaucratic infighting involved here, even when they observed the opposition of the Forest Service to the park proposal. Thus, E.D. Armstrong of Hailey in April 1916 published a half-page story in the Idaho Falls *Post*, in which he pointed out two major opponents, the woolgrowers and the Forest Service. While he recognized turf protection as the sheepmen's motive, he could find no "valid reason" for the forest rangers' opposition.[53]

Other commentators simply failed to grasp what was at stake and presumed that livestock interests were the only barriers. The editor of the Salmon *Recorder*, for example, noted the opposition of the grazing interests, and he also explained the difference between a national forest and a national park—the former is "a going business," while a park is "an open air museum" set aside by Congress to "preserve from commercial development beautiful scenery."[54] But he did not put two and two together; his editorial showed no awareness of the competing bureaucratic forces behind those differing uses.

Idahoans might conceivably have mustered the power to overcome the Forest Service's resistance to a Sawtooth National Park, but it would have taken more consistent focus and unity among political forces within the state than, in fact, existed. Mrs. Jean Conly Smith moved with her family to Omaha, Nebraska, in 1913, and while she continued her advocacy in a stream of newspaper articles, she could no longer mobilize and maintain the attention of the federated women's clubs in Idaho. Consequently, they did not play a role similar to the Columbian Club in the Payette Lakes issue.

Everyone at the time seemed to agree that a national park would be a great way to enhance the state's economy by attracting thousands of tourists, but the chambers of commerce and commercial clubs quickly fell to squabbling over how to channel that tourist traffic. Blaine County boosters predicted that the park "should make Hailey one of the greatest summer resorts in the entire West."[55] But Boiseans had another vision. The *Statesman* declared that the route from Boise to the Sawtooths by way of Lowman "is the most attractive and has the most fine scenery."[56] The Hailey newspaper took strong exception to this as "an evident attempt to put Boise in the foreground to the eclipse of Hailey."[57] Nevertheless, "the main gateway…is not to be taken from us. Nature has provided the gateway. It is Wood River."[58] Belatedly, a Sawtooth Park Association organized in 1921, led by E.W. Schubert, a prominent hotelman in southern Idaho, but it could not create a united front among the region's tourist interests.

Not even the prospect of a massive irrigation scheme that would flood much of Stanley Basin seemed able to rally scenic preservationists in defense of Sawtooth National Park. Beginning in mid-1921, reports began to surface that the state reclamation department had some notion of using Stanley Basin as a huge holding pond. A five-hundred-foot-high dam on the Salmon River, according to a September 1923 report published in the Pocatello *Tribune*, would put the town of Stanley under two-hundred feet of water and create a reservoir reaching all the way to Redfish Lake. A tunnel twenty miles long would then channel the water to irrigate 300,000–400,000 acres of desert lands near Mountain Home. This pipe dream, apparently thought up by S.H. Hays, a Boise promoter, never materialized, but certainly was not due to any local opposition. The Hailey paper, for example, blandly quoted Hays in April 1924, that "there is nothing to interfere with the success of this project."[59]

However, a Stanley Basin irrigation scheme, nor for that matter a Sawtooth National Park, never was to be. The area would remain under U.S. Forest Service control, eventually becoming the Sawtooth National Recreation Area. (For more about the Sawtooths saga, see later chapters, particularly IV and X.)

The story of the Craters of the Moon National Monument marks an almost complete contrast to the Sawtooth controversy. There was no debate over alternative uses of the Craters of the Moon. In fact, until about 1921, when Robert Limbert "discovered" them, they were virtually invisible, spurned as a "desolate, forbidden waste,"[60] without any developable natural resources. The movement to make the Craters a national park occurred only after the area was aesthetically redefined from one best forgotten to being a remarkable wonderland. Typical of this transformation, when Judge R.L. Givens spoke up in May 1924, favoring the national park designation, he recalled his first visit in 1901 "when I failed to receive a clearcut impression"[61] of the area.

The early history of the Craters area is conveniently presented in David Louter's *Craters of the Moon National Monument: Historic Context Statements* (1995). Until the turn of the century, it was only a blank spot on the map, avoided even by explorers. The first reported trip to the "Devil's Playground," as it was then called, came in June 1912, when a group of men from nearby Arco ventured into the area and marveled at the weird phenomena—deep craters; vents filled with snow, ice, and ash; and cinders covering the ground for thousands of acres. When the initial settlement boom of neighboring Lost River Valley subsided, Arco boosters, led by local newspaperman (and later governor) C.A. Bottolfsen, cast about for other sources of business and began to promote the area as a tourist attraction. To avoid confusion with California's Valley of the Moon, the Arco Chamber of Commerce in 1922 decided to adopt "something more appropriate and original," and gave the area the name it has since carried.[62]

Thus far, the story did not differ appreciably from others in Idaho, where boosters hoped to generate a large-scale tourist business by gaining national park designation for their local scenic attractions. In 1910 people in Coeur d'Alene and Sandpoint had suggested Priest Lake; in 1918, Sandpoint lauded the merits of Warren Island in Lake Pend d'Oreille; in 1925, the people of Shoshone would campaign for the Shoshone Ice Caves; while Twin Falls favored the City of Rocks; and the list could be continued.

A singular advantage of the Craters of the Moon was the involvement of Robert W. Limbert. The extraordinary promotional talents of this "protean" personality arose from a remarkable ability to catch and hold the interest of his audience. A friend described him as "a chap that can teach book scientists many truths, deeply interest all such as favor the outdoor life, and especially bring delight to hearts the thrill response to the song of a bird."[63] Hailing from Omaha, Nebraska, where he was born in 1885 and gained a basic formal education, Limbert worked for two years as a field naturalist for the Smithsonian Institution and arrived in Boise in 1911. He entered the taxidermy business and spent his leisure time exploring southern Idaho, either such well-known areas as the Sawtooths or little known spots, such as Bruneau Canyon. Within ten years, his articles, illustrated by his own photographs, began appearing in nationally distributed magazines.

Bob Limbert discovered the Craters of the Moon in 1921, and his passionate pleasure in its mysteries and geologic attractions converted the attitudes of southern Idahoans (those north of the Salmon River evinced little interest), convincing them that they had in their midst a scenic magnet unlike anything else in the whole world. Here "lies a miniature replica of the moon country," an editor wrote in an introduction to Limbert's massive feature story (running four pages with seventeen photographs), which the *Statesman* published in April 1921. It was "a vast expanse, silent, dead, except for an occasional bird, a country with cold volcanic mountains…a riot of color and fantastic shape so unearthly as to make one believe himself on another planet."[64]

Only a week later, the Idaho Falls *Times-Register* was already reporting that the Craters, "one of the greatest natural phenomena in the United States,"[65] might be set aside as a national park. In June, Limbert returned for another area exploration, this time accompanied by a group of scientists from the nation's capital and with the trip underwritten by the *Statesman*. Limbert already was expecting to do a major article for *National Geographic* magazine (which finally appeared in March 1924). In September 1923, Representative Addison Smith announced his intention to seek national park status for the Craters of the Moon. The following month Smith told the *Capital News*: "I feel that there is not the slightest doubt but what this area is national monument material of the highest interest."[66]

The movement enjoyed the solid support of people across southern Idaho, as can be seen in the establishment of the Craters of the Moon National Park Association. At its organizational meeting in Boise on November 16, 1923, the speakers included Governor C.C. Moore, and the officers were headed by Eugene Sherman, mayor of Boise, Arco's C.A. Bottolfsen, and E.W. Schubert, Pocatello hotelman. Without any opposition—the Craters had no appeal to stockmen, and the land already was controlled by Interior's Land Office—federal approval came easily. In May 1924, President Calvin Coolidge proclaimed it "Idaho's National Park," although, the *Statesman* conceded, "in the language of official Washington it is a national monument."[67]

This speedy conclusion surely had, as many commentators at the time noted, much to do with Limbert's inexhaustible enthusiasm. Typically, when he visited Pocatello for a week in June 1924, he spoke to the Bannock Sportsmen's Association, the local Kiwanis club, the chamber of commerce, and a gathering of college students.

Equally important, however, he emphasized the thrills of discovering what was previously unknown. Neither Idahoans or visitors from elsewhere were expected simply to stand in passive awe of the Craters' stark landscape. Instead, they were invited to enter the fun of finding something new. As Bottolfsen put it, "these places are just as Nature left them, without interference or improvement by man."[68] Anyone could make additional discoveries. Thus, several Boy Scout leaders, returning to Twin Falls from camping in the Sawtooths, stopped off for a brief visit in August 1927 and discovered two ice caves not previously mapped. In any case, visitors had a sense of discovering a whole new perspective. "One can almost see the hot liquid rock surging down the valley," Mrs. C. Russell Weaver of Gooding wrote her father. "What a paradise it is for those who are interested in the birth of this old globe we inhabit."[69]

Contrary to the hopes of those looking for an attraction comparable to Yellowstone National Park, Craters of the Moon developed only slowly and with visitations never more than a tiny fraction of Yellowstone's. The visitor count was up 25 percent in 1928 from the previous year, but that amounted only to 5,043 for the whole season. By 1929, even on a record-breaking August Sunday, only 220 visitors in 58 cars came.

Nevertheless, the Craters of the Moon marked an important change in southern Idahoans' attitudes toward their surroundings. Prior to its designation as a national monument, with all the publicity surrounding that event, southern Idahoans had seen almost nothing in their deserts worth saving. Deserts were thought to be valuable only if and when they could be irrigated and turned into farmland. Now, in the mid-1920s, there was at least one exception—at least one part of the desert to be celebrated and enjoyed for its own sake. It would still be a long step, taking several decades, before they could get behind something as extensive and as subtle in its appeal as the Snake River Birds of Prey Area near Mountain Home, but with the national recognition of Craters of the Moon, Idahoans began to move beyond the pioneers' purely utilitarian attitudes toward the landscape.

On the other hand, Idahoans in the 1920s continued to be all too ready to sacrifice scenic values for economic development when the two seemed to conflict. While it was true that, on occasion, they could move beyond such biases, as in the case of Payette Lakes, the story of Bechler Meadows provides a cautionary note against the assumption that Payette Lakes represented a complete change in local attitudes.

Bechler Meadows is an attractive wetland area on the upper reaches of the Falls River on the southwest edge of Yellowstone Park. It had no major scenic features, but it was an integral portion of the park. The fight over Bechler Meadows began in 1920 with irrigation interests wanting to build a dam with a reservoir that would flood the meadows. Idaho's Representative Smith introduced into Congress a bill that would permit this intrusion into the park, a scheme the Idaho Legislature supported by resolution in February 1921.

National conservation leaders, appalled by the proposal, published scathing critiques in *Literary Digest*, the *Saturday Evening Post*, and other widely circulated magazines. Several newspapers in southern Idaho fired back at these "Park

Faddists," as the Boise *Statesman* called them. Typical of the pro-irrigationist thinking was an article in the Idaho Falls *Idaho Register*, entitled "Highbrow Easterner Would Count the Bugs." The writer was incredulous (in those days, long before the Endangered Species Act) that a scientist would have the temerity to oppose the flooding of Bechler Meadows on the grounds that it would wipe out various bugs and insects there. As it stood, the article claimed, the area "represents nothing but dismal swamps which could be made much more beautiful by the making of a lake there."[70] If only the opponents would use "a little common sense," the Idaho Falls *Post* editorialized, they would concede the validity of the irrigationist position. "Yet this insane propaganda has been spread over the nation,"[71] and the Falls River dam seemed to be hopelessly blocked by forces too powerful for the irrigationists to fight.

Irrigationists' hopes for the dam were renewed in 1926 when Congress began considering expanding the boundaries of Yellowstone National Park to include the area that ultimately became Grand Teton National Park. At the same time, suggestions were made to make minor changes to other parts of Yellowstone's borders and tidy up management issues.

Why not, Idahoans asked, take this occasion to exclude Bechler Meadows? In March, a delegation of state leaders, including Commissioner of Reclamation Warren Swendsen, Game Warden R.E. Thomas, and John Thomas, then president of the Idaho State Chamber of Commerce and later U.S. senator (1928–33, 1940–45), went to urge the House Public Lands Committee to approve Smith's proposal to exclude Bechler Meadows from Yellowstone Park. They carried with them a resolution from the Driggs Chamber of Commerce favoring Smith's amendment. The Driggs businessmen summarized the arguments of the dam proponents, saying the area was "wholly outside of the line of tourist travel," "no road is maintained to this particular area," "nor is there anything of a scenic nature to attract tourists."[72] However, they found few sympathetic ears in the nation's capital. Opponents of the irrigationists did not debate the merits of the Idahoans' proposal. As the Pocatello *Tribune* noted, "opposition is based on the general proposition of not eliminating anything from the park, regardless of its economic value."[73]

Eastern Idahoans refused to take no for an answer. "There is," the Idaho Falls *Times-Register* sputtered, "a good deal of hypocrisy on the part of those self-appointed guardians of the east who would keep the national park from being 'deformed.'"[74] The "Reservoir Is Vital," a Pocatello *Tribune* editorial insisted:

> the protection accorded the lands striving for water and the preservation of the water itself constitute genuine conservation. The retention of waste spaces and pest-infested swamps is far from being equal in value to the other proposition.[75]

Addison Smith managed to get a joint House-Senate committee to visit the area in August 1926, holding a hearing at St. Anthony with some 800 to

1000 people attending. In December Governor Moore went to Washington to meet with Senator Frank Gooding to strategize over the issue. Former Senator Dubois spoke against the Bechler project, but, the Pocatello *Tribune* sniffed, "his interest in [Idaho] scenery is zeroically conoptious."[76]

In the spring of 1929, President Herbert Hoover appointed a blue-ribbon Boundary Commission to study the several proposed changes to Yellowstone Park. The commission visited Bechler Meadows in August, but its report failed to give the irrigationists any satisfaction. The decade ended where it had began, with obdurate opposition blocking the Falls River dam and its Bechler Meadows reservoir.

For Idaho as a whole, however, the next decade would open with far more ambitious scenic proposals. Scenic preservation prior to 1930 had victories and defeats—if the legislatively mandated preservation of Payette Lakes and the creation of Craters of the Moon National Monument could be counted as victories, the fates of Shoshone Falls, the defeat of the proposed Sawtooth National Park, and the *implications* of the Bechler Meadows case would have to be seen as defeats. But these issues tended to be focussed on relatively small areas. None but the Sawtooths involved more than a few square miles. The scale exploded into a whole new dimension with the creation of three Primitive Areas during the 1930s. With their boundaries spanning the center of the state, the Idaho, Sawtooth, and Selway primitive areas marked the beginning of what the Idaho Conservation League would eventually celebrate as the establishment of "Idaho—The Wilderness State."

ENDNOTES

1. Governor Stuenenberg's letter is reprinted in "Shoshone Reserve," Boise *Statesman* (October 31, 1900): p. 6. See also Jenny Emery Davidson, "Power Switches on the Middle Snake River: The Divergent Histories of Two Hydroelectric Projects." *Idaho Yesterdays* XLIV (Summer 2000): pp. 22–32.
2. See Carolyn Rhodes-Jones, "An Evolving View of the Landscape: Trappers, Tourists, and the Great Shoshone Falls," *Idaho Yesterdays* XXIII (Summer 1979): pp. 19–27.
3. "Great Shoshone Falls! Niagara's Idaho Rival," reprinted from Salt Lake City *Tribune* in the Salmon *Idaho Recorder* (January 10, 1889): p. 1.
4. "Snake River Cataracts," editorial in Boise *Statesman* (December 6, 1883): p. 2.
5. "Does the State Own the Falls?" Boise *Statesman* (March 29, 1891): p. 8.
6. "Where Are They?" editorial in Boise *Statesman* (March 31, 1891): p. 2.
7. "New National Park," Hailey *Wood River Times* (August 30, 1900): p. 1.
8. "W.A. Clark's Scheme to Harness Big Falls," Boise *Capital News* (October 16, 1903): p. 1.
9. "Possibilities Seen in Falls," Twin Falls *News* (April 19, 1924): p. 5.
10. "Shoshone Falls Presents Glorious Picture at Night," Boise *Statesman* (May 27, 1928): p. 8.
11. "An Eventful Week for Twin Falls," editorial in Twin Falls *Times* (May 21, 1928): p. 4.
12. "Shoshone Falls," editorial in Twin Falls *News* (May 29, 1925): p. 4.
13. "And Now It's 'Conservation' of Scenery—What Next?" editorial in Boise *Statesman* (February 15, 1911): p. 4.
14. "Protests to Preserve the Scenery of Idaho," editorial in Boise *Statesman* (June 23, 1911): p. 4.
15. "Want State Park on Coeur d'Alene," Boise *Capital News* (January 27, 1911): p. 8.
16. "Governor Hawley on Heyburn Park," St. Maries *Gazette* (July 21, 1911): p. 1.

17. "Ripe Timber in Heyburn Park to Be Sold," Boise *Statesman* (February 9, 1913): p. 2.
18. "Study Forestry in Heyburn Park," Boise *Statesman* (June 18, 1920): p. 4.
19. Bill Loftus, *Idaho State Parks Guidebook* (Lewiston, Idaho: Tribune, 1989), p. 36.
20. "Payette Lake Resort," Boise *Statesman* (May 22, 1900): p. 6.
21. Chapter 83 (S.B. 98), *Session Laws of 1925*.
22. "Establish a State Park," editorial in Roseberry *Long Valley Advocate* (January 12, 1905): p. 4.
23. "Payette Lake Park," editorial in Boise *Statesman* (January 17, 1905): p. 4.
24. "Why Not Idaho?" editorial in Roseberry *Long Valley Advocate* (February 5, 1905): p. 4.
25. "To Preserve State Lands at Lakes," Roseberry *Long Valley Advocate* (March 14, 1907): p. 1.
26. "Through Service to the Lakes," Boise *Statesman* (May 25, 1908): p. 2.
27. "Payette Lakes for Enormous Reservoir," Boise *Statesman* (May 12, 1911): p. 7.
28. "Will Not Mar Beauty of the Payette Lakes," letter from James B. Newport in Boise *Statesman* (May 22, 1911): p. 6.
29. "Payette Lakes Reservoir," letter from John F. Christiansen in Boise *Capital News* (June 19, 1911): p. 4.
30. "Payette Lakes Reservoir," editorial in Boise *Capital News* (July 8, 1911): p. 4.
31. "Land Board at Payette Lakes," Lewiston *Morning Tribune* (July 15, 1911): p. 5.
32. "Will Not Agree to Ruin Resort," Boise *Statesman* (July 16, 1911): p. 12.
33. "Payette Lakes Situation," editorial in Boise *Statesman* (August 6, 1915): p. 4.
34. "State Timber Sale Postponed 90 Days," McCall *Payette Lakes Star* (December 13, 1918): p. 1.
35. "Columbian Club Reviews Work during War Time," Boise *Statesman* (May 20, 1919): p. 5.
36. "Payette Forests Not Injured by Cutting," Boise *Capital News* (June 11, 1919): p. 5.
37. "Payette Lake Section Destined to Become the Greatest Playground in Northwest," Boise *Capital News* (January 19, 1920): p. 5.
38. "Investigate First," editorial in McCall *Payette Lakes Star* (February 27, 1920): p. 4.
39. "Recreational Loss," editorial in Kooskia *Mountaineer* (November 7, 1923): p. 2.
40. "Save Payette Lakes," editorial in Hailey *Times-News-Miner* (November 8, 1923): p. 6.
41. "Organization to Forestall Projected Reservoir Use of Payette Lake May Be Formed at a Mass Meeting," Boise *Capital News* (March 7, 1924): p. 9.
42. "Stanley Lake," Challis *Silver Messenger* (October 15, 1907): p. 1.
43. "Sawtooth National Park Bill to Be Introduced," Sandpoint *Pend d'Oreille Review* (February 18, 1916): p. 8. See also, Sarah E. Dant Ewert, "Peak Park Politics: The Struggle over the Sawtooths, from Borah to Church," *Pacific Northwest Quarterly* XCI (Summer 2000): pp. 138–49.
44. Jean Conly Smith, "Entrancing Beauties, Delightful Recreations in the Proposed Sawtooth National Park," Boise *Statesman* (January 2, 1916): Section 2, pp. 1, 13.
45. Jean Conly Smith, "Would Preserve Marvels and the Beauties of the Sawtooths," Boise *Statesman* (October 22, 1911): Section 2, pp. 1, 6. See also Dodd, "Preserving Multiple-Use Management," pp. 377.
46. "New Park Is Planned," Lewiston *Morning Tribune* (December 23, 1914): p. 7.
47. "Sawtooth Park Appears to Be Dead for Time," Boise *Statesman* (March 21, 1916): p. 7.
48. "Sheep, Scenery, Public Park or Pasture?" letter to the editor by Irwin E. Rockwell, in Boise *Statesman* (March 31, 1916): p. 6.
49. "Making It Easier," editorial in Boise *Statesman* (April 3, 1916): p. 4.
50. "Borah Favors Sawtooth Park," Twin Falls *Times* (July 27, 1915): p. 1.
51. William E. Borah, "In Rugged Grandeur and Scenic Wealth, the Proposed Sawtooth National Park in Idaho Surpasses Yellowstone and Yosemite," Boise *Statesman* (August 1, 1915): Section 2, p. 1.
52. "Houston Argues Against Park in Sawtooths," Boise *Statesman* (March 27, 1916): p. 7.
53. E.D. Armstrong, "The Sawtooth National Park," Idaho Falls *Post* (April 28, 1916): p. 3.
54. "Proposed Sawtooth National Park," editorial in Salmon *Recorder* (May 12, 1916): p. 2.
55. "Sawtooth National Park," reprinted from the Hailey newspaper in Challis *Messenger* (January 7, 1913): p. 1.
56. "Boise Should Be One of Sawtooth Gateways," Boise *Statesman* (August 13, 1916): Section 2, pp. 1, 2.
57. "An Injustice to Wood River," editorial in Hailey *Wood River Times* (January 5, 1916): p. 4.

58. "Let It Be Open to the World," editorial in Hailey *Wood River Times* (January 6, 1916): p. 4.
59. "Hays Tells about Gigantic Project," Hailey *Times-News-Miner* (April 17, 1924): p. 1.
60. "An Idaho Wonder Is an Immense Ice Cave in the Heart of a Lava Desert," Boise *Statesman* (October 12, 1914): p. 7.
61. "Givens Favors National Park in 'The Valley of the Moon,'" Boise *Statesman* (May 1, 1924): p. 7.
62. David Louter, *Craters of the Moon National Monument: Historic Context Statements* (Seattle: National Park Service, 1995).
63. Alford F. Grubb, "Interesting Character Is 'Bob' Limbert, Man Who Told World of Idaho's Famous Moon Crater Land," Pocatello *Tribune* (April 20, 1924): p. 5.
64. R.W. Limbert, "A Trip to the Moon Right Here in Idaho," Boise *Statesman* (April 10, 1921): Section 2, pp. 7–10.
65. "Lava Beds May Be Set Aside as Park," Idaho Falls *Times-Register* (April 15, 1921): pp. 1, 6.
66. "Congressman Smith Lays Plans to Get National Monument," Boise *Capital News* (October 4, 1923): p. 7.
67. "Idaho's National Park Dedicated," Boise *Statesman* (June 18, 1924): p. 1.
68. C.A. Bottolfsen, "Call of the Open Road Will Lead Tourist and Vacationer to 'Craters of Moon,'" Idaho Falls *Post* (June 7, 1924): Section 2, p. 1.
69. Letter printed in "Visit to 'Valley of the Moon' Is Interesting Trip," Priest River *Times* (June 6, 1929): p. 1.
70. "Highbrow Easterner Would Count the Bugs," Idaho Falls *Idaho Register* (May 28, 1920): p. 1.
71. "The Fall River Dam," editorial in Idaho Falls *Post* (February 9, 1921): p. 4.
72. "Driggs Is for Changing Park Lines," Idaho Falls *Post* (April 21, 1926): p. 1.
73. "Smith Making Strong Fight for Park Bill," Pocatello *Tribune* (April 25, 1926): p. 1.
74. "Congressional Delegation," editorial in Idaho Falls *Times-Register* (August 17, 1926): p. 6.
75. "Reservoir Is Vital," editorial in Pocatello *Tribune* (May 9, 1926): Section 2, p. 12.
76. "Bechler Project," editorial in Pocatello *Tribune* (December 18, 1927): Section 2, p. 8.

IV

Saving "The Last Frontier"

THE BIRTH OF IDAHO's officially designated and federally protected wilderness system could scarcely have been any easier. On November 14, 1930, the supervisors of three national forests, several officials from the regional office in Ogden, Utah, and "a group of local sportsmen" met in Boise to set the boundaries for the Idaho Primitive Area, covering one million acres within the Idaho, Payette, and Salmon national forests. They sought to keep the area roadless and thereby, "preserve a portion of Idaho in the unmolested condition as it was found by the first pioneers."[1]

This meeting was reported the following day by newspapers across the state without a single editorial caveat. Within a few days, several editors greeted the news with enthusiastic applause. The Idaho Falls *Times-Register* concluded that "the idea is good and will strike a popular chord."[2] Boise's *Capital News* called it a "Monument to Virgin Nature," a "hunter's paradise," and "a camper's delight."[3] "Splendid," also declared the same paper; this would preserve an area "where the honk of the automobile, the destruction by human hands, the accumulation of waste, the construction of modern highways, will be unknown."[4]

To demonstrate that the Idaho Primitive Area had the official blessing of Idahoans, Governor H.C. Baldridge convened a blue-ribbon committee to consider the proposal at an open meeting on December 20 at the statehouse. The governor began the meeting with a speech urging approval of the area, calling it "one of the most beautiful" sections in the state.[5] The committee heard the protests of several settlers within the area's perimeter, but voted in favor of establishing the area, although members explicitly cautioned against their action being taken as a precedent.

Stewart Campbell, the state mine inspector, was the only public official to voice opposition. His argument would be heard many times in future discussions about wilderness preservation: by prohibiting roads, the government was "reserving the area to the wealthy man only, be he miner or sportsman."[6] This brought so little public reaction that the legislature did not bother even to discuss the matter, and the Idaho Primitive Area was formally designated by the Forest Service on April 19, 1931.

How did this happen? From our perspective three-quarters of a century later, when wilderness issues not uncommonly drag on for decades, the ease with which the Idaho Primitive Area came into being seems almost magical. Nor can we assume that with the onset of the Great Depression, funds for new roads were so short that it was simple to set aside large roadless areas without argument. In point of fact, Depression-fighting measures, particularly Civilian Conservation Corps projects, accounted for the construction of thousands of miles of new roads in Idaho national forests during the 1930s.

National Forest leadership, particularly that of R.H. Rutledge, certainly is part of the answer. Although Rutledge, a quiet-spoken administrator, was far different in personality from the gregarious, politically savvy Major Fenn, they shared deep Idaho roots and an ability to relate to a people ever suspicious of anything that looked like federal strong-arming. In fact, Fenn appointed Rutledge in 1907 to his first "administrative" post within the Forest Service, as supervisor of the Coeur d'Alene National Forest. By that time, Rutledge already had accumulated an interestingly varied background. Born in 1873 in Kansas, he came to Idaho with his parents in a covered wagon in 1889. He attended the University of Idaho in 1895–96 and then spent ten years in Long Valley (near Cascade) ranching, teaching school, and learning something of the timber business. In 1905 he joined the Forest Service as a guard at Roseberry. Following his service for Fenn in Coeur d'Alene, Rutledge was assigned in 1909 to the regional office in Missoula, Montana. In 1920 he became the regional forester in Ogden, a position he held until 1938, when he became the first director of the Grazing Service (a forerunner of the Bureau of Land Management). That same year, the University of Idaho awarded him an honorary master's degree in Forest Administration.[7]

Rutledge was very careful in developing his plans for setting aside some of the remaining wilderness for the enjoyment of future generations. Although available records are thin and scattered, there is reason to believe that he spent years thinking about and promoting the idea. Take, for example, an April 1929 report in the Pocatello *Tribune* about Rutledge's talk to the Salt Lake County Sportsmen's Association: "the rib of mountains extending from Glacier park through the Grand Canyon is the last frontier. It is no longer possible to move on to untouched regions."[8] It was only the shortest of intellectual steps from that observation to the use he saw for designated wilderness areas. The Idaho Primitive Area "would make it possible," he told the governor's committee on December 20, 1930, "for people to detach themselves, at least temporarily, from the strains and turmoil of modern existence, and to revert to simple types of existence…for physical, mental and spiritual recreation or regeneration."[9]

Rutledge also did his homework. The U.S. Geological Survey announced in July 1930 that it would send a field party into the planned primitive area for the rest of the summer, the results of which would give some idea whether or not obvious ore deposits could be easily developed. On October 22, the Salmon *Recorder-Herald* reported that Rutledge and two members of his staff were "going over the proposed Middlefork Primitive area,"[10] a story possibly intended as a trial balloon to test local attitudes.

He also had the support of prominent Idahoans. According to an article in the Boise *Statesman* by Watson Humphrey, the whole movement for a primitive area originated when "a party of Idaho sportsmen, devoted hunters all of them, a few years ago made camp for the night on Big creek" one late October. Over the campfire, these men, including Governor Baldridge, Rutledge, and lumberman Harry Shellworth, heard Shellworth's idea for protecting "the land from the most dangerous enemy—the automobile."[11] This may appear a bit too cozy to be entirely believable, but undoubtedly the governor had a strong interest in such proposals. For instance, in December 1927 he told the annual meeting of the Nampa Sportsmen's Club that "Idaho's virgin hunting grounds which are dear to the heart of sportsmen should not be ruined by the building of roads into the state's interior."[12] It is also true that when he appointed the committee in December 1930 to consider the Idaho Primitive Area, he selected Harry Shellworth to be the chairman.

Nevertheless, a broad statewide consensus had to have existed for Rutledge, Baldridge, Shellworth, and like-minded men to gain such ready acceptance of the primitive area. The consensus *did* exist, based on the belief held by thousands of Idahoans that game preserves were essential for the continued viability of big-game hunting. For them, the primitive area was really a huge, permanent game preserve. After all, by the end of 1930, more than half of the land around the Middle Fork of the Salmon River to be included within the Idaho Primitive Area already was a game preserve. To many sportsmen, it appeared that the area simply expanded the game preserve boundaries and prevented over-hunting by blocking auto access. Thus, the Cascade *News* saw the "purpose of the proposed primitive area as not only to provide a game preserve for animals, but also to preserve a virgin country in its natural state for future generations."[13]

In the 1920s, the leading threat to game preservation seemed to be the automobile. The major concerns that had faced sportsmen in the first two decades of the century had been the lack of game laws and their effective enforcement. Now, the threat of ever-growing numbers of roads and the ease with which hunters could bag their quarry without ever leaving their cars was the new threat. Symbolic of this concern were two photos in the game warden's 1919–20 report. One showed an automobile on a mountain ridge, with a caption reading, "There Are Few Mountain Regions Now Unfamiliar to the Throb of the Gasoline Motor." The other photo focused on a car apparently stranded in a stream: "The Automobile Is Found in all Accessible Points Regardless of Obstacles Encountered."[14]

The solution favored by a growing number of Idaho sportsmen was to create game preserves. In 1923, fifty residents of the remote town of Elk City, sixty miles east of Grangeville, petitioned the game warden to close ten townships (i.e., 230,400 acres) on the grounds that with new highways, this area "will soon become such a popular hunting ground that the big game will quickly be exterminated unless new measures are taken for its protection at all times."[15]

The next year, the Wood River Fish and Game Protective Association proposed a game preserve in the Warm Springs Creek area encompassing six to seven townships. "So-called hunters have shot deer in the vicinity of Guyer Hot Springs from their automobiles; they have shot them down," the editor of the Hailey paper observed, "as they might have shot 'calves in a pasture.'" The editor undoubtedly spoke for many local sportsmen when he found this "revolting in the extreme."[16]

In 1928 the *Statesman* reported the opening of a road up the South Fork of the Payette River from Lowman to Grandjean, regretfully concluding, "another of Idaho's fast diminishing virgin game area[s] will be opened to the ubiquitous automobile and its loads of hunters."[17]

As early as March 1924, the Salmon Rifle Club began lobbying the legislature for a game preserve surrounding the Middle Fork of the Salmon River (the core of what became in 1930 the Idaho Primitive Area). "Under present regulations," according to the Salmon *Herald*, "the slaughter of this game has been terrific on the part of dude hunters, mainly non-residents, who come in autos…and kill vast numbers of the animals, mainly for their heads."[18]

Responding to these concerns, the state game warden (using the power vested in him by the 1919 legislature) designated more game preserves. By the end of 1926, according to Game Warden Thomas, Idaho led all states in the size of its game preserves. Of the twenty million acres of game preserves in national forests throughout the nation, three million were in Idaho.

Unfortunately, the designation of a game preserve did not, by itself, end the problem of the "dude hunter." Without a multitude of game wardens to protect the reserves, either hunters had to be dissuaded from coming to Idaho, or their access to prime hunting grounds had to be sharply curtailed. Neither option had any appeal to most Idahoans. The first was never given serious thought because it would threaten the very existence of a tourist industry, which state officials had attempted to foster since the first years of the century.

Typical of prevailing attitudes, State Game Warden J.B. Gowen was quoted by the *Statesman* in October 1914 as saying, "the tourist crop is…the best source of revenue and should be cultivated to the greatest extent" by making the state attractive to hunters.[19] Local sportsmen's organizations commonly shared the idea that tourism should be enhanced and frequently took on special projects to make the state more inviting to visitors. Thus, in 1923 the Boise Fish and

Game League dedicated a weekend to building campsites at Pine Flat on the South Fork of the Payette River, five miles from Lowman. State promotional literature usually featured hunting and fishing attractions, while the growing popularity of boat trips down the Salmon River commonly involved stops along the way for hunters to enjoy their sport. In short, Idahoans had no conceivable way to discourage visits by out-of-state hunters.

Nor could Idahoans imagine limiting hunters' use of public roads. After all, like most other Americans of the time, the state's residents were entranced with the pleasures of autotouring. Otto M. Jones, state game warden in 1919 (and occasional travel writer) put it this way:

> With a good motor, purring healthily into the open, an easy riding car, good companions and a swinging, ever changing mountain road that unfolds a never-tiring series of panoramic views to the motorist, there is nothing to compare to an early spring touring party of two or more cars.[20]

And, in case anyone was tempted to interfere with this passion, there remained the example of auto access into Yellowstone National Park. When federal authorities attempted to limit use of the park's roads to a couple of franchised transportation companies, motorists in eastern Idaho were outraged. "Exclusion of autos," fumed the editor of the Pocatello *Tribune*, "is about as reasonable [as excluding] a man with freckles or a lame leg."[21] Besides infringing upon motorists' freedom, the park policy hurt the tourist business. "The benefits" from a "great stream of traffic" out of Salt Lake City running through Pocatello and Idaho Falls to the park were practically un-limited, according to an Idaho Falls paper, and bounded only "by the scenery we have to show, investments we have in store, and the welcome we extend."[22] The opening of the park to auto traffic in 1916 turned out to be inevitable, and, seemingly, it also was inevitable in the mountains of Idaho that hunters would use whatever roads were available.

But why not leave some areas roadless? In February 1925, when S.B. Locke—on Rutledge's staff in the Forest Service's Ogden regional office—ad-dressed the Southern Idaho Fish and Game Association's annual meeting in Twin Falls, "he told of plans for wilderness projects which would be kept free of auto trails, permitting the sportsman who cared to get back into new country by pack to do so." Locke declared the area around the Middle Fork of the Salmon River "ideal for this purpose."[23] He expressed the same idea in a seven-page article included in the game warden's biennial report, which appeared in the spring of 1925. He pointed out that the difficulty of access into the Middle Fork area would be sufficient to limit the impact of hunters on wild game.

Locke's proposal did not represent any dramatic shift in Forest Service policy. It would continue to foster road building. The road from Lowman to Stanley, for example, was originally planned with the active cooperation of

Emile Grandjean and, in a 1924 talk to the Boise Rotary Club, Rutledge urged the road's completion to assist in the state's development.

On the other hand, the Forest Service's growing interest in preserving some wilderness areas by limiting access to trails for hikers and horsemen came in response to a rising regional public concern over the disappearance of wilderness. "We Need the Wilderness," the Coeur d'Alene *Press* titled an editorial appearing in the spring of 1929:

> Areas in which Nature has been left to do her worst and best; areas in which the forest is not burned and not improved and the streams are unpolluted and undammed offer a refreshment to modern man which he wants and needs.[24]

Occasionally, the role of such wilderness areas were seen, as in the above editorial, to be passively curative, or, as the Kooskia *Mountaineer* put it in March 1926: "Nature's own sanitarium offering seclusion, rest and recreation to the world weary."[25] More commonly, the emphasis was on the lack of the ugly, vulgar aspects of modern life. The Idaho Falls *Post* worried about,

> Just how far have the national forests been invaded with joyriding highways, polluted with the malodorous fumes of burned gasoline, strewn with the egg shells and other luncheon remains of careless and selfish throngs of tourists, degraded with the modern type of resort catering to a depraved taste for jazz, bathtubs, bridge, and dinner clothes?[26]

It seemed so much more wholesome to contemplate a simpler time, when, like the pioneers, one had to manage with minimum frills. A wilderness could be seen, as Rutledge phrased it regarding what later became Grand Teton National Park, as an area kept in its "present wild state as an outdoor museum and game and timber preserve."[27]

Many sportsmen might not have understood the notion of an "outdoor museum," but they had no trouble relating to Rutledge's emphasis, in his 1929 talk in Salt Lake City, on wild game and his distinction between the "sentimental" game enthusiast, who opposed killing any animal, and the "practical" game enthusiast, who "believes in game production, protection and utilization."[28]

Consequently, newspapers around the state dutifully printed the press release from the Ogden office announcing plans for the Idaho Primitive Area, which included a statement of its purpose: "in order to preserve a portion of Idaho in the unmolested condition as it was found by the first pioneers," in the words of the Kooskia *Mountaineer*.[29] The Idaho Falls *Times-Register* put it only slightly differently: "the tract will be kept as it was found by the pioneers."[30]

Nevertheless, left to their own devices, most journalists emphasized the attraction to hunters (a view, one suspects, shared by most of their readership). "It is," according to the *Statesman*, "in reality a glorious hunting ground";

in the opinion of the *Capital News*, "the state is interested mainly in the fish and game feature of the area"; "the primitive area…will be," the Lewiston *Morning Tribune* asserted, "the foundation upon which Idaho may build its greatest neglected industry—recreation."[31] Tellingly, almost none of them followed the lead of the *Capital News* in publishing Rutledge's statement to the Governor's Committee on December 20, 1930, where he articulated a far more sophisticated rationale for preserving wilderness (already cited earlier in Chapter IV, but presented here more fully):

> To make it possible for people to detach themselves, at least temporarily, from the strain and turmoil of modern existence, and to revert to simple types of existence in conditions [of] relatively unmodified nature [and] to afford unique opportunities for physical, mental and spiritual recreation or regeneration.[32]

Nor did the Idaho media pay much attention to the primitive area's precise location. They generally failed to publish maps, and the description of the boundaries mainly referred to watersheds, which probably very few readers could have accurately located. Thus, the *Morning Tribune* asserted that it included Lake Roosevelt and the site of the former Thunder Mountain gold rush claims, a statement unmentioned by most other papers. Contemporary Forest Service maps were too vague to verify the *Morning Tribune*'s assertion. The 1934 maps of the Payette and Challis national forests did not include any indication of the primitive area's location, while the 1938 and 1941 maps simply noted the presence of a primitive area, but not its border lines.

There was, in short, no immediate need to precisely define the boundaries of the Idaho Primitive Area, either geographically or functionally—nor pressure to decide whether it was a gigantic outdoor museum, as Rutledge envisioned it; or just a different kind of game preserve, as many Idahoans assumed; or "an enormous park for all the people," as the Twin Falls *Times* described it.[33] As the state and nation spiraled into the depths of the Great Depression, most people worried over far more pressing matters than what to make of a wilderness area in Idaho's remotest section. Not surprisingly under these circumstances, in 1931 a request by the Idaho State Chamber of Commerce for federal funding for a geological survey costing $48,000 was denied.

Consequently in 1936, when the primitive area was, in effect, tripled in size with the designation of the adjacent Selway-Bitterroot Primitive Area (its Idaho portion just north of the Salmon River encompassed 1.8 million acres, and also included a large part of adjoining western Montana), hardly anyone in Idaho even seemed to notice. The Salmon *Recorder-Herald* blamed the Wilderness Society, supported by "wealthy sportsmen, sentimentalists, and big game guides"[34] for the Selway-Bitteroot area's designation, but not even the Wilderness Society troubled itself about geographical details. Eager to save "the largest forest wilderness possibility in the United States," it lumped together the Idaho Primitive Area with the Idaho portion of the Selway-Bitterroot Primitive Area as the "Selway-Salmon River Wilderness."[35]

People throughout northern Idaho largely seemed to ignore this new development. The Lewiston *Morning Tribune* did devote a feature story to its creation, but thereafter usually made such references as the "Selway-Lochsa back country"[36] without any concern about where the officially designated primitive area fit in. Other area papers regularly published stories having to do with hunting in the Selway district, but almost never mentioned its status as a primitive area.

The same lack of concern continued with the announcement in July 1937 that 145,000 acres had been added to the Idaho Primitive Area. At most, newspapers noted that the addition included the Indian and Pistol Creek drainages, but, without maps or more detailed descriptions, the average reader had no idea where the area might be or what it looked like. It seemed as if the editors and their readers tended to share the view of the Twin Falls *News*, which had reported on the original creation of the Idaho Primitive Area by observing "there is something appealing about the idea," yet with the caveat, "most of us like nature primitive—but not too primitive."[37]

All of this dramatically changed with the creation of the Sun Valley resort north of Hailey, which opened in 1936 with a gala Christmas event attended by Hollywood stars and other national celebrities. "'Ware the Boom!" warned the Boise *Capital News*. "Something must be done quickly to prevent new public interest from overwhelming our primitive country."[38] Actually, this editorial, appearing in May 1937, served only as a reminder of the issues involved, which already had been in the public spotlight for more than a year.

In June 1935, the Hailey Chamber of Commerce had resurrected the idea of a Sawtooth National Park. This received a few polite nods—the Twin Falls *Times* termed it "worthy of serious consideration"[39]—but not until the following spring was it given full attention. The stimulus was a report in March 1936 that several thousand acres had been purchased near Ketchum for an exclusive winter resort. "A new era has begun," declared the *Statesman*, with the new resort giving an immense push to the tourist industry in central Idaho.[40] R.G. Cole, president of the Idaho State Automobile Association, urged the park's creation to capitalize on the tourist attractions of Sun Valley, since tourism, in his opinion, could be enhanced "even more actively than agriculture, mining or timber."[41]

Initially, public reactions tended to favor the proposal. After all, the editor of the Salmon *Recorder-Herald* reasoned, "as a national park" the Sawtooth country "would be converted to a more useful and profitable purpose than to continue using it for a sheep range."[42] More ruefully, the Twin Falls *News* thought it inevitable that the Sawtooths would become a "trippers' paradise." "We must resign ourselves to the new order, and if a National Park proves to be necessary to protect the country from spoliation, let us have it."[43]

But "Do We Want a Park?" asked the Twin Falls *Times*[44] in an editorial reprinted by the newspapers in Hailey and Jerome. To help answer that question, the State Planning Board convened the first Statewide Recreation Conference at Hailey on August 30–31, 1936. Will Simons, board chairman, opened the conference by insisting that its charge was to consider all options, not merely to decide on the question of a national park.

Guy Mains, supervisor of the Boise National Forest, pointed out in his address, "In Idaho, with the largest unbroken wilderness of any state, we have a wonderful opportunity for the development of recreation of all sorts." He went on to argue that "wild land must be studied, analyzed and placed under control on a basis which properly recognizes its perpetual importance."[45] Despite Mains' emphasis on the need for cool thinking, the *Capital News* reported that "violent opposition…broke into the open" at the conference over the park question, with the grange, representing grazers, and the Union Pacific Railroad, speaking for its interest in Sun Valley, as the most vocal opponents.[46]

Although not given any significant space by newspapers reporting on the conference proceedings, the most crucial presentation came from a National Park Service spokesman, who outlined the restrictions that would apply if the Sawtooths became a national park. Stockmen had already decided against the proposal because they would lose grazing land. But the Park Service presentation led to "a quick death" of support for the proposal in Ketchum, according to the Challis *Messenger*.[47] The Shoshone Chamber of Commerce decided that "the west should not be pastured off for the benefit of New York millionaires."[48] Noting the area's displeasure with Senator James Pope's failure to immediately withdraw his Sawtooth National Park bill, the Pocatello *Tribune* recapitulated all the things not permitted within a national park, and concluded: "the people of that district do not want any restrictions of that kind."[49]

The idea of a national park in the Sawtooths was done for, at least for another generation. The *Capital News* explained,

> We were afraid it meant an extension of the tin-can brigade into the untracked primitive country. We were afraid our little mountain heavens would be overrun by the uninitiated. We were afraid a uniformed man would stand by a gate demanding a ticket from us before we could enter into the wilderness we have cherished as our own all these years.[50]

The stage was set for the Forest Service to explain how it would manage the area. Senator Pope reported in April 1937 that he had withdrawn his park bill "because the forest service has assured me that it will improve the entire area."[51] The following month, R.H. Rutledge took the occasion of an invitation to speak to the Frontier Club in Shoshone to scope out what many in the area took to be a full-scale "Program for the Sawtooth-Salmon River Country."[52] He urged the need to consider the whole area, amounting to more than six million acres and reaching north from Sun Valley across the Salmon River and including the Selway-Bitterroot Primitive Area. He began by noting the challenge: "the power of effective advertising has been well demonstrated [by the creation of Sun Valley] and we are now faced with the problem of what to do with the sudden influx of people into our mountain playground." He concluded with an affirmation: "it is a plastic situation which, if we are wise enough, we can mold into something splendid and unmatched in our nation." The task he set for himself, and for his audience, was to consider all of the area's competing uses and to see how to fit them into a unified plan.

The only topic that Rutledge put aside unexamined was the notion that Stanley Basin ought to be flooded as an irrigation reservoir to serve the Boise area. He briefly noted that the region he was discussing served as a watershed for users from Boise to Butte, then moved on. One would never guess from his speech that the proposal to divert water from the Salmon River to the Boise Valley by way of a tunnel through the Sawtooths—a scheme noted in Chapter III as cropping up in 1923—continued to be pushed by Boise irrigationists and supported by Idaho's delegation. After the U.S. Geological Survey studied dam locations in 1925, the topic seemed to disappear, but it had only laid dormant.

With the appearance of many large-scale public works projects during the New Deal, many Boise Valley promoters renewed their pressure for the Sawtooths water scheme. It would redeem, they insisted, a tacit pledge that Boise irrigators would have adequate water, even in drought years. Senator Pope supported a request for $2 million to begin the work, claiming that it "is the very foundation for the development of southwestern Idaho."[53] Even though only $100,000 was allocated in February 1934 for preliminary studies, J.M. Lambert of the New York Irrigation District jubilantly announced, "the project is now assured,"[54] while the Reclamation Bureau blandly told the Salmon Chamber of Commerce that "such a project would never be approved if it would be detrimental to any other section of the state."[55] As it turned out, Secretary of the Interior Harold Ickes thrust the project back into limbo when he informed Governor C. Ben Ross in September 1934 that no funds were available even for a survey.

Therefore, Rutledge apparently saw no reason to give that grandiose proposal any consideration, but he did assure his listeners that "due consideration" would be given "to all economic factors that are related to the resources of the national forests." Thus, he noted that 671,000 sheep and 40,000 cattle grazed every summer in central Idaho's national forests. However, his speech focused on recreation as the most dynamic use and area maintenance of fish and game resources as the most demanding challenge to planning. He saw the Sawtooths as the Idaho Primitive Area's "Front Yard," being more accessible than, for example, Chamberlain Basin or the Middle Fork of the Salmon River, and yet needing protection from the more intensive use of the Stanley Basin and its many lakes. In other words, Rutledge hoped to establish a gradation of uses and development, with the most intensive being nearest to Sun Valley and then gradually diminishing to the north. He aimed to have his staff carefully work out plans for national forest lands in the area, but he suggested that the number-one objective of the Frontier Club was "the preservation of unsettled areas as a real frontier."

The Frontier Club had only very recently appeared on the scene. There is no known cache of its papers, so it can only be speculated at this point on why it suddenly emerged in the spring of 1937. It might well have resulted from a Forest Service attempt to foster a volunteer organization that would work with it as an equivalent to how sportsmen's clubs worked with the state Fish and Game Department.

In any case, the Frontier Club surfaced on May 9, 1937, in Hailey, when twenty-eight sportsmen met and elected officers. It intended to have representatives from the twelve central and south-central Idaho counties, ranging from Salmon, on the north, Arco and Burley to the east, and Mountain Home on the west. It was, the Hailey *Times* reported "the co-ordinated movement, entirely non-political, on the part of the citizens of Idaho to make Idaho perpetually one of the greatest outdoor states in the Union."[56] It apparently caught the interest of many other people in the area as well, since 150 attended the banquet in Shoshone on May 24 to hear Rutledge speak. Its aim of preserving the "interior wonderland" of Idaho "has so much behind it," the Shoshone paper editorialized a year later, "and is so different from park-building and exploitation schemes…that it can be made to appeal mightily to outdoor loving people" throughout the country.[57]

However, the club failed to gain consistent public attention in its own region. Every local weekly reported the meetings and resolutions of the local sportsmen's association, but coverage of the Frontier Club was distinctly hit or miss. The newspaper in Shoshone, where the club established its headquarters, could be relied on to give good coverage, and the Salmon *Recorder-Herald* paid close attention, but the Arco *Advertiser* only noticed the club when two of its representatives arrived to speak about its aims, and the Challis *Messenger* virtually ignored it.

Nevertheless, Frontier Club membership had increased to more than six hundred by August when it formally proposed the creation of a Sawtooth Primitive Area. Unlike in 1930 when an almost anonymous "group of sportsmen" suggested the formation of the Idaho Primitive Area, now a formally organized group, representing a substantial segment of the local population, stepped forth to start the deliberative process.

It is fair to assume that Rutledge influenced the process by which the Sawtooth proposal was handled. In sharp contrast to the decidedly internal way that the Selway-Bitterroot Primitive Area was created (administered from the Forest Service's Missoula regional office), in this case the general pattern of the 1930 process was repeated—a group of citizens made the proposal, it was publicly considered by a special committee appointed by the governor, and only then did the chief forester formally act. By 1937 a State Planning Board had replaced the special governor's committee of 1930. The board received a favorable report from its advisory committee at a public hearing of the proposal on September 10, noting that there was no opposition, since grazing would be allowed in the primitive area. It also recommended that the board study "the question of zoning the territory surrounding the proposed primitive area with a view to obtaining proper land use in order to preserve the frontier condition in the approach to the primitive area."[58] This clearly reflected Rutledge's idea of creating a gradation of area uses. "Primarily, we are seeking to protect the last frontier of America," according to Leo Bresnahan, a former assistant attorney general of Idaho, speaking on behalf of the Frontier Club, now counting eight hundred members.[59]

It surely gladdened the hearts of Rutledge and his colleagues in the Forest Service to hear L.F. Parson, secretary of the Idaho State Chamber of Commerce, support the proposal on the grounds that it would offset movements to convert the area into a national park. With Forest Service control, "an executive order would be amended from time to time to comply with the wishes of the people if changes appeared necessary in the future," he explained, "and it would eliminate restrictions imposed by federal park laws."[60] At the hearing's conclusion, the board approved the proposal, and on October 30, Rutledge announced the chief forester's designation of the Sawtooth Primitive Area. "We want," Rutledge declared, "to hold and maintain for future generations frontier conditions such as our forefathers met, with mystery, romance, freedom of use, and with inspirational qualities undiminished."[61]

Rutledge had set a tall order for himself and for users of central Idaho's primitive areas. Too tall, as it turned out. In the first place, they faced a contradiction that would always dog the steps of those wishing to preserve wilderness in America. How could one relive the frontier conditions of "freedom of use" when wilderness preservation inescapably required rules and regulations to prevent the wilderness from being developed out of existence? In addition, Rutledge was probably right in his belief that the primitive areas' periphery needed to be protected with zoning laws to maintain a gradation of uses, with intensity increasing only some safe distance away from the borders. But neither the State Planning Board in the 1930s nor any other public body since has evinced any intention of formulating and implementing such a zoning code.

The most fundamental dilemma of all, however, was what actually would be the preferred scenario for primitive area use. What does one do in a huge, artificially preserved frontier area? If it is seen as a vast, open-air museum, what is the story line for visitors to follow? Neither Rutledge nor any other partisans in favor of saving this last frontier answered that question in a way that the public found comprehensible and acceptable. In other words, the primitive areas were preserved, but their use remained undetermined.

The Frontier Club was unable to respond to the challenge of defining what visitors could do in this "last frontier." At the Shoshone meeting where Rutledge spoke, the final talk of the evening was by Troy Smith of Custer County, speaker in the State House of Representatives. Smith said, "we might just as well prepare for them," that is, "eastern 'dude' sportsmen" coming to the Sawtooths to fish and hunt.[62] But how? Four standing committees were established at this same meeting—Fish, Entertainment and Rodeo, Game Birds, and Frontier Area. The mixture of profound and trivial topics covered by the committees truly reflected the confusion that the club conveyed about its priorities.

Thus, on June 6, when two club officers appeared in Arco for a meeting to explain the club's aims, the local paper summarized their message as, "to promote the scenic and recreational resources of Idaho and to see to it that our streams are stocked with more fish than ever."[63] Similarly, at its October meeting in Twin Falls, Frank Moore, supervisor of the Sawtooth National Forest, described the new primitive area, but the major topic of discussion centered on screens to protect fish along the Wood River. Subsequent meetings focused on wildlife preservation and entertainment, without any sustained concern for the proper use of the "last frontier."

The Frontier Club's only lasting contribution, once the Sawtooth Primitive Area was designated, was an annual sixgun shooting match near Sun Valley, inaugurated in July 1938 in what was then "isolated" Elkhorn Gulch and continuing to the present. The month before, the club sponsored a "pioneer costume dance" in Ketchum, which, the Twin Falls *News* reported, "has caused a terrific amount of rummaging among attics and trunks...for authentic buckskins, broadcloths and flounces of early Idaho."[64]

In late June, Edward Worley, the founding president, died of a heart attack. While the club lingered on for another year, it seemed to have no clear and consequential purpose. In July 1939, it sponsored the planting of game fish by airplane in several mountain lakes, the annual six-gun shooting contest, with the winner receiving the Gary Cooper trophy, and a greased pig chase in "tin lizzies." Soon thereafter, the club quietly disappeared, without any comment from the press, pathetically ending the story of the first wilderness preservation organization in Idaho.

Meanwhile, Idaho's primitive areas received visitors with a wide range of motives. At the most atavistic, celebrators of raw masculinity saw the wilderness as the ideal place for rediscovering true manhood. Vardis Fisher published a piece in the September 1936 issue of *Esquire*, leaving no doubt as to his position by giving it the title, "An Essay for Men." His purpose, according to the subtitle, was to show how "the dudes start plump-bellied for Cougar Dave's wilderness, but they return looking changed."[65] Elsewhere, he shook his head, recognizing that "Frontiersmen Are Vanishing," with only a few surviving from the time "when the entire west was a physical frontier, with danger sitting at the table when they ate and darkening the cabins where they slept."[66] In a similar vein, the *Capital News* lamented the scene once roads came in, such as in Bear Valley: "here the yelp of the lady tourist in distress replaced the scream of the eagle."[67]

At the opposite extreme, scout troops ventured into the wilderness to practice their woodcraft, and Sun Valley had several pack teams for regularly scheduled trips for its guests. Responding to those protesting that this amounted to the primitive areas' commercialization, the editor of the Salmon *Recorder-Herald* retorted, "what good is the primitive area if no one is allowed to see it and to enjoy its natural beauty."[68]

Some tried to articulate the value of the wilderness experience as something that rose above mere tourism or he-man fantasies. Major Evan Kelley, regional forester in Missoula (and, therefore, the administrator of the Selway-Bitterroot Primitive Area) spoke at the Hailey conference in August 1936. He believed:

> many men, and women too, deep down crave association with nature in the rough, and where the environment compel[s] a mode of living shorn of the moral and physical softening effects of modern comforts and conveniences. They yearn for solitude to live in and listen to the wilderness.

He went on to define areas that provided such challenges as "sufficiently far-flung and wild that a person visiting them must undergo experiences in traveling and camping akin to those of the pioneers who first made their way into the Great West."[69]

Kelley's language came very close to that commonly used later by those advocating Wilderness Areas in the 1960s, but it was not at all typical in the 1930s. Nationally, the Wilderness Society had just been founded by Aldo Leopold, Bob Marshall, and others in 1935, and despite suspicions in Salmon that it had foisted the Selway-Bitterroot Primitive Area upon inattentive Idahoans, another couple of decades would pass before the Wilderness Society had any noticeable impact on Idahoans' attitudes about wilderness. Though a fairly extensive national dialogue about wilderness already had begun, only occasionally did some Idaho newspaper writer use language in Kelley's vein. The *Capital News*, for example, reported in April 1937 the availability of a new map for the Idaho Primitive Area, which, it went on to say, was for the "recreationist who wants to see 'life in the raw'...who wants to ride away into a vast timbered domain and be free from the things that man has done."[70]

The next year, McCall's *Payette Lake Star* dubbed central Idaho's wilderness as a "little kingdom" that "seems fresh from the Creator's hand."[71] The Coeur d'Alene *Press* summarized a primitive area as one where people could find a "mountain vacation 'far from the maddening crowd.'"[72] Nevertheless, these were uncommon exceptions to the way the Idaho press during the 1930s usually dealt with the subject.

Most Idahoans at the time viewed the primitive areas essentially as federally protected game preserves. Newspaper headlines frequently made this plain. The Idaho Falls *Post-Register* announced the creation of the Sawtooth Primitive Area with a headline reading, "Sportsmen's Paradise Established in Primitive Area of Idaho Woods," while Pocatello's *Idaho Examiner* put it similarly: "Sawtooth Area to Be Kept in Primitive State for Preservation of Wild Life."[73] Sometimes this was seen not as a way to re-experience pioneer ways, but to compensate for them. "It is gratifying," the *Statesman* editorialized in November 1938, "that we are partly making up for the folly of our pioneer and post pioneer ways" of slaughtering wild game without any concern for the future.[74] And an oldtimer in St. Maries concluded his comparison of the game scene in 1900 with that in 1939 by affirming the need for game preserves: "the only way to insure ourselves of game is to let a certain amount of the country revert back to its natural state."[75]

Special hunts in primitive areas were not always welcomed. Even though game authorities only declared those hunts to reduce herds that had grown too large for the available range, they could be lambasted as a "startling program of slaughter," to use the words of the *Kooskia Mountaineer*.[76] "What will the sons of today's sportsmen" think about the "wholesale slaughter" of elk in the Selway-Bitterroot Primitive Area, these "monarchs of the forest" being killed in an area "especially set aside for them?"[77]

Many hunters probably brushed aside such qualms, but few argued against getting into primitive areas as fast and easily as possible. Theorists might celebrate the rigors of hiking or packing into the backcountry, but most sportsmen welcomed a chance to fly in. It surely tantalized many readers of the Lewiston *Morning Tribune*'s report in July 1931 of three anglers who flew into the Selway region for a day's fishing. Leaving Lewiston at eight in the morning, it was only an hour's flight to Moose Creek Ranger Station, near which they enjoyed fishing for a few hours before returning home before nightfall. This was not an isolated stunt. As early as October 1928, guests flew from Grangeville to a dude ranch in Chamberlain Basin. In February 1931, Haddock Flying Service announced that it provided twice-a-week service from Cascade to Yellow Pine and other remote locations with a six-passenger, ski-equipped plane. The resort at Mackay Bar on the Salmon River had weekly service from Lewiston via Grangeville by May 1934. In October 1936, Vardis Fisher, the same man who had just published his hymn to machismo in *Esquire*, gave a rave review in the *Statesman* of his "Wings over Primitive Idaho" trip.[78]

Forest Service officials took a dim view of airplane intrusion into the wilderness. In 1933 Major Kelley attempted to ban airplanes in primitive areas, "in order to preserve [their] integrity and purpose."[79] But they could not stem the tide. "Riding the Sky-Trail to Moose Creek," Floyd Smith told readers of the *Morning Tribune*, was the way to "enjoy the undiminished pleasure of communing with nature in the raw…untrammeled by man and unscarred by cars" and the detritus of "modern picnic parties."[80]

And yet the Forest Service was partially the cause of airplane access into the roadless backcountry. "At every station in the wilderness there is an airport," the *Capital News* reported in 1936. "Most ranger stations find them indispensable."[81] The Forest Service earlier had accepted the use of airplanes for fire control, with Boise designated as a patrol base in January 1919. By the end of that year, a number of other aviation guard stations, including one near Grangeville, were being set up by forest officials. The Coeur d'Alene *Press* quoted R.H. Rutledge, then the district forester in Missoula, recounting after his first flight how impressed he was with the possibilities of aviation for fire spotting and suppression. Of course, that was long before any primitive areas were designated in Idaho, but throughout the 1930s, the Forest Service continued to develop remote airports, some within primitive area boundaries. Thus, in 1932, four new landing fields were announced, each large enough to accommodate the largest transport planes of the time. One was along the Middle Fork of the Salmon River in the Idaho Primitive Area.

Thus, hunters preferring to fly in, rather than take the time and energy to hike in, were not noticeably different in their thinking from the managers trying to take care of the primitive areas. Ideally, wilderness should be left in a "natural state." "Primitive Areas are virgin tracts," in the contemporary 1935 words of the Wilderness Society, that "preserve the native vegetative and physiographic conditions which have existed for an inestimable period."[82] And yet, the Forest Service felt it could not simply stand by and allow wildfires to burn forests (even though such conflagrations had occurred since time immemorial). Typically, in August 1939, confronted with a two-thousand-acre fire 112 miles north of McCall, the agency dispatched more than 500 firefighters and three airplanes dropping supplies by parachute, since the nearest road was twenty-nine miles away.

State Fish and Game authorities, responsible for managing wildlife in the primitive areas, also fostered landing fields there. Reporting on an inspection trip into the Idaho Primitive Area in 1940, the Coeur d'Alene *Press* noted that they had used three landing fields, since "flying has been encouraged by the fish and game commission as the cheapest transportation into the area."[83]

In conclusion, both users and managers of Idaho's primitive areas during the 1930s regarded those areas much more like vast outdoor museums than pristine samples of Mother Nature's work. Unlike later wilderness managers, who make every effort not to disturb native ecology, Idaho's early primitive area managers approached their charge more like museum directors, making changes as needed to enhance the "exhibit's" overall effect.

For example, the pioneers supposedly enjoyed turkey shoots. Since there were no wild turkeys native to Idaho, State Game Warden Amos Eckert in March 1937 proceeded to import twenty-six from Michigan as an initial breeding flock and expected to bring in some more from Texas for "the delectation of future generations," according to the *Statesman*.[84] The Challis *Messenger* put it more tellingly, so that "wild turkey shooting—a sport of pioneers—may return to Idaho."[85] The experiment failed. Even with a fulltime herder, the turkeys grew tame and refused to get out and find feed for themselves. Coyotes took several, and the rest were turned over to a local rancher. Nevertheless, this turkey caper remains a good example of prevailing attitudes toward wilderness in Idaho. The Forest Service chose to change its terminology in 1939, referring to wilderness rather than primitive areas, but more than two decades would pass before that change reflected significantly different thinking in Idaho.

ENDNOTES

1. "Idaho to Have Million Acre Primitive Area," Boise *Statesman* (November 15, 1930): pp. 1, 10.
2. "Idaho Primitive Area," editorial in Idaho Falls *Times-Register* (November 17, 1930): p. 6.
3. "Area Will Be Monument to Virgin Nature," Boise *Capital News* (November 17, 1930): p. 9.
4. "The Forest Primeval," editorial in Boise *Capital News* (November 21, 1930): p. 4.
5. "Idahoans Support Forester's Move," Twin Falls *News* (December 21, 1930): p. 1.
6. "Mining Chief Opposes Area," Boise *Statesman* (December 30, 1930): pp. 1, 2.
7. The best single source of biographical information is an obituary published in the Boise *Statesman* (November 26, 1956): p. 10.
8. "Frontier Area Makes It Hard for the Game," Pocatello *Tribune* (April 5, 1929): p. 3.
9. "Location of Primitive Area," Boise *Capital News* (December 21, 1930): p. 5.
10. "Notes from the Salmon Forest," Salmon *Recorder-Herald* (October 22, 1930): p. 1.
11. Watson Humphrey, "They Would Keep the State's Wildest Beauty Unspoiled," Boise *Statesman* (December 28, 1930): Section 2, pp. 1, 4.
12. "Roads Would Ruin Paradise of Sportsmen," Nampa *Leader-Herald* (December 16, 1927): p. 1.
13. "Idaho Forest Plan Approved," Cascade *News* (November 21, 1930): p. 1.
14. "Eighth Biennial Report of the Fish and Game Warden of the State of Idaho, 1919–1920."
15. "Game Preserve near Elk City, Citizens Plan," Grangeville *Idaho County Free Press* (January 18, 1923): p. 1.
16. "Will Protect Game," editorial in Hailey *Times-News-Miner* (February 19, 1925): p. 4.
17. "Big Game Area Open to Autos by November 1," Boise *Statesman* (September 28, 1928): p. 10.
18. "Rifle Club Memorializes Legislature," Salmon *Herald* (January 14, 1925): p. 1.
19. "Sees Money in Tourist Crop for Idaho," Boise *Statesman* (October 14, 1914): p. 12.
20. Otto M. Jones, "Spring Brings Itching Feeling to Palms Accustomed to Fish Rod or Steering Wheel," Boise *Statesman* (April 27, 1919): Section 2, p. 5.
21. "Autos in the National Park," editorial in Pocatello *Tribune* (July 11, 1913): p. 4.
22. "The Yellowstone Highway," editorial in Idaho Falls *Idaho Register* (March 28, 1916): p. 4.

23. "Many Attend Annual Dinner of Sportsmen," Twin Falls *News* (February 18, 1925): p. 3.
24. "We Need the Wilderness," editorial in Coeur d'Alene *Press* (May 28, 1929): p. 4.
25. "Advertise Aesthetic Resources," editorial in Kooskia *Mountaineer* (March 17, 1926): p. 4.
26. "Still Some Wilderness!" editorial in Idaho Falls *Post* (March 22, 1927): p. 4.
27. "Park Boundary to Be Changed," Pocatello *Tribune* (August 24, 1925): p. 1.
28. "Frontier Area Makes It Hard for the Game," Pocatello *Tribune* (April 5, 1929): p. 3.
29. "Virgin Area Set Aside," Kooskia *Mountaineer* (November 19, 1930): p. 1.
30. "Gem State Land Is Set Aside as 'Primitive Area,'" Idaho Falls *Times-Register* (November 15, 1930): pp. 1, 8.
31. Watson Humphrey, "They Would Keep the State's Wildest Beauty Unspoiled," Boise *Statesman* (December 28, 1930): Section 2, pp. 1, 4; "Primitive Area Meet Saturday," Boise *Capital News* (December 19, 1930): p. 12; "Neglected Wealth," editorial in Lewiston *Morning Tribune* (July 20, 1931): p. 4.
32. "Location of Primitive Area," Boise *Capital News* (December 21, 1930): p. 5, including a map.
33. "A Wise Program," editorial in Twin Falls *Times* (July 27, 1931): p. 4.
34. "The Primitive Area," editorial in Salmon *Recorder-Herald* (February 26, 1936): p. 4.
35. "Three Great Western Wildernesses: What Must Be Done to Save Them," *Living Wilderness* I (September 1935): pp. 9–10.
36. "Figures of Forest Show 2,990 Hunters in Primitive Area," Lewiston *Morning Tribune* (November 1, 1937): p. 6.
37. "Primitive Area," editorial in Twin Falls *News* (November 23, 1930): p. 4.
38. "'Ware the Boom!" editorial in Boise *Capital News* (May 18, 1937): p. 4.
39. "Sawtooth National Park," editorial in Twin Falls *Times* (July 3, 1935): p. 4.
40. "Stanley Basin Comes into Its Own," editorial in Boise *Statesman* (July 18, 1936): p. 4.
41. "National Park for Idaho," Twin Falls *News* (July 26, 1936): p. 3. See also Douglas W. Dodd, "Preserving Multiple-Use Management: The U.S. Forest Service, the National Park Service, and the Struggle for Idaho's Sawtooth Mountain Country, 1911–1972" (Ann Arbor, Mich.: UMI Dissertation Services, 2002.): pp. 78–129.
42. "A National Park," editorial in Salmon *Recorder-Herald* (July 29, 1936): p. 2.
43. "Tourist Paradise," editorial in Twin Falls *News* (August 23, 1936): p. 4.
44. "Do We Want a Park?" editorial in Twin Falls *Times* (July 31, 1936): p. 4.
45. "National Park Opinions Vary at Conference," Boise *Statesman* (September 1, 1936): pp. 1, 2.
46. "Sawtooth Park Battle Opens at Hailey Meet," Boise *Capital News* (August 31, 1936): p. 1.
47. "Pope's National Park Bill Opposed," Challis *Messenger* (March 3, 1937): p. 4.
48. "New Park Is Not Craved," Shoshone *Lincoln County Journal* (August 28, 1936): p. 1.
49. "One Thing They Don't Want," editorial in Pocatello *Tribune* (March 2, 1937): p. 4.
50. "No Sawtooth Park," editorial in Boise *Capital News* (May 6, 1937): p. 4.
51. "Pope Withdraws Park Proposal," Boise *Statesman* (April 29, 1937): p. 7.
52. "A Program for the Sawtooth-Salmon River Country," Shoshone *Lincoln County Journal* (July 16, 1937): p. 7. The full text of Rutledge's speech can be found in "Idaho Primitive Area—The Last Frontier of the Great West," Hailey *Times* (June 3, 1937): pp. 1, 11.
53. "Idaho Renews Argument for Water Supply," Boise *Statesman* (December 8, 1933): p. 1.
54. "Salmon River Diversion Approved," Boise *Capital News* (February 6, 1934): p. 1.
55. "Salmon Settlers Protest Tunnel," Boise *Statesman* (August 22, 1934): p. 8.
56. "Frontier Club Launched to Preserve Resources of Sawtooth Wonderland," Hailey *Times* (May 13, 1937): pp. 1, 8.
57. "Frontier Club, Inc.," editorial in Shoshone *Lincoln County Journal* (May 27, 1937): p. 2.
58. "Board Favors Rugged Area," Boise *Statesman* (September 11, 1937): pp. 1, 8.
59. "Keep Area Wild," Lewiston *Morning Tribune* (September 11, 1937): p. 1.
60. "Unit Plans for Primitive Area," Idaho Falls *Post-Register* (September 12, 1937): p. 8.
61. "Sawtooths Have Primitive Area," Boise *Statesman* (October 31, 1937): p. 9.
62. Harold J. Wood, "New Sportsmen's Organization Perfected," Twin Falls *Times* (May 25, 1937): p. 5.
63. "Frontier Club to Hold Meeting Here," Arco *Advertiser* (June 18, 1937): pp. 1, 8.
64. "Idaho Frontier Club to Revive Old Time Dances," Twin Falls *News* (June 10, 1938): p. 1.
65. Vardis Fisher, "An Essay for Men," *Esquire* (September 1936): pp. 35, 137ff.

66. "Frontiersmen Are Vanishing," Idaho Falls *Post-Register* (May 24, 1937): p. 7.
67. "Save Our Wilderness!" editorial in Boise *Capital News* (March 13, 1937): p. 4.
68. "Seeing the Primitive Area," editorial in Salmon *Recorder-Herald* (June 23, 1937): p. 4.
69. "Briefed Report" of the Hailey conference, p. 15. This summary of the proceedings may be found at the Idaho State Library in Boise.
70. "New Primitive Area Map-Folder Available," Boise *Capital News* (April 2, 1937): p. 2.
71. "Trail Riders of the Wilderness," McCall *Payette Lake Star* (June 16, 1938): p. 1.
72. "No Highways in Primitive Area," Coeur d'Alene *Press* (April 3, 1933): p. 4.
73. "Sportsmen's Paradise Established in Primitive Area of Idaho Woods," Idaho Falls *Post-Register* (October 12, 1937): p. 13; "Sawtooth Area to Be Kept in Primitive State for Preservation of Wild Life," Pocatello *Idaho Examiner* (September 11, 1937): p. 1.
74. "Increase in Game," editorial in Boise *Statesman* (November 30, 1938): p. 4.
75. "Local Man Gives Sportsmen's View," St. Maries *Gazette-Record* (April 20, 1939): p. 8.
76. "Thousand Elk Must Go," editorial by "Mr. Ordinary Citizen," in Kooskia *Mountaineer* (August 19, 1937): p. 2.
77. Floyd L. Smith, "Killing Elk to Save Their Lives in So-Called 'Mercy Hunt' Brings Condemnation of Idaho Sportsmen," Lewiston *Morning Tribune* (September 1, 1937): p. 9.
78. Vardis Fisher, "Wings over Primitive Idaho," Boise *Statesman* (October 11, 1936): Section 2, pp. 1, 8.
79. "Ban Airlines in Primitive Areas," Grangeville *Idaho County Free Press* (March 9, 1933): p. 6.
80. Floyd L. Smith, "Riding the Sky-Trail to Moose Creek," Lewiston *Morning Tribune* (August 25, 1935): Section 2, pp. 1, 3.
81. Saxton E. Bradford, "They're Taking to the Air in Idaho's Primitive Area," Boise *Capital News* (October 12, 1936): p. 5.
82. *Living Wilderness* I (September 1935): p. 2.
83. "Deer and Fish Plentiful in Idaho Primitive Area," Coeur d'Alene *Press* (October 30, 1940): p. 3.
84. "26 Wild Turkeys Will Test Gem State's Primitive Area," Boise *Statesman* (March 12, 1937): p. 20.
85. "Game Warden Taking Turkeys to Middle Fork," Challis *Messenger* (March 31, 1937): p. 8.

V

Mustangs and other Varmints

W HILE IT IS FAIR TO SAY that Idahoans gradually accepted more of a conservationist attitude as the twentieth century wore on, it came at anything but an even pace. As already related, scenic preservation gained some notable successes as early as the 1920s and wilderness preservation was well underway in the 1930s, but when attention turns to some other topics, there was almost no significant change prior to the 1960s.

For example, Idahoans almost never took an environmentalist view of wild animals until the late 1960s. Rather than thinking about them on their own terms, Idahoans' concern for wildlife generally focused on protecting a few species they liked to hunt or fish and getting rid of predators. In other words, for most people of the time, only two kinds of animals and fish existed—those that fit in with humanity's needs and interests, and all others. The latter commonly fell under the catch-all category of "varmints," which in the West included not only vermin and rodents, but also any creatures that got in the way.

The case of the trumpeter swan marked a rare exception to this generalization. In the 1960s, newspapers throughout the state took pleasure in reiterating the story of how the trumpeter swan had reached the brink of extinction by the early 1930s, with only seventy-three left concentrated in about sixty square miles in Idaho and Montana bordering Yellowstone National Park. Thanks to careful protection by federal agencies with the support of local sportsmen, the swans began to flourish, increasing to 1,500 by 1957 and more than 4,000 at the end of the 1960s. When a swan was killed in 1964, the Boise *Statesman* noted it was "a reminder of a shameful waste and also a major accomplishment in wildlife preservation."[1] And why save the swans? "Well, why not?" replied the Twin Falls *Times-News*. "Man proved long ago he could eliminate any particular species. Now, he's also proving he can save and perpetuate a bird that has no peer for size, beauty and grace. That's enough incentive."[2]

But this was an exception, and perhaps the attitude toward eagles might be another, as Warden Amos Eckert found out in 1937. In March, along with his attempt to plant turkeys in the Idaho Primitive Area, Eckert declared war on eagles in the same area, sending out five professional hunters to shoot as many as possible. Eckert was responding to a complaint from Elmer Purcell, a trapper in Salmon, that golden eagles were attacking deer, mountain goats, and mountain sheep. Their kills were so great that they couldn't even be estimated, according to Eckert, and "I propose to stop this slaughter."[3]

This provoked an outcry from near and far. "I never saw enough eagles in this state to do harm to anything," scoffed Gus Keefe, a banker and "pioneer sportsmen" in Shoshone.[4] The *Statesman* objected that no real evidence proved that eagles were actually bothering sheep or goats. The Oregon Audubon Society denounced Eckert as "a bum sport," and letters flooded into the governor's office from all over the country protesting the killing of eagles. Governor Barzilla Clark found it convenient to replace Eckert in April, although he denied that this had any connection with the eagle controversy.

Nevertheless, not everyone condemned Eckert's war on eagles; many reports in Idaho newspapers appeared without editorial comment, possibly suggesting tacit approval. Eckert received letters praising his efforts, such as one from Elmer Keith of North Fork, agreeing that eagles "are the worst predator of all to young mountain sheep, goats, antelope and deer."[5] The Salmon newspaper asserted that if eagles were allowed to go "unmolested, mountain sheep and goats are doomed."[6]

The following year, the local sportsmen's association urged placing a bounty on golden eagles, declaring them "Predator No. 1."[7] In December 1939, George Booth of Burley, chairman of the Fish and Game Commission, also suggested a bounty on eagles. While the bald eagle was given protection in 1940 by an act of Congress, golden eagles remained vulnerable to hunters. In 1966 the *Statesman* reported that twenty-eight golden eagles were killed in Idaho. Not until the creation in 1971 of the eighty-mile-long Snake River Birds of Prey Area west of Mountain Home did eagles finally have a safe haven in Idaho.

Nothing more clearly demonstrates the obsessive utilitarianism of Idahoans' attitudes in those years toward wildlife than the attempt to wipe out wild mustangs in the state. When President Richard Nixon signed a 1971 law banning the hunting of all unbranded horses, he said they deserved protection as "a matter of ecological right—as anyone knows who has ever stood awed at the indomitable spirit and sheer energy of a mustang running free."[8] There may not be any clear idea of what an ecological right is, but most people today probably would not quarrel with Nixon's sentiments, and they almost certainly would agree with the law's statement that mustangs are "living symbols of the pioneer spirit of the West."[9] Yet for the previous half-century, numerous wild horse roundups were explicitly staged in Idaho and throughout the Great Basin to rid even the most remote areas of what were then called "knotheads" or "outlaws," condemned as "scrubby, mangy, unfit for anything but chickenfeed."[10]

It remains far from clear why so many Idahoans began to do everything in their power to wipe out mustangs in the late 1920s. It may be true, as a 1926 report in the Idaho Falls *Times-Register* claimed, that "war has been declared for a long time on the stray horses of the western states."[11] But, as far as can be determined from the scattered and infrequent press coverage, the war in Idaho had been a distinctly desultory affair until the mid-1920s. Apparently what then changed was an order from the Department of Agriculture to rid public lands of them. They "are increasing rapidly, are useless, consume the grass that is needed for livestock and in other ways make themselves a nuisance."[12]

Ironically, none other than R.H. Rutledge, the man who would lead the quest to save the last frontier only a few years later, pushed the order's enforcement. He announced in January 1927 that 2,117 wild horses were eliminated from the national forest lands in his district during the previous year (including 779 in Idaho), along with 2,788 the year before. That would, he believed, free up range for ten thousand sheep. Nor did Rutledge limit his effort to national forest lands of Idaho and Montana alone. "If these pests are not cleaned up on the deserts," the Pocatello *Tribune* quoted him as saying, "they continue to drift upon the forests and ruin the breeding for many valuable domestic animals."[13]

This was a sharply bittersweet enterprise. "The cowboys who hunt wild horses are mostly in the game for the love of the sport," stated an article in *Popular Mechanics.* They actually hated the brutality with which sheepmen shot horses at watering holes.[14] "Boiseites generally were totally unmoved," according to the *Statesman*, "by reports that wild horses are being sent to canneries and fertilizer factories."[15] But only three weeks later, the *Statesman* published a meditation on "The Passing of the Wild Horse" by Glenn Balch, an author whose horse stories later gained regional fame. Balch was convinced that wild horses soon would follow the dodo bird and passenger pigeon into extinction. "The death knell of the wild horse has been sounded… He has no place in our economic system." There was no arguing the matter; "to get right down to bed rock facts, free from all sentimentalism whatever, the wild horse is worthless." Still, seen in the wilds of Idaho, "they make a stirring sight as they come, in single file through the brush." One was tempted to "weep tears of regret" watching them trot "sadly to extinction."[16]

Rounding up all the mustangs turned out to be a much bigger job than anyone at the time had imagined. Many herds, each numbering in the hundreds, were scattered around southern and central Idaho, near Pocatello, near Mackay and Challis, southeast of Twin Falls, near Council, and as far north as Craig Mountain, some fifty miles south of Lewiston. In each case, an initial roundup captured a few hundred horses, but the cagiest and fastest evaded their would-be captors.

The largest number—perhaps ten thousand in 1930—ran free in Owyhee County (the southwest corner of Idaho) and intermingled with another thirty thousand in neighboring portions of Oregon and Nevada. That spring, more than one hundred riders from ranches in all three states set out to clear the range of all of them. By late May, more than two thousand were caught and shipped in some eighty carloads from Murphy and Mountain Home to Butte and Portland to be ground up into chicken and fox feed.

But neither that roundup nor the many that followed over the next three decades succeeded in wiping out the wily mustang. The same pattern reoccurred time and again: roundup followed by assertions of the demise of mustangs in an area, followed a year or two later by yet another roundup. "Large droves of the horses remain," the *Statesman* acknowledged in May 1931.[17]

In August another major shipment left Bliss, and the paper passed along the ranchers' belief that the area's mustangs had been thinned to a mere handful. Disgruntled ranchers could say what they would about wild horses being diseased, deteriorated by inbreeding, and generally inferior to domestic stock, but "a wild horse, untrammeled by rider and saddle, can make a roundup a pretty tough job," as Grover Knight of Caldwell ruefully conceded in the summer of 1936.[18] The answer, he and several other roundup organizers in the mid-1930s believed, was aviation. Knight hired an aviator from Los Angeles, while Lemoine Stevens of Twin Falls flew the plane himself. This, they thought, would surely do the trick. "The wild horse situation is well under control," E.R. Greenslet assured a *Statesman* reporter, after a roundup in November 1936 assisted by an airplane.[19] But herds of mustangs continued to roam thereafter.

Part of the problem was geographical. The spaces involved were simply too vast and thinly populated for anyone to impose tight controls or eliminate the herds. Owyhee County encompasses eight thousand square miles (roughly the same size as Connecticut), and even today is without a single town except along its northern border, with only isolated ranches scattered in the interior mountains and "breaks" (the arid backcountry, cut by ravines and ridges). The mustang haunts elsewhere in Idaho were on a smaller, but still imposing, scale.

But motivation also was a problem. While government officials kept urging the need for roundups, they offered no financial incentives. Consequently, ranchers only planned roundups in off-seasons, which sometimes meant times of unfavorable weather, and cowboys lost interest when the market price for horseflesh fell off, which it frequently did in the Depression-ridden 1930s. Furthermore, it sometimes seemed like a bad business at best. The Twin Falls *Times* concluded a roundup report in June 1930 with the wistful observation that the mustangs would probably follow "the trail of the buffalo and be driven completely out of the rangeland, taking with them another reminder of the old pioneer west."[20] In 1938 the *Statesman* noted that "they all have to go… It may be a shame that another page is being torn out of the old west, but it's got to be done."[21]

That is not to say that any substantial movement emerged in Idaho to save the mustangs. Periodic roundups continued. Sometimes the cowboys won; sometimes the mustangs got the better of them. Perhaps the most notable example of the latter occurred in May 1944 when eighty riders in the Owyhee Mountains out of Jordan Valley, Oregon, spent three days crowding wild horses into a box canyon. Exactly how many were in this would-be corral depends upon which story can be believed. According to a report at the time, it was six hundred, but a few years later they were said to number two thousand. In any case, just as the cowboys thought they finished the job, their reserve mounts bolted into the herd, stampeding the wild animals into "inaccessible canyons."[22] The cowboys had to go home with nothing but the thrill of the chase. As one told a journalist two years later, "the craziest excitement a man can know in this life is running wild horses. The country is wild and the horses are wild and you got to be wild too."[23]

Fearing that the mustangs could not survive the repeated attempts to end their existence, Pete Lenz of Boise spoke up on their behalf. "I'm still enough of westerner," he told the *Statesman* in October 1945, "that I like to see an occasional band of wild horses out on the range…and I hate to think of these horses being killed off… They represent to me an era of the west that will never live again except in memory."[24] Unwilling simply to indulge in sentimental nostalgia, Lenz tried to do something to save them. He and a few like-minded Boiseans proceeded to organize the Idaho Humane Society, with one of their original goals to end the rounding up of mustangs. Lenz wrote Glen Taylor, Idaho's "Cowboy Senator," asking his intervention to "put an immediate stop to the ruthless and needless killing."[25] Taylor sidestepped the issue by asking Idahoans to write him about how they felt about it. The humane society quickly settled down to the mundane task of caring for stray dogs and cats.

The fight to save the mustangs was waged by people in other states without Idahoans paying much attention, let alone giving any noticeable support. Velma Johnson, a secretary in Reno, organized an unrelenting campaign that earned her the title of "Wild Horse Annie" and national attention. Her efforts to end the use of airplanes culminated in a 1959 federal law prohibiting that practice, legislation that was ignored by Idaho newspapers. They did give some notice to the first wild horse refuge—established in 1963 on 435,000 acres in Nevada's Nellis Air Force Base. They also reported the battle of Lloyd Tillett and several other ranchers in the Pryor Mountains along the Montana-Wyoming border, which forced the Bureau of Land Management to end its efforts to wipe out that area's mustang herd and to set aside thirty thousand acres for the horses to roam without harassment. But this never led to any concerted effort toward protecting Idaho's remaining mustangs. That only came with the enactment of federal legislation in 1971 outlawing the hunting or killing of any unbranded horse or burro.

Idahoans' lack of interest in saving the mustangs arose not from their insensitivity to conservation, but rather from their belief that conservation required a rational, persistent protection of natural resources (in this case, the range lands). "Wild horses," according to the *Statesman*, "merely are stage sets on the western scene."[26] In other words, they were at best ornaments rather than producers, which the Challis *Messenger* reminded its readers, "add little, if anything, to the economy of the state."[27]

This marked a major change in local thinking, however. It was noted in Chapter I how fiercely the Forest Service's early conservationist thinking was opposed by much of the public, particularly in the northern part of the state. Although rangers managed to win over most critics by 1920, that had not yet carried over into a general acceptance of conservation. The editor of the Coeur d'Alene *Press* spoke for many when denouncing conservation in September 1930: "the west has listened too long to the swan song of the conservationists... The west has been conserved to death... Most 'conservation' is bunk!"[28]

It took the traumas of the 1930s—not only the Great Depression, but also repeated natural catastrophes, including the Dust Bowl and the flooding of the Mississippi River—to convert Idahoans to a commitment to conservation. It forced recognition that the old easy-come easy-go approach to the land had to be put aside. "The old pioneers never thought about waste," the Sandpoint *Bulletin* conceded. "If they saw a forest, it did not occur to them that those trees were going to be needed." Now, "we must watch carefully over the remainder."[29] The Twin Falls *News* agreed. In an editorial titled "Reversing the Pioneers," it concluded that Americans were now moving beyond simply talking about conservation and "beginning to do something practical about it."[30]

By 1936 the Coeur d'Alene *Press*, too, had completely reversed its editorial stance, applauding the Idaho Wildlife Federation for its recognition that wildlife preservation required concern for habitat, which in turn required attention to stream purification, reforestation, and replacement of native grasses. "The fact that more is being done now than ever before for conservation and preservation of all natural resources," it concluded, "is very encouraging."[31] Even the Lewiston *Morning Tribune*, the most hidebound of all the anti-conservation papers in the state, had joined the bandwagon by the end of the 1930s. Noting that to be called a "conservationist" once was a term of opprobrium, an editorial at the beginning of 1940 admitted, "the nation has come to realize [conservationists] were right." Conservation "is a battle and a continuing one, which must be carried forward consistently" if society was to avoid the accusation of having wasted its heritage.[32]

Very little backsliding occurred after World War II. In 1954 a movement arose in Lemhi County against accepting the Soil Conservation Service, and the Salmon *Recorder-Herald* published editorials supporting the cause. But even there, no one argued against the importance of soil conservation. The whole fight erupted over whether federal controls were needed or whether local people could do it better themselves. The localists lost, and few tears were shed over the outcome.

However, wildlife conservation measures could have Draconian implications, as demonstrated by the attempted extermination of mustangs, and in the emphasis on protecting a few favored big game species (deer, elk, mountain sheep, and mountain goat), while neglecting other animals. It generally was asserted that big game was a major state resource attracting many tourists, although there is no evidence that anyone did a cost/benefit analysis to confirm this. Beyond these favored few species, wild animals in Idaho definitely were at risk of being harried off the land, unless they could be shown to be of some value to humans.

Sometimes it was done. Take beaver, for example. When trappers had hunted them to the verge of extinction by 1905, the legislature restricted beaver trapping to Fish and Game officials (and only when local populations became so large as to menace farms and ranches). Generally, beaver were seen as "natural conservationists," whose dams and ponds enhanced soil conservation by slowing runoff in mountain streams. According to William Welsh, the Boise River watermaster, beaver had been "of tremendous value" in the Boise River drainage; "we need them."[33] The trouble was that beaver flourished only in a few areas, particularly in the three northern counties of Benewah, Kootenai, and Bonner, and did not naturally spread elsewhere. Therefore, beginning in a limited way in the late 1920s, and then far more ambitiously in 1937, state and federal conservation personnel began transplanting beaver. With costs underwritten by federal game preservation funds (under the Pitman-Robertson Act), thousands of beaver were transplanted, 3,673 for the years 1938–42 alone. By 1945 they were even being relocated by air into the primitive areas.

However, it was not long before the situation changed. Beaver are naturally prolific and their numbers increased to roughly forty thousand in Idaho by 1940. Consequently, trappers began in 1941 to campaign for the reopening of a beaver season. Under the tireless leadership of David Brazil of Boise, the Idaho Trappers Association repeatedly lobbied the legislature and started an initiative campaign in 1945. Despite the opposition of the Fish and Game Department and the Idaho Wildlife Federation, the trappers (and farmers not persuaded by the transplanting program) finally won. Dismissing the department's caretaker/trapper program as either ineffective or unfairly limiting access, proponents of a regular beaver season gained legislative approval in 1957.

One might conclude from the story of beavers that other creatures might also have been considered to be useful. "There must be various animals in danger of extinction," the editor of the Twin Falls *News* speculated, "that would be glad to tackle some of our other conservation jobs."[34] But this was not a notion shared by many Idahoans at the time. Much more typical was the position taken by the Kooskia *Mountaineer*. Beaver and muskrats were not, the editor observed, destructive to other animal life, as opposed to martens, fishers, and weasels that were, and "which may well be hunted off entirely."[35]

Hunting some creatures off "entirely," however, might upset the balance of nature, a concept not completely unfamiliar to people at the time. Newspapers occasionally published editorials reminding readers of the dangers of overruling Mother Nature, who then "strikes with swift reprisal."[36] In November 1928, for example, the *Statesman* warned of "Nature Meddling": "when man invades the forest and says, 'these animals I shall let live…and these others I shall exterminate,' there is trouble ahead."[37] The Twin Falls *News* worried about the tendency of hunters to kill hawks because they preyed on game birds: "it is not a sensible thing, according to many naturalists. Even birds of prey serve a useful purpose," particularly that of keeping rodents in check.[38] Even T.B. Murray, head of the Biological Survey in Idaho and, in effect, the chief warrior against predators, told the Stanley Basin Wildlife Society that civilization's advance had disturbed nature's balance, and "man must assist nature in restoring a balance."[39]

Nevertheless, in Idaho for much of the twentieth century these efforts tended to be like Sunday school truisms, which most people paid lip service to while continuing to do business as usual. It was not nearly as easy to follow the example of Henry David Thoreau, striving to observe wildlife without disturbing it, as it was to go out and kill animals, preferably in large numbers. The prevailing imagery was one of warfare, not that of unobtrusive observation or even of a gardener selectively just pulling weeds. Tellingly, the Idaho Falls *Post-Register* reported in 1936 that the Works Progress Administration "has declared 'war' on Idaho's predatory animals and rodents."[40] Two years later, the Twin Falls *Times* gave front-page coverage to "Bombing Warfare" aimed at eliminating fifty thousand crows along the Snake River near Burley. A large crew installed more than three hundred small bombs in a rookery to be set off electronically, a method developed in Canyon County several years previously.[41] Only about ten thousand were killed, far less than what the same method had achieved two years before on Lake Lowell near Nampa. "Boom! Boom! 40,000 Crows Are Blasted into Eternity," was the way the editor of the Shoshone paper headlined the story. [42]

Also in 1936, Bonner County resumed its "War on Predatory Pests," with the county extension agent and the local sportsmen's association sponsoring prizes for youngsters helping in the battle to "stamp out the squirrels."[43] The following year, the sportsmen in Shoshone declared "War against Magpies."[44] "The fight to keep rabbits and squirrels from materially damaging our crops," the county extension agent in Twin Falls ruefully admitted, "seems to be an everlasting battle."[45]

The war on jackrabbits was a particularly ugly one. Rabbit drives had been organized in southern Idaho farm communities since the first years of the twentieth century. They were herded into enclosures, then clubbed to death. This was not "nice" or "pleasant," the *Capital News* conceded, but it was "a necessary act of self defense."[46] Nevertheless, it made a poor impression elsewhere. Reporting that sixty-five thousand rabbits had been killed in Lincoln County during June 1934, the *Statesman* noted that back east, "it is termed by various leagues, associations and other astute bodies, as nothing short of cruelty, slaughter, decimation of game and the like." Idahoans were being called merciless, and "so they are…an item of self defense to the farmer."[47] Why, the *Statesman* writer snorted, one might as well protest killing grasshoppers.

Without denying the threat and impact of rabbit infestations on crops, one still has to wonder about those drives—too many people participated and seemed to take too much pleasure for them to be merely a grim necessity. For example, in February 1951 in two drives near Idaho Falls during one weekend, 5,500 rabbits were corralled and killed by some five hundred people. This was, in fact, something of a recreational activity, with the added benefit that pelts were sold to pay for community projects.

As a "war," it really was never-ending, "a good bit like pushing back the ocean," according to Beth Rhodenbaugh, a writer for the state Fish and Game Department.[48] Even when federal rodent control workers went at it as hard as they could—ninety men working fulltime in early 1937 and killing about 750,000—no noticeable long-term impact was made on the rabbit population, and drives continued unabated into the 1970s.

Although state and federal wildlife authorities were involved and should have known better, those attempting to control the rabbits failed to make even the most basic ecological analysis. If they had asked about the rabbit's natural enemy, they would have found it was the coyote. And yet the rodent control people also killed coyotes as frequently as possible. In the spring of 1937, in addition to the 750,000 rabbits, they bagged more than two thousand coyotes per month. With the coyotes gone, the rabbits reproduced faster than all efforts to kill them off.

Curiously enough, the same ecological blindness characterized most other predator control policies until well into the 1960s. Chapter II noted how agricultural interests initially fostered those policies, but by the early 1920s that changed. In January 1922, the *Statesman* quoted Emile Grandjean: "the forest rangers are carrying on an active campaign in the exterminating of predatory animals by trapping and poisoning and are co-operating with the Biological Survey [predecessor to the U.S. Fish and Wildlife Service] and the state fish and game department in the work."[49] The results were terrific. In 1922, 49,149 animals were killed: 44,541 coyotes, 3,579 wildcats, 676 lynx, 143 wolves, and 225 cougars. This continued year after year. In the fiscal year ending June 30, 1937, 18,819 predators were killed, including 17,897 coyotes, 83 bobcats, 76 bears, and 716 badgers. "Predatory animal destruction is a perfectly feasible thing," the *Morning Tribune* believed, "and the only requirement to make it a success is an adequate financial return to the expert trappers" by providing sufficient bounties or salaries.[50]

The standard argument was that predators killed more big game than did hunters. In 1929 the Twin Falls *News* quoted C.K. McHarg, Jr., supervisor of the Coeur d'Alene National Forest, who said 2,358 hunters came to northern Idaho in 1927, killing less than one big-game animal apiece, whereas predators had killed an estimated 3,810 deer. Sportsmen felt justified in joining ranks with farmers and ranchers. In 1928 the Challis Rod and Gun Club wrote to Salmon, asking Lemhi County sportsmen to support a war of extermination on cougars. The men in Salmon responded by resolving to ask Congress to rid stock and game ranges in the West of these "predacious pests."[51]

Hardly anyone for many years protested the killing of predators by shooting or trapping, but the frequent use of poisons eventually evoked organized opposition. As early as 1931, concerns were published about the dangers of poison to other animals. In the spring of 1935, the Twin Falls *News* printed an angry critique by rancher and trapper Ned Foster, blasting the "pernicious activities" of the Biological Survey: "its wanton destruction of wild life in Idaho is an abortive attempt to exterminate predatory animals," killing fox, marten, and other fur-bearing animals, while coyotes continued to thrive.[52]

Others vigorously defended the poison program. "The mink, weasel, and marten are ferocious little killers," asserted the editor of the Kamiah *Progress*. He believed they caused as much destruction to game birds and other small animals, as cougar and coyote did to deer and elk.[53] The Lewiston *Morning Tribune* published an editorial titled "Man vs. 'Varmints,'" applauding an increase in the federal budget for predator control.[54] Even Ted Trueblood, the nature writer living in Nampa who was gaining a national following for his articles in *Field and Stream* and other outdoor magazines, saw little reason to argue about the poison program. "I don't object so much to the occasional fur bearers that are poisoned," he wrote Arthur Carhart in 1948, "nor the dogs—as long as it isn't my dog," but he wondered if the money for the program was well spent "from the standpoint of the deer."[55]

In April 1950, the newly formed Idaho Outdoor Association (IOA), representing professional trappers and hunters rather than avocational sportsmen, began circulating petitions to outlaw the use of poisons for predator control. The association insisted that too many other animals were killed, but it found little support. Farm and sportsmen's organizations united in defense of the poison program. The Ada County Fish and Game League dismissed the IOA's evidence as "exceedingly flimsy,"[56] while Eddie Pederson, long-time president of the Bonneville Sportsmen's Association, stated that he could "definitely point to many splendid results of the predator poisoning program which have benefited sportsmen and others."[57] R.G. Cole, a state Fish and Game commissioner, said predator control agencies "should be privileged to use all modern devices, including poison."[58] Although the IOA continued its campaign for the next several years, it never gained enough signatures to bring the issue to a statewide initiative ballot.

The Citizens' Rights Association (CRA) fared no better. Formed in Boise in mid-1956 to protest the use of the poison "1080" (sodium fluoroacetate) on the grounds that it represented a hazard to human life, all it got for its efforts was a statement from the Fish and Wildlife Service spelling out in detail the procedures it believed kept the poison within safe limits. The CRA disappeared within a few months.

Not until the 1960s did anything like a movement questioning predator control appear. In April 1961, the Twin Falls *Times-News* asked editorially whether this was the "Right Approach?"[59] It noted that many thousands of coyotes were killed every year, and yet they continued to exist in large numbers. Furthermore, if coyotes were effectively eliminated from a particular area, then a plague of rabbits followed. By 1964 the pressure had become so great and so widespread that the Secretary of the Interior appointed an advisory board to study the whole issue. The board's report highly criticized the predator control branch and recommended limiting its involvement to only the most critical cases. In Idaho, the state Wildlife Federation finally addressed the issue at its annual meeting in 1966. It recommended classifying cougars as a game animal, to which the *Post-Register* added its "Amen." But even then, there was no implication that predator control should be completely terminated. "We are only suggesting we be more discriminating—particularly with bear and cougar."[60]

Bears even today continue to have a problematic place in Idaho, but cougars have long since disappeared from the predators' list to become a big game animal protected by Fish and Game Department rules and regulations. The transition began in the later 1960s. In May 1967, Ladd Hamilton, a Lewiston editorial page writer, composed a long "think piece": "The Cat: Good Guy or Bad?" Originally appearing in the *Morning Tribune*, [61] it was reprinted by the *Statesman* and the *Post-Register*. Hamilton used Billy Reed, a government trapper, as the prosecutor, while the defense was presented by Ferris Weddle, an environmentalist living in Stites whose columns were beginning to appear in a number of Idaho papers. No verdict was rendered in the article, but public opinion increasingly favored the defense. In June 1967, the *Post-Register* took the editorial position that "Idaho Should Sustain the Cougar." Its argument typified the emerging pro-cougar position in mixing scientific and aesthetic arguments. Cougars "serve a purpose—as a nature balancer and as one of the most interesting and beautiful animals in our mountains."[62]

Papers throughout the state delighted in covering the research of the University of Idaho's Maurice Hornocker, who was in the midst of a multi-year study of cougar life patterns and habits in the Big Creek section of the Idaho Primitive Area. Hornocker traveled the state, telling service clubs, newspaper editors, and anyone else willing to listen about the cougar's ecological and aesthetic merits. The Sandpoint *News-Bulletin* quoted Hornocker as saying the cougar is "a splendid animal—an integral and important part of our wilderness environment and a true vestige of primitive America."[63] He had shown, according to the *Post-Register*, that the cougar "is not the nemesis to wildlife and livestock he has been thought to be in Idaho."[64] "The Cougar Needs Protection," the Lewiston *Morning Tribune* editorialized in December 1969; it "has been the victim of an elaborate mythology that gradually is being disproved."[65]

Hornocker was more than an able speaker; he also brought back stunning photographs from his trips into the wilderness (as evidenced by a November 1969 article in *National Geographic*[66]). Used as slides to illustrate his talks, these photos may have documented his scientific analysis, but they also had a powerful aesthetic impact, which surely helped his cause with the many people who had only the most modest interest in scientific analysis.

Idaho by 1970 was just about ready to follow the example of a growing number of other western states and change the cougar's designation from predator to game animal. The Idaho Wildlife Federation recommended it, and, the director of Fish and Game told a legislative committee, the cougar "deserves that status."[67] The legislature was reluctant to act, with stockmen still loudly voicing their fears, but it eventually did so in March 1971. The story of the cougar, nevertheless, was an exceptional case, rather than typifying a fundamental attitudinal change toward wild creatures in Idaho.

Far more typical was the fate shared by lowly squawfish, carp, chub, and other so-called "trash fish." (Never mind how they came to be there. Carp originally were planted in the 1880s—the same decade that pheasants were introduced—with the idea that they would be a useful food source. Utah chub, which bedeviled much of eastern Idaho, were derived from fishermen's use of live minnows. Squawfish, on the other hand, apparently were native to Idaho.) Anglers were not interested in finding possible ways to make some practical use of these spoilers of sport-fishing waters. Enterprising commercial fishermen, however, seined and sold them to private hatcheries as fish food. In 1968 more than two million pounds were taken for a total value of $45,000, but such was not the stuff of sports page stories.

The modern chemical industry offered an alluring answer to the question of how to get rid of trash fish. A stream or body of water could be "treated" with a poison that killed all the fish, after which preferred varieties of fish could be replanted. In 1942, Tolo Lake near Grangeville and Soloman Lake in Bonner County were treated with powdered derris root, but the statewide campaign against trash fish really got underway after World War II. Beginning in 1948, several streams and bodies of water were treated each year, totaling sixty by 1960, usually with rotenone, which prevented fish from using their gills, but left dead fish safe to eat. Commonly, local sportsmen took this as a festive occasion. They might even set up hamburger stands to serve the crowds (sometimes running into the thousands) who came to watch and salvage the fish.

Rarely was there any objection when Fish and Game officials selected a stream, lake, or reservoir to treat. Even when some local people did protest, they hardly got any satisfaction, since officials felt so secure in the righteousness of their mission to maximize sport fishing. In July 1957, residents around Cocalalla Lake south of Sandpoint became so irate over the proposed treatment of their lake that they sent a petition to Governor Robert Smylie with more than four hundred signatures. Raymond Taylor, their spokesman, argued that the trout being planted in the area were "soft and mushy," and were far less desirable than the local perch and whitefish. Nevertheless, the department overruled these objections, and treatment of Cocalalla Lake occurred in August.

St. Maries sportsmen managed to get a much more attentive hearing regarding treatment of the St. Joe and St. Maries rivers. After putting it off for a couple of years because of local concerns, department staff went to St. Maries in January 1959 to explain their plans. The following month, sportsmen voted 40 to 72 against treatment. "The principal objection," the local paper reported, "came from those who believe pan fish to be of equal importance to trout, and noted that no provision for their replacement was made."[68] In March they reluctantly approved a compromise where just a few creeks would be treated as an experiment. Gradually, sportsmen in the St. Maries area accepted a "spot trash fish eradication program,"[69] while Fish and Game officials acceded to continued local opposition to full-scale treatment of the St. Maries and St. Joe rivers, since the spiney rays in those rivers were popular with local anglers.

Development of poisons focusing on specific species seemed the new hope in the 1960s. Squoxin, for example, invented by Craig MacPhee of the University of Idaho to kill only squawfish, was greeted by the Twin Falls *Times-News* as "a breakthrough of utmost importance… The time may come when man will be able to eliminate many or all unwanted forms of plant or insect life without upsetting the balance or endangering other forms of life."[70] Squoxin tempted the editor of the St. Maries *Gazette-Record* to foresee a time when "days of idyllic fishing can be restored."[71] Nevertheless, the decade ended with the fight against trash fish continuing unabated.

There seemed no end to the war on varmints, no matter what new technologies might be developed.

ENDNOTES

1. "Trumpeter Swan Story Mirrors Same and Accomplishment," Boise *Statesman* (June 18, 1964): p. B1.
2. "Up and Away," editorial in Twin Falls *Times-News* (December 12, 1963): p. 4.
3. "Declares War on Eagles," Boise *Capital News* (March 11, 1937): p. 3.
4. C.G. Sumner, "Sportsmen Scoff at Idaho's War Against Eagles," Boise *Statesman* (March 21, 1937): p. 8.
5. "Mountain Resident Accuses Eagles of Killing Livestock," Boise *Statesman* (April 1, 1937): p. 1.
6. "Saved the Eagles," editorial in Salmon *Recorder-Herald* (May 5, 1937): p. 4.
7. "Salmon Seeks Game Preserve," Idaho Falls *Post-Register* (April 3, 1938): p. 9.
8. "Nixon Signs Wild Horse Bill Instigated by Oregon Pupils," Boise *Statesman* (December 18, 1971): p. 1.
9. The language of the act is quoted in "Act Protects Wild Horses," Salmon *Recorder-Herald* (February 8, 1973): p. 1.
10. "Wild Horses," editorial in Boise *Statesman* (November 28, 1936): p. 4.
11. "Range Horse Imported for Meat Purposes," Idaho Falls *Times-Register* (July 30, 1926): p. 1.
12. "Wild Horse Steaks for Europe Tables," Idaho Falls *Times-Register* (December 14, 1926): p. 10.
13. "Elimination of Wild Horses Is Problem of Forest Service," Pocatello *Tribune* (January 13, 1927): p. 8.
14. Kathleen Caesar, "With the Wild Horse Hunters," *Popular Mechanics* XLVI (July 1926): pp. 76–80.
15. "Idaho's Mustang Doomed, Boise Inquiry Indicates," Boise *Statesman* (March 1, 1928): p. 12.
16. Glenn Balch, "The Passing of the Wild Horse," Boise *Statesman* (March 25, 1928): Section 2, pp. 1, 2.
17. "Range Riders' Cut in Wages May End Wild Horse Roundup," Boise *Statesman* (May 28, 1931): p. 1.
18. "Jordan Valley Cowboys Roundup Horses Via Plane," Idaho Falls *Post-Register* (July 17, 1936): p. 12.
19. "Wild Horse Roundup Ends; Plane Is Locked in Hangar," Boise *Statesman* (November 25, 1936): p. 1.
20. "Idaho's Ranges Fine Combed in Wild Horse War," Twin Falls *Times* (June 28, 1930): p. 5.
21. "Wild Horses Surrendering to Campaign by Airplane," Boise *Statesman* (October 28, 1938): p. 1.
22. "Wild Mustangs Refuse to Be Rounded Up," Idaho Falls *Post-Register* (May 28, 1944): p. 6.
23. Quoted in Jean Muir, "Wild-Horse Roundup," *Saturday Evening Post* (September 28, 1946): pp. 24–25ff.
24. "Boisean Voices Sharp Protest at Roundup of Wild Horses," Boise *Statesman* (October 25, 1945): p. 5.
25. "Boisean Urges 'Cowboy' Senator to Spur Aid for Wild Horses," Boise *Statesman* (November 6, 1945): p. 1.
26. Doug Lovelace, "West's Famed Wild Horses Disappearing," Boise *Statesman* (April 30, 1945): p. 10.
27. "Surplus Horses Will Be Removed," Challis *Messenger* (June 16, 1943): pp. 1, 8.
28. "Conservation," editorial in Coeur d'Alene *Press* (September 17, 1930): p. 4.
29. "The Conservation Movement," editorial in Sandpoint *Bulletin* (March 25, 1936): p. 2.

30. "Reversing the Pioneers," editorial in Twin Falls *News* (March 26, 1939): p. 4.
31. "We Must Rebuild," editorial in Coeur d'Alene *Press* (August 25, 1936): p. 4.
32. "Progress of Conservation," editorial in Lewiston *Morning Tribune* (January 2, 1940): p. 4.
33. "Watermaster Defends Beaver," Boise *Statesman* (February 4, 1945): p. 5.
34. "Busy Beavers," editorial in Twin Falls *News* (July 22, 1938): p. 4.
35. Untitled editorial in Kooskia *Mountaineer* (April 26, 1922): p. 2.
36. "Out of Balance," editorial in Boise *Statesman* (May 26, 1936): p. 4.
37. "Nature Meddling," editorial in Boise *Statesman* (November 30, 1928): p. 4.
38. "Unbalancing Nature," editorial in Twin Falls *News* (April 26, 1930): p. 4.
39. "Stanley Basin Wildlife Society," Challis *Messenger* (May 11, 1938): p. 1.
40. "PWA 'Wars' on Idaho Coyotes," Idaho Falls *Post-Register* (January 14, 1936): p. 1.
41. "Bombing Warfare Mapped to Eliminate 50,000 Crow Pests in Burley Territory," Twin Falls *Times* (February 19, 1938): p. 1.
42. "Boom! Boom! 40,000 Crows Are Blasted into Eternity," Shoshone *Lincoln County Journal* (January 3, 1936): p. 1.
43. "Resume War on Predatory Pests," Sandpoint *Northern Idaho News* (May 15, 1936): pp. 1, 5.
44. "Sportsmen War Against Magpies," Boise *Statesman* (April 3, 1937): p. 9.
45. Henry S. Hale, "Pest Poisoning Drive Advised," Twin Falls *Times* (February 7, 1934): p. 3.
46. "Idaho Jackrabbit Population, Ump Million, Somewhat Reduced," Boise *Capital News* (August 3, 1934): p. 10.
47. Charles G. Sumner, "Eastern Sportsmen Misguided about Idaho's Jack Rabbits," Boise *Statesman* (July 25, 1934): p. 7.
48. Beth Rhodenbaugh, "Jackrabbit Population Declines during Strange Wildlife Cycle," Boise *Statesman* (March 1, 1953): p. 10.
49. "Grandjean Tells of Idaho's Game," Boise *Statesman* (January 22, 1922): p. 4.
50. "Game Big Asset," Lewiston *Morning Tribune* (January 7, 1925): p. 7.
51. "Sportsmen's Club Transacts Some Timely Business," Salmon *Recorder-Herald* (February 29, 1928): p. 1.
52. Ned Foster, "Coyote and Rodent Control Called Menace to Wildlife," Twin Falls *News* (April 28, 1935): p. 7.
53. "Defends State's Poison Program," Kamiah *Progress* (March 26, 1931): p. 1.
54. "Man vs. Varmints," editorial in Lewiston *Morning Tribune* (February 2, 1934): p. 4.
55. Ted Trueblood to Arthur Carhart, June 15, 1948, in Ted Trueblood Papers (Boise State University Library Special Collections), Box 10, File 6.
56. "Anti-Poisoning Move Opposed," Boise *Statesman* (June 14, 1950): p. 11.
57. "Anti-Poison Move Rapped at Idaho Falls," Boise *Statesman* (June 2, 1950): p. 20.
58. "Chamber, Farm Bureau Hit Anti-Animal Poison Move," Idaho Falls *Post-Register* (June 2, 1950): p. 12.
59. "Right Approach?" editorial in Twin Falls *Times-News* (April 15, 1961): p. 4.
60. "Predator and Wildlife," editorial in Idaho Falls *Post-Register* (April 5, 1966): p. 4.
61. Ladd Hamilton, "The Cat: Good Guy or Bad?" Lewiston *Morning Tribune* (May 7, 1967): Section 2, p. 1.
62. "Idaho Should Sustain the Cougar," editorial in Idaho Falls *Post-Register* (June 15, 1967): p. 4.
63. "Idaho Cougar Study Subject of National Magazine Story," Sandpoint *News-Bulletin* (November 27, 1969): p. 12.
64. "Grazing Fees and the Cougar," editorial in Idaho Falls *Post-Register* (January 28, 1969): p. 4.
65. "The Cougar Needs Protection," editorial in Lewiston *Morning Tribune* (December 23, 1969): p. 4.
66. Maurice G. Hornocker, "Stalking the Mountain Lion—to Save Him," *National Geographic* CXXXVI (November 1969): pp. 638–54.
67. "F and G Director Urges Cougar Game Status," Boise *Statesman* (February 1, 1969): p. 10.
68. "Vote Says 'Keep Yer Rotenone-Pickin' Hands Off Them Rivers,'" St. Maries *Gazette-Record* (February 5, 1959): p. 1.
69. "Sportsmen Urge Ambitious Plans," St. Maries *Gazette-Record* (February 7, 1963): pp. 1, 10.
70. "Wide Possibilities," editorial in Twin Falls *Times-News* (October 14, 1966): p. 4.
71. "Tremendous Future Ahead," editorial in St. Maries *Gazette-Record* (July 1968): p. 12.

VI

Entr'acte

A FTER THE CREATION OF THE Sawtooth Primitive Area in 1937, an interlude of a dozen years or so followed when little of significant consequence occurred in the development of conservation concerns in Idaho. The 1930s marked a decade of primitive area designation; the 1950s saw the emergence of a strong, statewide movement demanding the end of dredge mining, air pollution, and other environmental transgressions. On the other hand, the 1940s, if one reads the state's newspapers correctly, seemed to be mostly a do-nothing decade.

It might have been quite different. The Idaho Wildlife Federation organized in the spring of 1936 and gained more than ten thousand members within five months. R.G. Cole of Boise, the first federation president, set forth an ambitious agenda: "Sportsmen are now demanding a hearing in all matters wherein wildlife is affected."[1] In preparation for the federation's first annual meeting in January 1937, Cole announced that discussion topics would include over-grazing, which was "making deserts out of our big game winter range." And, he went on, "how about the pollution of streams by mining companies, municipalities, and what not? We must attack this problem vigorously."[2] Cole staked out territory that the Idaho Wildlife Federation would, in fact, claim as its own, but not until the early 1950s.

Similarly, changes in Forest Service regulations pertaining to primitive areas did not have any noticeable immediate impact. In 1939 the so-called L-20 Regulations for primitive areas were replaced by the U Regulations, which provided much more protection for wilderness areas, as they were now called. The U Regulations prohibited timber cutting, road construction, and issuance of special use permits for such things as summer homes and hunting camps. Ultimately, the regulations' ramifications would be wide ranging, but again, not until the 1950s.

During the 1940s, primitive areas were, in effect, being domesticated, with state and federal authorities treating them like vast game preserves. Each year groups of game management specialists traveled through them to take game censuses and study range conditions. Finding that the systematic eradication of predators led to a growth in deer herds beyond the habitat's carrying capacity, special two-deer hunts were initiated as early as 1942.

No effort was made to limit flying access into primitive areas. Airplanes planted remote lakes with the most desirable varieties of fish. In July 1944, Moose Creek Ranch was developed in the Selway Primitive Area, one hundred miles east of Lewiston, as an "up-to-date dude ranch and hunting headquarters" with accommodations for fifty guests.[3] Financed by Johnson Flying Service of Missoula, Montana, and Cascade and Zimmerly Air Transport of Lewiston, Moose Creek offered "spacious lawns and even a concrete swimming pool" for the enjoyment of those who flew in for a day or two of hunting and fishing.[4] It was, one travel writer declared, a "tiny bit of civilization" in a wilderness "which must be similar to that which our forefathers saw when they entered Idaho."[5] Other wilderness resorts were built on a more modest scale, such as Tom McCall's Ranch on the Middle Fork of the Salmon River and the Stonebraker Ranch in Chamberlain Basin.

In 1946 airplanes were banned from the Bob Marshall Wilderness in Montana, but Idahoans showed no inclination to follow suit. In fact, they preferred to increase aerial access into Idaho's primitive areas. In late 1946, the Fish and Game Department obtained a permanent easement for the seventy-nine acre Hood Landing Strip on the Middle Fork of the Salmon River, and announced intentions to expand it. The 1947 legislature considered applying some controls on out-of-state flyers into primitive areas, and rumor had it that the Idaho Wildlife Federation would favor something similar at its annual meeting in December 1947. But nothing came of it. At the meeting, everybody agreed "the airplane is beneficial to the orderly harvest of game."[6] Meanwhile, with the entry of smokejumpers, forest fires in primitive areas were fought just the same as elsewhere. Beginning in August 1946, when they were dropped into a blaze near Sawtooth Lake, smokejumpers fought fires in primitive areas each summer.

Occasionally, someone thought that it might be best to "Leave It Primeval," to quote a Boise *Statesman* editorial of May 1948, "to conserve primitive conditions of environment."[7] A September 1950 story out of the nation's capital, which was printed by many Idaho papers, speculated that a time would come when travel into wilderness areas might have to be curtailed. This caused a noticeable shudder amongst Idahoans. "Surely, someone must be in charge," Grangeville's *Idaho County Free Press* conceded, "but 'controls' are something that must be watched closely in this day and age."[8] Even when visitor overcrowding became actually observable, Idahoans were extremely reluctant even to ponder the possibility of limits on their accessing primitive areas as they wished.

By 1950 Idaho already had become second only to California in "man-days" of visits to primitive areas of one-hundred thousand or more acres. The

Challis *Messenger* reported in August 1952 that George Lowers, a pilot from Pocatello, stopped by its office, telling of traffic at the Indian Creek field in the Idaho Primitive Area. When he flew in his wife and her friend, nine planes were parked on the strip, and he saw planes coming and going throughout the day. The Salmon River was "practically lined with fishermen" for four miles beyond the landing strip.[9] Two years later, the Salmon *Recorder-Herald* noted the great increase in visitors, both hunters and sightseers, to the Bighorn Crags, totaling eight hundred, "heretofore an unheard of amount of traffic" for that area.[10] By the mid-1950s, new administrative arrangements would have to be implemented if the wilds of Idaho were to retain some wildness.

This was not a case of a handful of preservation-minded foresters being overwhelmed by an indifferent public. Apparently, Forest Service officials made little, if practically any, effort to persuade Idahoans to give up aerial access into primitive areas to avoid disturbing the natural ecology, or to protect the pristine purity of those areas.

The River of No Return Highway project, too, demonstrated that Forest Service personnel saw Idaho wilderness with the same split vision typical of most Idahoans. Paradoxical as it may seem today, Idahoans for much of the twentieth century regularly held two contradictory attitudes toward the most outstanding natural attractions. Unlike the case of Shoshone Falls, where people had to choose between preserving the falls or developing the Snake's water for irrigation, it often seemed that Idahoans thought they could do both. They could cherish the natural scenery while, at the same time, push through major development projects. In that sense, Governor Don Samuelson's later attitude toward the White Clouds merely reflected a traditional approach in Idaho.

Take, for example, the main Salmon River, running westward across the state from just north of Salmon City to Riggins, and commonly called the River of No Return. Its popularity as a venue for white-water boating gained national attention well before *National Geographic* sponsored a fall 1935 trip to the area and published a profusely illustrated article in its July 1936 issue. The very essence of floating down the River of No Return lay in its undeveloped setting—the primary appeal was that this was the only way one could see these sights. And yet many local people, including Captain Harry Guleke, the most famous Salmon River boatman, dreamt of a day when the Salmon would be improved to the point where it no longer was a river of no return, when people could easily travel up and down its length by power boat and car.

As early as 1904, commercial interests in Salmon City began campaigning for congressional funding to improve the river channel. In the Salmon *Idaho Recorder*'s opinion, "a few well directed blasts" would enable exploitation of mineral and timber resources along the river.[11] By 1909 it hoped that the Pittsburg and Gilmore Railroad would lay track along the river from Salmon to Riggins. When nothing came of the scheme, pressure was renewed for navigational improvements. In 1918 the *Statesman* published an article that typified attitudes of the time. "As for landscape picturesqueness, the canyons of the Salmon river are unexcelled anywhere," but the area's people want the channel cleared because it "is the only way whereby commerce reaches the interior of the state."[12] Although Congress appropriated $20,000 for engineering studies in 1919, no follow-up work resulted. Small-scale mining operations and a handful of ranches along the river were supplied by Guleke and other boatmen, but the 1920s came and went without any major change in the River of No Return.

However, the Forest Service quietly and without much public attention began work on a road that might eventually run all the way from Salmon to Riggins. In May 1928, the Salmon *Recorder-Herald* published a photograph with a caption noting that the agency had constructed a "good automobile road" along the river for the nineteen miles from North Fork to Shoup, and "is endeavoring to secure funds for additional work down the river."[13] R.H. Rutledge, already in charge at Ogden's regional office, favored the project. "Give me a couple of CCC [Civilian Conservation Corps] crews for the next five or six years," he was quoted in 1938 by a reporter in Washington, D.C., "and we will open up the Salmon country."[14] This seems like strange talk from the man who pushed for the creation of primitive areas in Idaho as a way to save the "last frontier." On the other hand, he was, as the *Post-Register* noted when it printed the story out of Washington, the "hardy product of the Long valley country of Idaho."[15] Rutledge shared Idahoans' attitudes toward the backcountry, both cherishing naturalness and dreaming of development. That double vision, when applied to the Salmon River country, projected it as an idyllic remnant of the last frontier that should be claimed and developed.

This contradiction is exemplified by James Herndon, an attorney in Salmon, who originally had arrived in the area by stagecoach from Montana. In 1928, Herndon painted a pen portrait of the "last frontier":

> For those who long for the freedom of a new land, this, the last frontier, is a place you would love, with its sparkling streams and wild rivers, the air laden with the perfume of forest glades. The people are hospitable and free hearted, and here in this little mountain country they dream the years away in contentment, mingling intimately together.[16]

Yet, Herndon and his son, Charles, devoted much of their time over the next thirty years to gaining completion of the River of No Return highway.

The road did not have much chance of getting funded until the Depression created the need for work-relief projects. Even then, the area was too remote (and the project possibly too low in priority) for a commitment of really large-scale funds. However, hundreds of young men in the Civilian Conservation Corps spent their winters along the relatively sheltered river, slowly blasting a roadway and hauling out rock and debris. By 1937 the road extended to the mouth of the Middle Fork, while another crew carved out some twenty miles of road upstream from Riggins. By 1939 the road was gaining only about five miles a year, and a gap of sixty-seven miles remained unbuilt when the onset of World War II drained away all available funds and manpower. Despite the untiring pleas of its supporters, the road never found a sufficient following after 1945 to obtain further funding. It remains today as the truncated stumps it was at the end of the Depression.

Any suggestion at this late date that the River of No Return Highway should be completed surely would be drowned out by a roar of protest from those committed to wilderness preservation, but those concerns remained unvoiced in the 1930s and 1940s. Proponents occasionally referred to some unnamed opponents, but the issue was apparently little more than game preservation; some people feared that if the road was completed, wild game in the Idaho Primitive Area would be imperiled. But the press carried no stories of anyone speaking on behalf of preserving the area's natural integrity.

Not until the early 1960s did the question of wilderness preservation come up. Afraid the designation of the Selway area as a wilderness would put a permanent end to the road project, people in Salmon persuaded the North Idaho Chamber of Commerce to endorse funding a feasibility study. William Bacon, the assistant regional forester from Ogden, lamely mumbled that the Forest Service "cannot take a position on the project at this time."[17] The *Post-Register* editor conceded that "there is high purpose" in the project, but, admitting to "our unprogressive attitude," he concluded that it did not fit the primitive area, that "the sheer audacity of its unconquered mountains, is something we hate to see compromised by a highway regardless of the admitted purpose."[18]

Ultimately, the reason the Salmon road did not receive sufficient funding to be completed had nothing to do with environmental concerns, but, rather, it largely was because sectional interests in northern and southern Idaho tended to spin off in divergent directions. Initially, there was not any particular sectional issue when proponents, such as W.H. Simons, the state mine inspector, talked about the opportunities for resource development that the road would open up. According to Simons, it was "probably the greatest undeveloped mineralized region in the United States."[19] But that line of argument failed to generate much interest in a Depression-ridden decade, when the country already had more available natural resources than it had the means to fully exploit.

However, what excited chambers of commerce across southern Idaho, particularly in the southeast, were the implications of a whole new transportation network if commerce could easily cross the state's midsection, greatly reducing the mileage and driving time between Spokane and Salt Lake City. Representatives from the Salmon, Pocatello, Idaho Falls, and Blackfoot chambers of commerce met in Blackfoot in May 1933 to talk about the possibilities. They received supportive telegrams from the chambers in Weiser, Payette, Caldwell, and Nampa. The following month, another meeting in Blackfoot attracted members of sixteen chambers. "The demand for the construction of the Salmon river highway," the Salmon City newspaper chortled in September, "is growing every day."[20]

But that was only true if one ignored the doubts being expressed in northern Idaho. Emphasizing its commitment to the Lewis-Clark Highway along the Lochsa River (eventually US 12), the Lewiston Chamber of Commerce voted on May 9 not to support the Salmon delegation's position. Besides a difference of opinion about which highway to build first, there was a fear that somehow the Salmon highway was yet another plot by the south to thwart the north's interests. As Lewiston's R.G. Bailey put it, "Salmon City was being made the cat's paw to pull the chestnuts from the fire by southern Idaho interests who wish to enter the Lewiston country by the back door and draw all the resources of this section in an eastern direction."[21] In April 1935, the Lewiston chamber responded to a delegation from Grangeville, which "reported the forest service on the south side of the Salmon heartily in accord with the plan,"[22] and voted to back the project. But it did so without noticeable enthusiasm, and neither the Lewiston *Morning Tribune* nor any other northern Idaho newspaper gave it much space or backing.

In connection with plans for postwar development, the legislature in March 1945 passed a resolution urging congressional funding to complete the Salmon River road and authorized the governor to appoint a committee to push along the project. The Forest Service responded by telling Idaho's congressional delegation that it was too low a priority to have any chance for funds, given the critical need for roads that could quickly contribute to the exploitation of timber for postwar housing. And federal highway officials, Representative Henry Dworshak had to tell the Idaho Falls Chamber of Commerce in May 1946, believed that it was up to the state to take the initiative and prioritize the project high enough to get it built. Quite clearly, there was no adequate intersectional consensus to support this, and the River of No Return Highway remained an unrealized "dream 150 miles long."[23]

Two other non-events of the 1940s also had substantial implications for the pace and range of conservation in Idaho. In both cases, they demonstrated important aspects of Idahoans' perceptions of their state's scenic attractions and the legal constraints hampering efforts to protect some of those attractions.

Chapter III told how the fight to save Payette Lakes ended with an affirmation by the legislature in 1925 that scenic preservation could be more important than lumbering or irrigation. That remained an isolated policy pronouncement until the end of the 1930s; it is important to note that the three primitive areas designated between 1930 and 1937 all had outstanding scenic characteristics, but none had seriously competing economic uses. Scenic resources, as the Pocatello *Tribune* reflected in June 1938, had only recently become of economic consequence for many Idahoans:

> Nature bothered the pioneer rather more than she delighted him… Not until a good deal of the country side was tamed could we really enjoy the wildness of the remaining part… Well guarded [scenic resources] will feed the soul of man forever. It is the highest type of conservation that preserves them.[24]

Consider the Snake River Canyon near Twin Falls. The dramatic scenery of Shoshone Falls had, of course, been recognized since the time of the first settlers. But during the area's original pioneering stage, the harshly jagged, dark, volcanic rimrock, barren of any trees or even large shrubs, had no positive, aesthetic appeal for local residents. For most, these lands simply were barriers difficult to cross or venues for possible agricultural development. Not until the late 1930s, did anyone begin to see their austere yet intrinsic beauty. And then it was a very short step, at least for some people, to question the zeal with which the middle reaches of the Snake River had been developed. By November 1939, the Twin Falls *Times* editor could ask "Why So Much Power Development?" The Snake River, "one of the foremost streams in the world from the standpoint of natural grandeur is gradually falling prey to a ruthless commercialism." Idahoans, in the editor's opinion, needed to "come to their senses," evaluate these natural riches, and raise "their voices in protest against further plunder."[25]

Protestors first engaged the issue in January 1940, after the Idaho Power Company asked for permits to develop the hydroelectric potential of Box Canyon and Crystal and Niagara springs along the north edge of the Snake River in Gooding County, some twenty-five miles downstream from Twin Falls. An immediate hue and cry arose, probably to the great surprise of Idaho Power, which had no warning of any public concern over this latest effort to exploit the river's power possibilities. After all, this project would generate about $25,000 in new taxes for the county at a time when it only collected $81,000 from all other sources. And the additional power would contribute to the area's economic growth. "You have to clear away the obstructions," Burton Driggs told the Gooding Chamber of Commerce, "so that we can go forward and build a real city here."[26]

Not so fast, cried many in the Magic Valley. The Twin Falls *Times* imagined trying to explain to a visitor in 1950 who asks, "what has become of that grand and glorious Snake river" he'd heard of in the past? "Will we close our eyes under the humming hypnotism of power—or will we think?"[27] Even if one conceded the value of previous development at Shoshone Falls and Thousand Springs, the Twin Falls *News* wondered "where are we going to draw the line?… Why should Magic Valley, already over-burdened with major power plants, be expected to give up its few remaining small springs and streams?"[28]

On January 3, 1940, at a meeting in Burley, fifty representatives from nine sportsmen's organizations had voted unanimously to protest the Idaho Power project. Meanwhile, A.L. Swim, chairman of the Twin Falls County Planning Board, announced that he was writing the governor, noting that the board in 1935 had recommended preserving such natural attractions as Box Canyon. His letter, printed by the Twin Falls *News*, argued that it was not in the public interest "to permit too rapid appropriation of such resources."[29]

On the other hand, Idaho Power arranged a tour of the sites for Southern Idaho, Inc., a regional chambers of commerce association; those on the tour voted to support the company on the grounds that "we shouldn't stand in the way of progress."[30] Besides, as Harry Elcock, manager of the local sugar company plant, told the Twin Falls Chamber of Commerce, "comparatively few [people] have an opportunity to avail themselves of these natural attractions."[31]

Dismayed by the hornet's nest of controversy inadvertently stirred up, C.J. Strike, Idaho Power's president, informed Southern Idaho, Inc., on March 18 that the company was withdrawing its proposal. The Gooding *Leader* lamented what appeared to be the loss of a major development in the county because of the opposition from "the Twin Falls chamber of commerce and others of that city."[32] But as it turned out, Idaho Power had not given up; it had only decided to take some time to study ways of addressing concerns for scenic preservation.

Ralph Carpenter, manager of Idaho Power's Twin Falls division, announced in January 1941 revised plans: "special consideration has been given to the preservation of fishing and the natural beauty of these springs."[33] Under the new plans, while water would still be diverted from Box Canyon near its source, the power plant would be placed inconspicuously in the canyon itself, tucked away behind a natural ridge, eliminating the need for any pipes and allowing the water to flow naturally from the plant into the river.

Initially, it seemed that the issue had been laid to rest. Both the Twin Falls *News* and the *Times* announced that they had no argument with this new arrangement, while the Gooding *Leader* reiterated that "we are for it."[34] But public concerns remained. By the end of January, eighteen protest petitions were circulating in Twin Falls and Jerome counties, and the Twin Falls papers had renewed their critiques. "These springs in this natural area are more valuable and beneficial to the citizens of Idaho," the *News* declared on January 30, "than the power plants that would destroy them forever."[35] Although the Gooding *Leader* found the argument "frivolous when the whole Sawtooth range of mountains lies to the north of us and most of it still primitive,"[36] hundreds of area residents signed petitions and supported a movement to preserve thirty-two miles of the Snake River canyon from Shoshone Falls to Thousand Springs. Save Scenic Idaho, with Harold Harvey of Buhl as its spokesman, prepared a bill to create a recreation area, which was introduced in the legislature on February 17. The bill called for "preservation, protection and perpetuation of all natural scenic, recreational and sporting assets of the area."[37]

Many other people failed to see what all the shouting was about. For these "scenic enthusiasts," the Gooding *Leader* sniffed, "Idaho's natural beauties seem to be in a lava crevice." The *Leader* thought they should spend their time focusing on the state's beautiful lakes and forests. "There lies Idaho's scenic spots, not out here on a sagebrush-flanked lava rut."[38] The Filer *Citizen-Democrat* agreed that the issue "is more or less a case of making a mountain out of a mole hill." Construction according to Idaho Power's plan "is almost certain to have a salutary effect on this whole area."[39] The Buhl *Herald* quoted J.W. Taylor, former Idaho attorney general, addressing the Buhl Kiwanis: "for the life of me I can't see what we are losing from a scenic standpoint." Crystal and Niagara springs "are not of sufficient scenic magnitude to cause great concern."[40] It seemed like a dog-in-the-manger ploy to the Wendell *Irrigationist*; the Twin Falls people developed their own resources and were now trying to thwart Gooding County's chance to do the same.

The argument over the scenic merits of Box Canyon and its neighboring springs turned out to be moot. Failing the preservationists persuading the legislature to create a recreation area—a proposal that never showed much chance of success—the issue had to be phrased in terms of natural resource development, because no general law in Idaho pertained to scenic preservation. Thus, it fell to the state reclamation commissioner, E.V. Berg, to hold the public hearings.

Although one might imagine that the case of Payette Lakes and the legislature's action in 1925 to preserve the attractions of that area could serve as a precedent for saving Box Canyon, no one seems to have brought that up. This is even more puzzling, given the fact that in 1927 the legislature declared that preservation of the scenic beauty of Priest, Pend Oreille, and Coeur d'Alene lakes in northern Idaho to be a beneficial use (see Chapter VII). Comparisons between the large, tree-bordered lakes of north Idaho and Box Canyon may have seemed too strained, just another example of what the Gooding *Leader* saw as arguments "so frivolous that the sincerity of the agitators is questioned completely."[41] And the cases were, in fact, sharply different. While the beauties of the Payette and northern lakes had been generally acknowledged for decades, no similar consensus existed regarding Box Canyon. Its world-class standing as a spring, remaining to this day sixth in the world in flow, was never mentioned.

Harold Harvey and his preservationist friends tried to make the case that Box Canyon and Niagara and Crystal springs had greater value as tourist attractions than as sites for hydroelectric power generation. "Tourists and travelers,"

Harvey told Berg at the initial hearing in Boise at the end of February, "do not spend their money looking at power plants."[42] Vardis Fisher joined the fray with a letter to the Twin Falls newspapers: "a beautiful park along the Snake river as proposed would return to Gooding county, and to all other counties adjacent, much more in tourist and other revenues than the handful of taxes which certain persons are clamoring for."[43] This argument received no encouragement from Berg, but giving in to the hundreds of petitioners asking for a hearing in Magic Valley, he scheduled a second meeting in Jerome at the end of March. Harvey reiterated his argument: "I...still maintain that scenic, recreational and sporting uses for water are beneficial uses."[44] Berg still did not grant the legitimacy of that position. But he delayed making a decision until hearing from a disinterested engineer on the technical merits of Idaho Power's proposal.

While waiting for Berg's decision, the preservationists busied themselves with plans for a recreational area from Shoshone Falls to the Malad River. On April 2 the Snake River Recreation and Parks Association held its organizational meeting in Jerome. Ten days later, they obtained the Fish and Game Commission's endorsement for the "recreational and sports area in the Valley of Thousand Springs."[45]

By the end of the month, the game was over. On April 22 Berg issued his decision. Idaho Power received the permit it needed to develop Box Canyon, but Berg found that insufficient time remained for the company to complete the plants at the two springs, so he denied those permits. The preservationists immediately announced that they would appeal the decision in district court, but there seemed to be little reason to hope for a different finding there.

Remarkably enough, the protests of the scenic preservationists ended successfully. Without those protest delays, Idaho Power might well have completed its projects prior to the onset of World War II, but as it turned out the war came before construction could begin. Following 1945 Idaho Power focused on other developments, and Box Canyon remained unharmed. After almost sixty years, Box Canyon became a state park in December 1999, with financial assistance from the Nature Conservancy and (a sign of how times had changed) Idaho Power.

The final "non-event" of the 1940s was a different kind. Unlike the Salmon River highway and the Box Canyon power plant, which were only worrisome "might-have-beens," the creation of gunnery and bombing ranges at several locations in southern Idaho set precedents that would haunt later conservationists. There was a complete lack of environmental alarm when the ranges were established, then maintained long after the end of World War II.

Almost no military presence had existed in Idaho after the closing of frontier Army posts, such as Fort Boise, but this changed in the late 1930s as World War II approached. Then, as military planners began exploring the need for various kinds of installations, promoters of Idaho cities and counties, like those throughout the nation, sought whatever might be forthcoming in federal funds and jobs. What Idaho got was air bases at Boise, Mountain Home, and Pocatello, a naval gun retooling facility at Pocatello, and a naval training camp at Farragut on the south end of Lake Pend Oreille. All had numerous impacts on the surrounding localities, but the air bases and naval retooling facility, in particular, required extensive acreage for gunnery and bombing practice and testing. These bases had to be located in unpopulated areas, on what generally were viewed as worthless lands.

The desert of southern Idaho seemed ideal. "Nothing out there could be damaged," as Dr. L.F. West put it, speaking as chairman of the Boise Chamber of Commerce aviation committee.[46] That wasn't entirely true. Stockmen quickly reminded everyone that the sagebrush desert actually provided grazing for thousands of sheep and cattle. They vigorously protested a bombing range in southern Ada County, which would take "the very heart out of spring and fall grazing."[47] A proposed bombing and gunnery range on a million acres south of Craters of the Moon elicited similar complaints from stockmen in the Magic Valley. The *Statesman* dismissed these protests as being "a flimsy argument," concluding that "the crux is that every one must sacrifice for defense."[48]

In practice, the Army Air Force negotiated training schedules so that stockmen could continue grazing their herds during the few spring and fall weeks when grass was best. But other than the stockmen, no one seemed to have any concerns about the military's use of the desert. The general attitude was reflected in a description by one public official of the area south of Orchard (twenty miles east of Boise): "the site is of absolutely no other value because it is an uninhabited stretch of lava with no use as grazing land."[49] This applied not only to a few thousand acres in Ada County, but also to areas measured in miles, such as the naval proving ground east of Arco, extending five by twenty miles.

After all, as the Pocatello *Tribune* explained, "the principal inhabitants are coyotes and jackrabbits."[50] It seemed to be waiting for some meaningful use: "This area that has lain in desolate quietness since the miocene period, when it was torn by intermittent volcanic eruptions," according to the *Tribune*, "again will rock with explosive shocks."[51] The change was actually cause for celebration; the Arco *Advertiser* welcomed it as "Time Marches On": "today the desert is teeming with activity… The desert is no longer a desert. It is a vital, important…area."[52]

Nor was hardly any public concern expressed at the end of the war about the environmental ramifications of enormous ordnance experiments conducted at the naval gunnery facility. In particular, vast explosions of 250,000 and 500,000 pounds of TNT (larger than any blasts that the world had ever seen, save New Mexico's Trinity atomic test and the two atomic bombs dropped on

Japan) used up outdated ordnance for testing ammunition storage facilities. Newspapers throughout the state reported on the massive physical aspects of these great explosions, with little inkling about possible damages to the land, aquifer, air, or wildlife. The Pocatello *Tribune* rated the explosion of August 31, 1945, however, as a "dud" in Pocatello, since "nobody felt the jar and nobody heard the blast,"[53] while the *Morning Tribune* reported that the one a year later "failed to provide the display that had been expected."[54] The notion that the tests might be harmful rarely cropped up, and when it did, it received scant attention. In 1947 Judge Chase Clark dismissed for lack of evidence a case brought by the Era Mining and Development Company of Rexburg, seeking damages alleged to have been done at the company's mine near Arco as a result of the tests.

There seemed to be almost nothing that the military could do to upset the locals. In 1944 the Navy obtained state permission to hold anti-aircraft gunnery practice at Farragut by shooting across Lake Pend Oreille into the opposite hillside. In 1949 the Air Force established a new bombing and gunnery range south of Mountain Home without even publishing a detailed description of the location. Press reports simply located it south of Glenns Ferry and west of Hagerman.

However, by the early 1950s, things were changing. The Navy must have been shocked when in February 1952 its proposal to conduct deep-water bomb testing in Lake Pend Oreille stirred up a storm of protests. Spokane's acting mayor worried about the impact on the city's water supply. "You cannot possibly imagine how serious this would be," Idaho's Senator Herman Welker expostulated. "These tests will be the equivalent of atomic explosions in their terrific force."[55] He feared that it would "completely eradicate all fish" in a lake world renowned for its Kamloop salmon.[56]

This controversy came at a time when atomic testing in the Nevada desert was so enveloped in secrecy that authorities would only later confirm that a test had occurred (even though the blasts were clearly observable to residents in four states). Public officials were totally unprepared for the outcry over ordnance testing at the bottom of Lake Pend Oreille. Idaho's Governor Len Jordan blandly announced that the Navy had the state's permission for the tests, since Fish and Game files showed that no "irreparable" damage would result. Tom Murray, director of Fish and Game, confirmed that the department had given its approval to the Navy the previous August. In fact, it was soon disclosed, the Navy had set off charges in the lake in 1950 and 1951, although not as large as those now proposed.

But times really had changed. Opposition was not only vigorous, but also statewide. The Coeur d'Alene Wildlife Federation convened a February 7 meeting of sportsmen from the Idaho panhandle; the 150 who attended voted their strong disapproval. This was given front-page coverage in the

Idaho Falls *Post-Register*. The proposal "makes us more than a little sore," editorialized the *Statesman*. "We'd be willing to wager our shirts that the entire scheme…was dreamed up by a group of the customary bullet-headed brass-hats in Washington who don't give a hoot one way or the other about Idaho's natural resources."[57] The Salmon *Recorder-Herald* editor agreed:

> Who in the world sits back there in Washington dreaming up all these wild and stupid schemes? Do they like to see everyone get "up in the air" over some of these crazy plans, or are they just so blamed ignorant that they don't know any better?[58]

The Navy hurriedly brought in Captain A.G. Mumma, an ordnance expert, to try and allay local concerns. He told Sandpoint sportsmen the explosions would be no more than the equivalent of three sticks of dynamite, so it only would kill fish within one hundred yards.

The Fish and Game Department tried to patch up some acceptance of the Navy's proposal. Director Tom Murray and Oliver McConnell, the commission chairman, spent an afternoon in Sandpoint meeting with sportsmen. McConnell thought the tests were "being accepted much better."[59]

It didn't work. On February 18, the Bonner County Sportsmen's Association renewed its opposition and authorized a delegation to visit Spokane to meet with sportsmen there. Three days later, the Spokane County Sportsmen's Association voted to join the fight opposing the Navy, which had become so vociferous that CBS News reported it nationally. Belatedly, Governor Jordan retracted his earlier support and even denied that there had been any formal state approval. By February 29, the Bonner County sportsmen sent the governor petitions containing five thousand signatures calling for an end to the proposal. On March 4, Jordan wrote Secretary of the Navy Dan Kimball, urging him to cancel the tests, "in view of the overwhelming protests" in northern Idaho.[60] Within a week, the Navy announced that it had indefinitely suspended the tests at Lake Pend Oreille.

The ease with which opposition to the tests was mobilized revealed something that only recently had begun to emerge in Idaho. For the first time, there was a statewide conservationist lobby. Led by the Idaho Wildlife Federation, relying on its many constituent local organizations, this conservationist lobby still had a limited range of issues on which it could bring its power to bear. Continued use of southern Idaho deserts for gunnery and bombing ranges, for example, evoked no comment from the sportsmen at that time. Consequently, and unlike the retreat the Navy was forced to make at Lake Pend Oreille, the Air Force gained renewal of its lease on state lands south of Mountain Home. The Land Board ruefully admitted, "it was probable that the federal government would take possession of the land" if the state resisted.[61]

Nevertheless, beginning in the early 1950s, public policy makers in Idaho, at least in some cases, had to deal with the force of a conservation-minded public. How that came to be, how the deep, sectional differences within the state were first bridged to gain a unified statewide position on conservation issues, is the subject of the next chapter.

ENDNOTES

1. "Guard Wildlife," Lewiston *Morning Tribune* (September 13, 1936): Section 2, pp. 1, 5.
2. "Game Men Meet," Lewiston *Morning Tribune* (December 14, 1936): p. 6.
3. "Hunting Lodge to Be Built in Primitive Area," Lewiston *Morning Tribune* (July 29, 1944): p. 8.
4. "Primitive Area Camp to Offer Air-Borne Comfort," Lewiston *Morning Tribune* (October 8, 1944): Section 2, p. 1.
5. Don Feris, "Moose Creek Is Oasis of Civilization in Wilderness," Lewiston *Morning Tribune* (September 16, 1945): Section 2, p. 1.
6. Dave Johnson, "State Game Commission Wins Praise," Boise *Statesman* (January 12, 1948): pp. 1, 2.
7. "Leave It Primeval," editorial in Boise *Statesman* (May 28, 1948): p. 4.
8. "This Bears Watching," editorial in Grangeville *Idaho County Free Press* (September 28, 1950): Section 2, p. 2.
9. "Primitive Area Is Popular Place Now," Challis *Messenger* (August 13, 1952): p. 1.
10. "Trekking into Wilderness Area Indicates Mountain Spirit," Salmon *Recorder-Herald* (February 4, 1954): p. 1.
11. "To Open Salmon River," Salmon *Idaho Recorder* (January 22, 1904): p. 1.
12. E. K. Abbott, "Central Idaho People Want Salmon River Cleared for Boat Traffic," Boise *Statesman* (February 17, 1918): Section 2, pp. 1, 4.
13. Salmon *Recorder-Herald* (May 2, 1928): p. 1.
14. John L Wheeler, "CCC to Finish Salmon Road," Lewiston *Morning Tribune* (May 22, 1938): Section 2, p. 1.
15. "Workers Blast Gorge," Idaho Falls *Post-Register* (May 22, 1938): p. 11.
16. James A. Herndon, "The Salmon River Country: Our Last Frontier," Boise *Statesman* (August 12, 1928): Section 2, pp. 1, 5.
17. "Salmon River Highway Linking Lewiston and Eastern Idaho Suggested to Chamber," Lewiston *Morning Tribune* (May 28, 1961): pp. 12, 7.
18. "Price of Progress," editorial in Idaho Falls *Post-Register* (September 2, 1962): p. 4.
19. "Salmon Highway Project Lauded," Boise *Statesman* (May 9, 1933): p. 8.
20. Untitled editorial in Salmon *Recorder-Herald* (September 13, 1933): p. 2.
21. "Salmon City-Lewiston Highway on River Route Fanciful, Says Bailey," reprinted from the Lewiston *Morning Tribune* in Salmon *Recorder-Herald* (September 28, 1932): pp. 1, 4.
22. "Back River Road," Lewiston *Morning Tribune* (April 24, 1935): p. 12.
23. Clayton Darrah, "Invading Idaho's Unconquered Wilderness," Boise *Statesman* (October 8, 1933): Section 2, pp. 1, 5.
24. "And Our 'Scenic Resources,'" editorial in Pocatello *Tribune* (June 23, 1938): p. 4.
25. "Why So Much Power Development?" editorial in Twin Falls *Times* (November 29, 1939): p. 4.
26. "Driggs Urges Vigorous Year for Development of Gooding," Gooding *Leader* (February 29, 1940): p. 1.
27. "A Stranger Sees Us in 1950," editorial in Twin Falls *Times* (January 5, 1940): p. 4.
28. "Something to Think About," editorial in Twin Falls *News* (January 5, 1940): p. 4.
29. "Planning Board's Chairman Protests Power Site Grab," Twin Falls *News* (January 7, 1940): p. 1.
30. "Power Plants vs. Natural Beauty," editorial in Twin Falls *News* (February 25, 1940): p. 4.
31. "Chamber Strikes at Endorsement of Power Plans," Twin Falls *News* (March 9, 1940): pp. 1, 2.
32. "Twin Falls Opposition Kills Program," Gooding *Leader* (March 21, 1940): pp. 1, 12.
33. "New Studies Made for Proposed Power Sites," Twin Falls *Times* (January 8, 1941): pp. 1, 8.
34. "Have Always Been for It," editorial in Gooding *Leader* (January 16, 1941): p. 2.
35. "Opposition Rises to Power Harness of Scenic Springs," Twin Falls *News* (January 30, 1941): pp. 1, 2.

36. "Gooding County Supports Project," editorial in Gooding *Leader* (February 6, 1941): p. 2.
37. "Recreational Area on Snake River Proposed," Twin Falls *News* (February 18, 1941): p. 1.
38. "Have Overlooked Scenic Environs of Idaho State," editorial in Gooding *Leader* (February 13, 1941): p. 1.
39. "Mountain-Molehill," editorial in Filer *Citizen-Democrat* (February 20, 1941): p. 4.
40. "Taylor Talks on Power Sites," Buhl *Herald* (February 27, 1941): p. 1.
41. "Hearing on River Sites to Be Held Friday," Gooding *Leader* (February 27, 1941): p. 1.
42. "Decision Delayed on Canyon Power Plants," Twin Falls *News* (March 1, 1941): pp. 1, 2.
43. Letter to the editor from Vardis Fisher, Twin Falls *Times* (March 6, 1941): p. 6.
44. "Spirited Claims Mark Hearing on Canyon Property," Twin Falls *News* (March 29, 1941): pp. 1, 2.
45. Idaho Fish and Game Commission Minutes, April 12, 1941. The Minutes are archived in the Director's office in Boise.
46. "Idaho May Be Bomb Target," Boise *Statesman* (January 11, 1940): p. 1.
47. "Grazing District Board Opposes Establishment of Bombing Range," Boise *Capital News* (January 22, 1940): p. 10.
48. "Bombing Versus Grazing," editorial in Boise *Statesman* (July 12, 1941): p. 4.
49. "Plans Pushed for Gowen Bomb Range," Boise *Statesman* (December 12, 1941): p. 6.
50. L.E. Spalding, "Blackfoot Hopes to Benefit from Pocatello Gun Plant," Pocatello *Tribune* (March 23, 1942): p. 5.
51. "Famous Volcanic Region near Arco Soon to Become Big Gunnery Range," reprinted from the Pocatello *Tribune* in the Arco *Advertiser* (August 14, 1942): p. 8.
52. "Time Marches On," editorial in Arco *Advertiser* (July 16, 1943): p. 4.
53. "They Heard the Arco Blast," editorial in Pocatello *Tribune* (August 31, 1945): p. 4.
54. "Half Million Pounds of Explosive Goes Off on Purpose at Arco, but Show Disappoints Observers," Lewiston *Morning Tribune* (October 2, 1946): p. 1.
55. "Spokane Protests Underwater Tests," Coeur d'Alene *Press* (February 5, 1952): p. 1.
56. "Welker Protests Navy Plan to Drop Bombs in Idaho Lake," Lewiston *Morning Tribune* (February 5, 1952): p. 8.
57. "The Threat to Pend Oreille," editorial in Boise *Statesman* (February 8, 1952): p. 4.
58. "Navy Still Wants to Bomb Lakes," editorial in Salmon *Recorder-Herald* (February 14, 1952): p. 6.
59. "Fish and Game Official Says Protests Ease," Boise *Statesman* (February 19, 1952): p. 9.
60. "Governor Asks Navy to Halt Bombing Plans," Boise *Statesman* (March 5, 1952): p. 6.
61. "Bomb Range Lease Renewed by Land Board," Boise *Statesman* (October 7, 1952): p. 6.

VII

Protecting Our Water

ONSERVATION ARRIVED AS A statewide political force on November 2, 1954, when voters overwhelming approved an initiative to control the impact of dredges on Idaho's rivers and streams. Sponsored by the Idaho Wildlife Federation, but largely ignored by the press, the dredge initiative represented, according to Eddie Petersen, a prominent "wildlifer" and future Idaho Falls mayor, "a significant example of how an aroused population can handle a serious problem on the grassroots level."[1] He observed that the anti-dredge movement was not just the work of sportsmen. It also relied on the support of woolgrowers, cattlemen, and irrigationists. It also marked the beginning of a sustained public concern about water pollution that, in less than ten years, saw the virtual end of municipal dumping of raw sewage into nearby bodies of water.

How did this come to be? How did Idahoans become persuaded that they should unite politically, and reverse practices that had littered many mountain valleys with ugly mounds of tailings and converted most of the state's rivers into open sewers?

Dredges were working more or less continually in various parts of Idaho since the beginning of the century with relatively little public concern voiced for the landscapes being ravished. Dredges were busy mining gold by 1901 near Idaho City, at Pierce in 1906, Stanley Basin by 1920, and the Salmon River just below the mouth of the Middle Fork by 1926. They also were used by 1907 to extend Coeur d'Alene's waterfront, and in 1913 to clear navigation of the Kootenai River and reclaim land for farming near St. Maries. Press coverage was not particularly frequent, and little in the way of criticism can be found prior to end of the 1930s. Quite the contrary. The dredges' sheer power fascinated many observers. In 1912 the Salmon *Idaho Recorder* commended the new dredge on Kirtley Creek as "one of the attractions" of the area.[2] In 1922 a large dredge on the Feather River was admiringly described by the Boise *Statesman*: "a gold-hungry monster is greedily devouring hundreds of tons of gravel a day."[3]

During the Depression-ridden 1930s, John Finch, University of Idaho's dean of the School of Mines, assured newspaper readers that "vast deposits of the old gravel" from previous mining operations around the state held the promise of "large-scale dredging operations producing millions of dollars."[4] In fact, during those years, dredge operators found it profitable to rework the old mining ground at Warren, Pierce, Dixie, Stanley Basin, and (most lamentably in the view of later critics) along the Yankee Fork of the Salmon River.

The first real sign of opposition to dredge mining came in January 1939, when the grange introduced into the state legislature a bill to regulate dredging, claiming it was becoming a menace to irrigation districts by causing excessive silting in canals and ditches. E.T. Taylor, master of the Idaho Grange and a Kootenai County representative, told the legislature that grangers were not opposed to dredge mining of gold, but insisted that settling ponds needed to be used to minimize silting damage to farms downstream. Although nothing came of the bill, it is notable that dredge control was even then linked in the minds of its proponents with broader water pollution issues. A Coeur d'Alene *Press* editorial also noted that the bill would lead to state regulation of pollution in the Coeur d'Alene River caused by the Silver Valley's smelters and deep hard-rock mines. Denying any wish to "legislate our neighboring mines out of business," the *Press* argued that Shoshone County hard rock miners needed to develop other means to limit pollution rather than simply dumping wastes in the river.[5]

This *Press* editorial was the latest in a long, and thus far unsuccessful, effort to gain adequate statewide political clout to force Shoshone County silver mining companies to stop polluting the Coeur d'Alene river and lake. In 1905 more than sixty farmers along the Coeur d'Alene River from Cataldo to Harrison brought suit against the mining companies for polluting the river with tailings containing minerals that, they claimed, gravely damaged the farmlands watered by the river. After visiting the scene, Judge James Beatty denied the farmers' petition for a temporary restraining order, finding the "wild assertions of complainants...without justification."[6] The following year, the judge again decided against the farmers, asserting that if they had their way, they would close the mines and be "the ruination of every line of business in the Coeur d'Alenes."[7] Appeals proved fruitless; in 1908 the U.S. Circuit Court of Appeals sustained Judge Beatty's decision, as did the U.S. Supreme Court in 1909.

In 1930 the Kootenai County Farmers Union resurfaced the issue, resolving to fight the "mine slimes and debris" that polluted the Coeur d'Alene River.[8] Members succeeded in having the county Republican convention in August pass a resolution supporting the union position. In addition to impacting farmlands, mining pollutants were "increasingly a menace to the use of the lake from a beauty, health and recreational standpoint."[9] This pressure brought a group of state officials to examine the situation in November, but the report of W.V. Leonard, the state chemist, minimized the harm done by mine effluents in the river and lake. "We don't care," the Coeur d'Alene *Press* editor angrily retorted, "whether the debris is going to make the lake a total loss tomorrow or 100 years from now… It is our lake and we are going to fight to preserve it, as far as possible, from unnecessary and unsightly pollution."[10]

The 1931 legislature approved the creation of a special commission, chaired by the attorney general and including the chairmen of the Kootenai and Shoshone county commissions, to look into the matter and report to the next session. During its investigations, four different teams of federal authorities visited the area. Max Ellis, a University of Missouri physiology professor and director of interior investigations, led the final investigation in July 1932 for the U.S. Bureau of Fisheries. His report, issued in December, did not support the mining companies. For the fifty miles of river from above Wallace to its mouth near Harrison, Ellis found "a barren stream, without fish, fauna, fish food or plant life and with enormous lateral supplies of potentially toxic materials which will continue to pollute the waters…for a considerable time."[11] Following this report, the *Press* hoped that "the wrong will be righted by the mine owners"[12]

Ironically, the silver-mining companies' plan was to install a dredge at Mission Flats near Cataldo to move mine tailings from the river into a series of settling ponds. Without flumes from the mineshafts to the settling ponds, much effluent continued to flow into the Coeur d'Alene River, only a portion of which the dredge could remove. Unsatisfied by the mining companies' response, Gus Nelson, state senator from Kootenai County, introduced a bill in the 1933 legislative session prohibiting pollution of Idaho streams by industrial wastes. This "would close every mine in the Coeur d'Alene district," proclaimed Representative Donald Callahan of Shoshone County.[13] The Coeur d'Alene Chamber of Commerce voted 19-3 against the bill's passage, fearing that it also would require the city to stop dumping sewage into the Spokane River. The bill quickly died, and Idaho would have to wait another generation before seeing any significant abatement of its water pollution problems.

The moral to this story is that, even when confronted with as undebatable a case of pollution as that of the Coeur d'Alene River, there was no way to gain passage of state legislation to rectify the problem. Frank Lafrenz, senator from Kootenai County, tried again in 1939 and was voted down 30-9. In addition to the mining companies' opposition, many communities feared the costs of treating their sewage water. Senator William Holden of Bonneville County, for example, said it would be "financially ruinous to the city of Idaho Falls."[14]

The anti-dredge movement continued to gain some support at the beginning of the 1940s. Sportsmen's groups in Valley County resolved in May 1940 to "concentrate effort to reduce the havoc caused in fishing streams by mine dumps."[15] In November, Dick d'Easum reported that fishermen in the Boise Valley, who were worried about dredging impacts on the Yankee Fork and at Atlanta, had become "thoroughly disturbed" by the reports of dredges coming to the Middle and South Forks of the Boise River. "The time has come," d'Easum concluded, "for a loud and vigorous squawk."[16]

It seemed as though the issue would come to a head at the annual meeting of the Idaho Wildlife Federation in January 1941. W.J. Smith, president of the Oregon Wildlife Federation, came to speak on how Oregon had dealt with water pollution, particularly in the Willamette River. According to the Boise *Statesman*, Smith showed slides to make his point that the "pollution of streams is a result of a lack of intelligent planning."[17] The IWF called for a study of stream pollution by the Fish and Game Department and then to work out a program with "interested industrial and municipal groups to overcome harmful effects."[18] This obviously was a very tall order, and one the commission chose not to accept. The commission did, according to its minutes, finally appoint a committee on January 12, 1942, but limited its task to investigating dredge pollution on the Boise River and to report its findings to the U.S. Reclamation Service. Even though the Ada County Fish and Game League had joined with Boise Valley irrigators and threatened to fight "tooth and toenail" a gold dredge on the Middle Fork of the Boise River,[19] the issue quickly vanished from the local press.

Opponents of dredging and water pollution could not drum up any continuing sense of urgency in the public at large. Idahoans had become adept at denying the consequences of water pollution. "The danger from the flow of tailings is a mere conjecture based on statements which do not bear the test of experience," so reported the *Statesman* in 1888.[20] Forty-five years later, the same song was being sung. Even after the Ellis report's publication, state chemist W.V. Leonard persisted in denying any great health hazard due to chronic lead poisoning from the public using Coeur d'Alene water. Similar denials regularly appeared from dredge operators. The Challis *Messenger* in April 1941 noted continued "agitation among sportsmen" along the Salmon River blaming the Yankee Fork dredge for muddy water. After describing the settling ponds created by the dredge company, the editor concluded that no chemicals were used to clarify the water; since "the roily water which is turned out of the dredge has absolutely nothing in it but natural dirt."[21]

In the first years after World War II, there seemed no reason to hope for anything much different. In 1948 the Land Board did deny a dredging permit for the South Fork of the Clearwater, but primarily because, according to Land Commissioner Edward Woozley, "river bed dredging has been very disappointing from a royalty point of view."[22] With the discovery of major deposits of monazite (a source of plutonium) in central Idaho, the economics quickly changed, and dredges were churning up land south of Cascade by 1950.

What about the great piles of rock tailings the dredges left? Many shrugged them off as nothing more than the cost of doing business. "Gold dredges may mess up the scenery," as Elvin Fisher of Elk City said in the Grangeville paper, "I grant you that, but so do sugar beet factories, stock yards and sawmills. Yet they are necessary to the welfare of the people."[23] Commending the Land Board in 1950 for denying a dredging application in Stanley Basin, the Twin Falls *Times-News* thought the legislature ought to do something about this kind of threat to Idaho's scenery: "some rigid code should be established to control all unnecessary damage even in those exceptional cases where dredging privileges might be permitted."[24] But there was no sign at that time of anyone really trying to pass dredge-control legislation.

The broader issue of water pollution seemed almost as hopeless. A bill to control stream pollution, sponsored by the Idaho Department of Public Health, was introduced in the 1945 legislative session, but soon was buried in the House Appropriations Committee. The Idaho Chamber of Commerce volunteered to coordinate a statewide survey, and, in 1947, the legislature created the State Water Pollution Advisory Committee, but without either funding or any real mandate other than to gather information. Evidence of water pollution could be found without much effort. As late as 1947, a *Statesman* editorial expostulated about a pipe dumping raw sewage into the Boise River between Julia Davis Park and what was then Boise Junior College. In May 1949, A.L Biladeau, acting director of the city/county health unit in Boise, told the Idaho Public Health Association convention in Twin Falls that stream pollution in Idaho was probably the worst in the whole country The legislature had earlier that year passed a law changing bonding limits so communities could finance sewer treatment systems, but that legislation received little press coverage, and Idaho cities and towns made no immediate rush to use it.

And yet, despite the environmentally gloomy situation in 1950, a movement soon arose that produced the dredge-control initiative, and, within ten years, most of Idaho's municipalities had passed bond issues and built at least primary sewage treatment plants. (New matching federal subsidies, too, had become available for wastewater treatment.) This was an extraordinary and dramatic turnabout.

There's nothing like the threat of loss to enhance something's value. Idahoans might abuse their water by dumping sewage and industrial effluents into streams, but they had no intention of allowing the water to be taken away from them for use by others. Any question of control crystallized a unified opposition throughout the state, regardless of the differences between the well-watered north and the semi-arid south.

In 1927 came the first demonstration of how protective Idahoans could be when water became an issue. The Bureau of Reclamation had developed plans for a vast irrigation project in central Washington, which proposed to use the large northern Idaho lakes—Priest, Pend Oreille, and Coeur d'Alene—as reservoirs. A large delegation from the Spokane area arrived at Boise in January 1927 to request the legislature's cooperation. It met a brick wall. Governor H.C. Baldridge already had secured an evaluation from Warren Swendsen, former state reclamation commissioner, strongly discouraging Idaho's approval unless "absolute public necessity…exists."[25] Baldridge then convened, according to a report in the Idaho Falls *Times-Register*, an informal caucus of all legislators, asking them for protective legislation. H.B. 43 immediately passed on January 24, unanimously by the House and by a large majority in the Senate. It authorized the governor to hold in trust on behalf of the people of Idaho all unappropriated water in those three lakes. "The preservation of said water in said lakes for scenic beauty, health, recreation, transportation and commercial purposes necessary and desirable for all the inhabitants of the state is hereby declared to be a beneficial use of such water."[26]

The press in all corners of the state applauded the act. "Idaho does not want," as the *Times-Register* had put it the year before, when it first reported the Washington project, "to have its natural heritage prostituted through the diversion of its water to another state."[27]

However, the battle had barely begun. The irrigation project for central Washington was only the beginning of what would soon become a comprehensive plan for regional development. The construction of the Grand Coulee and Bonneville dams on the Columbia River had initiated a regional power grid, as regional planners saw it, that could become the basis of a Columbia Valley Authority (CVA) modeled after the Tennessee Valley Authority.

Few Idahoans found it an appealing vision. They feared that the power grid would bleed off Idaho's inexpensive electricity for use by large coastal cities and sharply increase power rates in Idaho. Even worse, CVA would "hand over control of the Snake River and all of its tributaries" to federal authority, according to the Pocatello *Tribune*. It warned of the danger of "the tentacles of the federal octopus."[28] "We shouldn't be the tail to a kite in some of these large developments," U.S. Senator John Thomas warned the Idaho Reclamation Association, "and furthermore we shouldn't be having our resources tied up in control of some bureau."[29] "A Thousand Times No," the Arco *Advertiser* cried. "We want no one except our courts to have the last say in Idaho's water distribution."[30]

The CVA's proponents commonly argued that the issue was public versus private power and attributed Idaho's opposition primarily to the machinations of private power interests. That seriously underestimated Idahoans' almost obsessive fear that some other, more populous, area would try to wrest away local control of water rights. When the Coeur d'Alene *Press* termed a dam at Albeni Falls (on the Pend Oreille River between Sandpoint and Priest River) as "a sort of a Frankenstein monster,"[31] that was not because of its size or impact upstream, but because it would serve out-of-state interests. The Idaho Chamber of Commerce expressed its opposition to "any form of federal legislation designed to interfere with, or which would permit interference with the right of the various states to the waters within their boundaries," a position widely reported throughout Idaho, including the Coeur d'Alene *Press* and the Boise *Statesman*.[32] The following day, the *Statesman* reinforced the point in an editorial lambasting the "Columbian Octopus," concluding that the Bonneville Power "Administration's lust for power must be jerked up short."[33]

The only section of Idaho that found the CVA initially appealing was the Lewiston area. It seemed that the CVA and its proposed series of dams would finally realize hopes for an "Open River"—that is, for the Columbia and Snake rivers to become navigable, making Lewiston a port city. Not surprisingly, when Representative Compton White and Bonneville Power administrator Paul Raver scheduled a hearing on postwar plans for Pacific Northwest development, they picked Lewiston. On August 31, 1943, at the Lewis-Clark Hotel, Raver presented his hopes for the production of "ample power" and the development of inland waterways that would "bring the resources locked in the hills of the region into production of useful goods."[34] The following year, Raver issued a "blueprint for a Pacific Northwest industrial wonderland," entailing the construction of twenty-two new dams in Oregon, Washington, and Idaho.[35]

The intermittent skirmishes over a scheme discussed but not really pushed during the previous fifteen years now became a full-scale battle. For the next six years, the proposal for a region-wide, comprehensively planned Columbia Valley Authority consumed an immense amount of printers' ink and countless hours in heated debates throughout Idaho. Governor Bottolfsen attempted to minimize water users' fears with the argument that "the Snake River has plenty of water to take care of both interests," that is, irrigation and navigation.[36]

But that was never the issue. The Idaho Farm Bureau Federation quickly reminded everyone that questions of priority and control were crucial, that water users must guard against any encroachment on their rights. On the other side, those fears seemed just like an "old bugaboo," in the words of the Lewiston *Morning Tribune*. It went on to articulate the new, regional viewpoint: "the dominant interest should not be the priority for irrigation, navigation, hydroelectric power, flood control or other separate problems but the whole welfare of the entire Snake-Columbia basin."[37] "CVA Bad for Idaho," replied the Idaho Falls *Post-Register*. It "sounds the death knell for states rights... It is bureaucracy at its very worst."[38]

Opposition to the CVA was adamant and statewide. "Control is getting too far away from the people," stated Ephraim Ricks of Rexburg.[39] Donald Callaghan, a Wallace mining executive, feared that the CVA would "extend into the lives of all the people."[40] William Welsh, Boise River water master, was indefatigable in his protests, speaking frequently throughout the state. "We do not want jurisdiction over water rights taken from state courts… We do not want a federal agency which can practically nullify existing water rights."[41]

Control of water rights seemed so fundamental to life as Idahoans knew it that they saw any threat to that control as a conspiracy. The *Statesman* believed that proponents of "such governmental projects should get over on the other side of the fence called Americanism and identify themselves as out-and-out socialists believing in statism."[42] Even Lewiston quickly cooled to the idea. After hearing an adverse report on the CVA bill from its waterways committee, the Lewiston Chamber of Commerce board of directors voted in October 1945 to oppose it. The resolution found the bill "too far reaching," that it gave too much power to the authority's board of directors. The chamber joined the position held by most Idaho business groups that development was best served by the Corps of Engineers and the Bureau of Reclamation.[43] The following month, even the Inland Empire Waterways Association, the heart of the Open River movement, voted at its Lewiston convention against the CVA, fearing that it might thwart congressional support for navigational improvements.

Not everyone in Idaho opposed the hope for planned regional development as envisioned by the CVA. Senator Glen Taylor campaigned vigorously on its behalf, even though he acknowledged that it was not in his political interest to do so. He saw himself as an exemplar, leading the fight against the "private power boys," which he claimed, "are controlling this movement" in opposition.[44] This was also a dominant argument of the CVA Information League, organized in Boise in September 1945, with Clayton Davidson elected as president. "We are battling the power interests and ignorance," Davidson told the Ada County Agrarian Club.[45] A handful of groups in Idaho found this a plausible argument, including some labor unions and local chapters of the Farmers Union. But most saw it as a paranoid refusal to recognize the strength of the forces opposing CVA. When the Idaho Reclamation Association passed a resolution against the passage of any CVA bill, Davidson retorted that the association had "lost its identity and does not accurately reflect the views of a majority of Idaho agriculturists."[46]

The North Idaho Chamber of Commerce passed a resolution in October 1945 affirming that the people of the Northwest have "demonstrated their ability to take care of their natural resources, working with and through these existing agencies."[47] Many groups in Idaho took this position. The CVA Information League could not counter it. Instead, it complained that it faced "an unbreakable, unscalable stone wall of suspicion and misunderstanding," as Harry Wood of Boise put it.[48]

The CVA became a major issue in the 1946 election, but it turned out to be no real contest. Proponents were overwhelmingly defeated. The Lewiston

Morning Tribune lamented that "common sense was snowed under," with victory won "by frightening bogeys bred in the minds" of the voters.[49] In any case, the Boise *Statesman* believed the issue was "dead as a doornail in Idaho."[50]

If that had, in fact, been the CVA's end, the history of conservation in Idaho might have been appreciably different. Rather like a rocket building up to exit speed, Idahoans concerned about protecting their water needed greater momentum than they had yet achieved. The 1947 legislature authorized Governor C.A. Robins to appoint a committee to survey the water situation in Idaho to determine beneficial use and how to avoid unnecessary pollution. The governor did not get around to making appointments until May; then the committee disappeared into obscurity.

Federal authorities, however, were not yet ready to give up. The Bonneville Power Administration continued to push its vision, and in January 1949, President Harry Truman urged Congress to pass legislation creating a Columbia Valley Authority. As he told Boiseans during a brief visit in May 1950, without it, "we will continue to have a scatter-shot approach to resource development."[51]

No noteworthy shift in Idaho opinions about the CVA occurred between the 1946 election and June 1950, when the outbreak of the Korean War shelved further thought of major new domestic programs. The Lewiston *Morning Tribune* spoke for advocates: "the dream of thus harnessing great basins is not easy to discard."[52] But "We Can Be 'Ignored,'" replied the Twin Falls *Times-News.* "We'd be at the mercy of those who carried weight politically. And how would we like that?"[53] Those attending the 1949 annual meeting of the Idaho Reclamation Association in Pocatello were assured that Congress would not pass the CVA bill. Alex Coleman of St. Anthony, a member of the powerful Committee of Nine (which decided irrigation policy in the Upper Snake River Valley), spoke for most Idaho water users: "are we going to let some dreamers come in and tell us how to handle our problems?"[54]

However, those same years saw an important buildup in water protectionism in Idaho, which was a mixed blessing for conservationists. On the negative side, it led to the creation of a state water administration that, as will be seen in Chapter IX, would oppose the wild rivers program. Governor Robert Smylie, who headed the movement to create the Water Resources Board, told an audience at a Corps of Engineers hearing in February 1955 that he wanted "the ways and means of developing, comprehensively, every drop of water that tumbles from the snow packs of the Snake River watershed."[55] Followed to its logical conclusion, such an attitude could lead to a policy as all encompassing and leaving as little water to nature as in the Netherlands. On the other hand, concern for ending the fouling of Idaho's streams would lead, in less than twenty years, to a policy favoring the permanent protection of wild rivers from dams or most other kinds of development.

The extended CVA controversy made possible the passage of an anti-dredge initiative by politicizing the Idaho Wildlife Federation and giving it a statewide network that reached far wider than its core constituency of sportsmen. Democrats pushed the CVA, with its many dams possibly endangering wildlife habitat. Therefore, when the IWF rather belatedly entered the political fray, it backed the Republican opposition. In March 1949, the North American Wildlife Conference and its subsidiary National Wildlife Federation passed a resolution opposing the CVA. Tom Murray, Director of Idaho Fish and Game and Theo Wegener, IWF president, attended the conference. In December at the annual IWF convention in McCall, members voted unanimously for a resolution condemning the CVA. The Lewiston *Morning Tribune* chided the sportsmen for "staring so intently at the trees that they have overlooked the forest," which, in the *Morning Tribune*'s opinion, was the overarching fact that "the rivers are going to be developed, come what may."[56]

Not by the CVA, if the Idaho Wildlife Federation had anything to say about it. Its 4th District had already passed a resolution at a Sun Valley meeting in November, labeling the CVA in typical early Cold War era rhetoric as "un-American in purpose, communistic in design and an encroachment on state management of its wildlife and natural resources."[57] This closely followed the comments of IWF president Theo Wegener, who also was a leader in the state Republican party, and chairman of the Idaho Development Association, formed in March 1949 to oppose the CVA. As Wegener traveled around the state lambasting any kind of regional planning authority, it was not clear whether he was speaking as IDA chairman or IWF president, but sportsmen didn't seem to care. And he received great press coverage in the process. His speech before a combined meeting of the Caldwell and Homedale Kiwanis clubs in June 1949 received an extensive report in the St. Maries *Gazette-Record*, including his conclusion: "we must make our choice now between economic freedom and dictatorial serfdom; between capitalism and socialism."[58] That may sound like strange talk coming from a conservationist, since today we are so accustomed to the idea that environmentalists tend to be politically liberal. But it anticipated the position the IWF would take a few months later, and it went over well with the Kiwanis in Caldwell, as it did with IDA supporters in Challis, Rexburg, and Coeur d'Alene.

Unlike some later environmentalists, who questioned the compatibility of private enterprise and ecological protection, most wildlifers and their political friends in the early 1950s had no quarrel with mining as such. But they insisted that the public at large should not have to tolerate heavy and widespread environmental damage resulting from dredge mining in Idaho's rivers and streams. It was one thing for dredges to work in selected and remote areas, such as Florence and Elk City (which were never protested), but quite another when they threatened to tear up the state's rivers.

With the high value of monazite and a strong gold market in 1950, dredges were active, or being proposed, in all parts of the state—along the Snake River from Blackfoot to Hells Canyon, in Stanley Basin, on the Clearwater River above Lewiston, along the St. Joe River above St. Maries, on the Salmon River near Lucile, and in mountain meadows near Cascade and in Bear Valley.

Sportsmen and their political allies worried not only about the impact of dredges on fishing and the silting of waters downstream, but also the destruction of scenic values. Officers of the IWF's 2nd District and Fish and Game conservation administrators met in Lewiston on September 10, 1950, organizing a protest over a Land Board hearing on proposed dredges for the North and Middle Forks of the Clearwater River. They opposed them because of permanent damage to fish life and streambeds, and argued that "recreational values will be destroyed."[59]

One of the most frequently cited and photographed examples of dredge destruction was along the Yankee Fork of the Salmon River above Clayton. Seth Burstedt, a rancher near Challis and recently elected senator from Custer County, told the *Statesman* in January 1949 that one of his goals was to protect Idaho's scenery. On the Yankee Fork, "they just went through that once beautiful meadow and stream and left it a desolate waste. Something should be done about it."[60] That refrain sounded repeatedly for the next five years during the campaign for an effective dredge-control law. "Once one of the finest stretches of trout fishing waters in the entire country," according to the Twin Falls *Times-News* in May 1954, twelve miles of the Yankee Fork was "turned into an eyesore that makes the blood of sportsmen run hot every time they think of it."[61]

Those lamenting the dredgers' depredations frequently found themselves apparently powerless to prevent an endless replication of the devastation. Fred Baumhoff, whose dredges had worked the Yankee Fork, turned his attention in 1950 to Big Creek near Cascade for its monazite deposits. Current state law did not extend to dredges working on private land, and Baumhoff showed little remorse for his previous work or any inclination to minimize the impact his dredges were now having in Long Valley. In 1954 he conceded that the Yankee Fork "doesn't look good," but "given a little time and patience, we can work out an agreement satisfactory to all."[62] Such an agreement did not seem likely to curtail damages anytime soon, since Baumhoff was estimating that the monazite deposits were extensive enough for his dredges to work there for "many, many years."[63]

The IWF talked about the need for stronger controls on stream pollution at its annual meeting in McCall in December 1950, and there seemed to be some hope that the legislature might take needed action. Custer County's Seth Burstedt introduced a bill in the 1951 session that would require dredging companies to level off their tailings and build settling ponds to reduce downstream siltation. "You all know," Burstedt told his colleagues in the Senate, "how these dredges leave nothing but desolation and waste behind them."[64] However, Harry Nock, senator from Valley County (where Baumhoff's monazite dredges were then working) protested that Burstedt's bill was too far reaching, and the Senate passed Nock's resolution for indefinite postponement.

The following summer, the rapidly emerging statewide movement for dredge control made itself heard in protests against an application to the Land Board to dredge the Salmon River only eighteen miles from Stanley. The hearing in August received press coverage from Coeur d'Alene to Idaho Falls. G.P. Lee of Portland, an investor in the proposed venture, claimed, "if private investors don't take out the monazite, the government will take it out and your good river will be torn up anyway." To which Glenn Brewer, Custer County state representative, replied by noting that in 1949 the state received just $1,600 in royalties from dredgers, only two of which avoided losing money for that year.

Not only did Tom Murray, director of the Idaho Fish and Game Department, oppose the proposal because it would injure salmon and steelhead spawning areas, but local cattlemen also complained. If dredging was permitted, testified Pierre Piva, president of the Stanley Basin Cattlemen's Association, "it'll leave us just a pile of rocks." Recreation and tourism "are permanent sources of income to Idaho," Burstedt observed, "but dredging takes out all the money in a short time, leaving the ground a tremendous loss."[65] The Twin Falls Chamber of Commerce, Boise's Ada County Fish and Game League, and local residents also filed protests. "Don't Let 'Em Dredge," the Twin Falls *Times-News* pleaded: "everyone in southern Idaho who enjoys the natural grandeur which abounds in Stanley basin should fight this particular move with every weapon at his command."[66] The Land Board quickly decided to deny the application, with Land Commissioner Edward Woozley explaining, "the board has no desire that the Salmon be used as a thoroughfare for dredging areas above the high waterline."

Opponents might have congratulated themselves on this victory, but there was cold comfort in hearing Woozley note the difficulty in determining the merit of particular cases "when so many dredging operations are being carried on in direct violation of good conservation practices."[67] Perhaps all dredging ought to be stopped. "Keeping in mind the stupid depredations of the past and thinking of coming generations," the *Statesman* admitted that it could not "help wondering if any kind of royalty arrangement can justify a continued wholesale plundering of the Idaho outdoors as yet unspoiled."[68] A week later, the Salmon *Recorder-Herald* threw down the gauntlet: "let's stop all dredging…by these greedy operators" unless absolute national necessity required otherwise.[69]

That position would have faced overwhelming opposition, of course, and the IWF always denied that it hoped to drive all dredgers out of business, but its leaders found growing support for the idea of forcing dredgers to clean up their operations. By November 1951, the *Statesman* reported that Bruce Bowler, a young Boise attorney and avid environmentalist, would submit to the IWF annual meeting a proposed dredge-control initiative modeled after the bill that failed to get out of committee during the last legislative session. When the 4th District met in Shoshone in early December—hearing Senator Robert Ransom of Blaine County report that the legislature had failed to act because of heavy pressure from a few lobbyists—the organization voted to support the initiative for the 1952 general election. The following week, Bowler submitted his initiative proposal to the IWF meeting in Boise for consideration by voters in 1954. It appears that the IWF planned to wait until after the legislature (which met only in alternate years) had one more chance to pass a dredge-control bill.[70]

Waiting until January 1953 for the legislature to meet must have tried the patience of men like Bowler. Dredgers continued their work, blandly turning aside protests with excuses like that offered by Baumhoff: "now we think we have the problem solved."[71] Meanwhile, the Land Board approved new dredging proposals, including a scheme of mind-boggling dimensions conceived by S.A. Atkinson. He aimed to dredge the length of Hells Canyon, using ten dredges over an eighteen-year span to move 528 million cubic yards, with an estimated cost of $95 million to recover $171 million in minerals. Since the reservoirs of the Hells Canyon dams would later cover all the tailings, opponents could only focus on the disruptions of salmon spawning beds and the probable destruction of Snake River sturgeon. They could not persuade the land board to deny Atkinson's request and thereby avoid those dire but hard-to-see consequences. Secretary of State Ira Masters, the only board member to vote against it, saw it as a subtle ruse to sidetrack the construction of dams. In August 1952, Idaho Mining Inspector George McDowell predicted that more dredges would soon be working monazite deposits throughout central Idaho.

Finally, the 1953 legislative session convened, and on February 10, Burstedt introduced a bill drafted by Bowler requiring dredgers to create settling ponds and smooth over any disturbed areas, so that they would be "reasonably comparable with the natural contour of ground prior to such disturbance."[72] Burstedt thought such a bill should have been enacted a generation ago to avoid the "ruthless wasting of recreational and scenic areas by uncontrolled dredging operators."[73] However, even though Ben Wherry, chairman of the Senate Fish and Game Committee, said the introduced bill excluded reference to replacing topsoil in hopes of minimizing opposition, dredgers howled in dismay. "This will absolutely end dredging in this state," stated Harry Murphy of the Idaho Canadian Dredging Company.[74]

Unable to get his bill out of committee, Burstedt reluctantly conceded the need to compromise and introduced less-stringent language, requiring settling ponds only "as far as reasonably possible."[75] He warned colleagues that dredging opponents would put the issue on the 1954 ballot by initiative unless the legislature acted. The dredgers' friends were unimpressed. Harry Marsh, secretary of the Idaho Mining Association, reiterated the accusation that the bill's proponents wanted to end dredging in Idaho. He sneered, these are people "who would halt the Russians by hitting them in the face with a fish."[76] Bruce Bowler countered: "if it isn't economically feasible to justify putting the land back where it was, the dredging should not be done in the first place."[77]

The Senate voted 37-3 in favor of the mining industry for a version opposed by Burstedt, and which, Bowler claimed, "completely neutralized" the IWF's aims.[78] After a confusing flurry of activity, during which the House voted both for a bill sponsored by mining interests and one sponsored by the IWF, the legislature finally settled on the one miners said they could live with. The bill was condemned as "a gutless wonder" by Representative Robert Faris, while Senator (later Lieutenant Governor) Jack Murphy said it would "do nothing for the dredging problem."[79]

Sportsmen immediately began planning for an initiative campaign, with those in Bonneville County approving the move at a meeting on April 10, 1953. Wildlifers were not persuaded by George McDowell, the state mining inspector, who claimed that dredgers were making a sincere effort to comply with the law passed by the legislature. What worried them was McDowell's admission that the problems of leveling and seeding dredged land "has not definitely been solved."[80] The *Morning Tribune* reflected the IWF position when it argued, "it is not good business to ruin a stream worth an almost infinite amount of money in order to dredge out minerals worth a great deal less."[81]

The IWF approved the initiative drive during its annual meeting in Boise in January 1954. After a false start, with a faulty petition having to be replaced, the drive proceeded in earnest in early May. The task was imposing; 20,750 voter signatures needed to be secured and turned into the Secretary of State's office by July 1. Four of the five initiative proposals that year failed to reach the required goal, but the dredge-control initiative made it handily, with over 1,500 signatures to spare. Clearly, the IWF had a strong following all around the state.

The initiative aimed to put more teeth into dredge controls and focused on four changes from the 1953 act—(1) moving administrative control from the mining inspector to the Land Board; (2) requiring settling ponds to "reasonably clarify" water, rather than just "where reasonably possible;" (3) require a performance bond of $300 per acre, rather than having operators billed for restoration after the fact; and (4) reduce the minimum size of the dredges to be controlled by law down to those working 500 cubic yards per day (the previous lower limit had been for dredges working 1,000 cubic yards a day).[82]

The initiative received overwhelming acclaim in Idaho except from most people in the mining industry. The Dredge Operators Association was organized in May to lead the opposition. Fred Baumhoff, its president, argued that the initiative was "designed to eliminate dredging and discourage industrial production of Idaho's resources."[83] He also denied that dredging ruined fishing downstream and urged voters to give the 1953 law a chance to prove itself. An occasional letter to the editor favored leaving miners alone to pursue their trade. "It is quite true we all hate to see nature torn up," Forrest Williams wrote in the *Statesman*, "but I would sure hate to give up all the benefits we have received from the mines of the world, too."[84] A few days before the election, the Wallace *Miner* complained that few outside the mining industry actively opposed the initiative, "which seems to be determined to maintain Idaho as a primitive area."[85]

Most newspapers were remarkably reticent to take a stand. The *Morning Tribune* published a favorable editorial in March, but nothing thereafter. The *Statesman* in July carried an editorial observing that "adoption of the measure is by no means assured," but faced a "lively fight."[86] A few other papers ran editorials like that of the Arco *Advertiser* on October 15, briefly summarizing arguments for and against the measure and suggesting that voters should consider the matter. Over all, however, press coverage was so muted as to be implicitly against the initiative.

Nevertheless, spokesmen for the initiative remained confident that they were on the winning side; the Dredge Control Act Committee, which had been organized to respond to miners' criticisms, insisted it was not opposed to dredging, but only the permanent scars "needlessly left on Idaho's beautiful mountain valleys." The initiative, according to the committee, intended nothing more onerous than to require operators "to take every reasonable measure to minimize the damage" done to an area where they worked.[87] As Pierre Pulling, a prominent Pocatello conservationist, put it: "immediate progress must sometimes be slowed to attain a reasonable safety. Some sacrifices are essential for other types of progress."[88]

The backers' confidence was borne out by the November 1954 election results. The initiative was the most popular item on the ballot, winning by a 5-to-1 margin. It also enjoyed strong support in the mining counties, as well as in the most-urbanized ones. Bonneville County, containing Idaho Falls, voted 9,910 to 1,191 in favor, but Lemhi County also came in with 1,356 to 372, and Custer County (with the Yankee Fork), 952 to 227.

Enforcing the new law, however, was quite another matter. Although Governor Len Jordan signed the act in December, months passed before the Department of Lands made any attempt to enforce it. On March 9, in an article appearing in newspapers around the state, Mining Engineer O.T. Hansen reported the measure had not yet been put into effect because of differing interpretations of its language. "We want to strike a medium between sportsmen and dredge operators," Hansen explained, and he announced a forthcoming meeting to discuss the matter with dredgers.[89] IWF representatives were not invited, which hinted at Land Department attitudes.

Hansen and Land Commissioner Arthur Wilson offered various excuses, saying, "the only way we can enforce it is by public opinion."[90] Regarding the Porter Brothers dredge in Bear Valley, Hansen added that it was on federal land and fulfilling a contract with the Atomic Energy Commission. That same spring, sportsmen throughout northern Idaho protested a proposal to dredge twenty miles of the St. Joe River, but Wilson said the dredge might have a capacity below 500 cubic yards, therefore the new law did not apply. "Where's the Dredge Law," the Salmon *Recorder-Herald* asked editorially on May 12, wondering why it was still not being enforced. Wilson did not answer, perhaps for the same reason he had not answered a letter from Frank Roberts, IWF district president: "very frankly, I didn't know the answer," he told Roberts at a public meeting in Grangeville. "Wording of the act makes it very difficult to enforce—or even to approach in many respects."[91] Hansen tried to explain to the Lewis-Clark Wildlife Club in Lewiston his problem with the law: "we must be able to prove some damage has been done due to turbidity…where is the proof coming from?"[92]

Contrary to their public pretense of impartiality, neither Wilson nor Hansen accepted the dredge-control law, nor did they intend to fully enforce it. A revealing letter can be found in the Land Department files from Wilson to Clair Finch, whose Crooked River dredge so upset Frank Roberts and other area sportsmen. On May 19, 1955, Wilson wrote to the Clearwater Dredging Company:

> Sportsmen feel that they have accomplished a great benefit to the state and to mankind through this Dredge Initiative. The Department feels hesitant as to the value of the Initiative unless we can get full cooperation from the operators. If you do the best you can under our supervision, we will then be willing to take a lot of abuse from the sportsmen. However, if we have trouble getting you to do the minimum requirements we do not hesitate to say that the sportsmen may be able to close your operation.[93]

For his part, Hansen thought the law unreasonable. "He said he has tried to determine the exact meaning of the word 'reasonable' in the Act, without success," states the Land Board Minutes. Hansen went on to complain that the protests over Finch's dredge were frivolous: "the stream isn't used for drinking water, there is no boating, no swimming, no irrigation and everyone will tell you that you can catch more fish there than in a clear stream. So the question is, what is the basis of the Hearing?"[94] Publicly he argued that Finch was excluded from the dredge law because, as he told a gathering in Grangeville, of loopholes "in the loosely worded act."[95] It was becoming increasingly apparent to sportsmen that the main loophole was Hansen's bias toward dredgers.

Other dredging controversies cropped up at the time, but the one revolving around Finch's dredge on the Crooked River turned out to be crucial. With the collusion of Land Department staff, Finch managed to put off enforcement for several months. At a November hearing, the Attorney General's office agreed to draw up a complaint to be sent within thirty days to Frank Roberts for review, but that did not happen. Another hearing was held on March 5, 1956. The defense used an argument sounding like it came from Senator Heyburn fifty years before: dredgers "have a constitutional right to use the water in Idaho streams because it belongs to the people and that right cannot be abridged."[96] The allegation that Finch was being arbitrarily harassed seemed stronger when Hansen testified that, fifteen months after the law had supposedly gone into effect, the Land Department had never adopted any regulations for dredge operators or set any water clarity standards. "A muddy stream has a certain jar on the senses," Hansen explained, and "it is true that the eye appeal has its place, but how much credit must be given is difficult to evaluate."[97]

Finally in August, the Land Board declared that Finch violated the dredge-control law. "I had hoped that it would not be necessary," Hansen wrote Finch, "but some of the Board members and Mr. Wilson have been under tremendous pressure from the sporting element of the State, and this is the consummation of the sportsmen's pressure."[98] Finch appealed to the Idaho Supreme Court, which in September 1957 reversed the Land Board decision, finding unconstitutional the law's provision for appeals directly to the supreme court.

With the Finch case concluded, Hansen's earlier assertion that the law's enforcement depended upon public opinion had, indeed, become fact. Finch ended his operation in May 1957, but protests over dredges continued to require Land Board deliberations. However, until the law changed in 1970, protesters had no recourse to the courts and could only hope that public condemnation would force dredgers to obey Land Board decisions.

The force of public opinion, however, had an immense impact on eliminating raw sewage from Idaho streams by the end of the 1950s. At the beginning of the decade, most cities and towns dumped untreated sewage into the nearest stream. The Snake River was a "filthy sewer," according to a Lewiston sanitarian,[99] while the Clearwater River seemed like a grim misnomer by the time it flowed into the Snake. The scene looked no better with the Portneuf River in Pocatello, Rock Creek below Twin Falls, the Boise River below the capital, or the Spokane River downstream from Coeur d'Alene.

Federal and state incentives did not by themselves persuade people to change their ways. Congress, beginning in 1948 with the passage of Public Law 845, provided matching grants to communities for construction of sewage treatment plants. In 1949 the Idaho Legislature approved a constitutional amendment expanding local bonding limits for sewer improvements. This along with federal matching funds made municipal sewer treatment plants affordable. At the same time, Governor Robins, a physician in private life, urged Idahoans to cooperate with the Water Pollution Advisory Committee.

Only a sustained public campaign, however, persuaded Idahoans to stop dumping raw sewage into their rivers. Again, sportsmen led the way. While they pushed for an effective dredge-control law, they also urged the need to recognize the health hazards of untreated sewage. They began individually in their own communities. For example, Dr. W.R. Jacobs in Lewiston, Bruce Bowler in Boise, and Eddie Petersen in Idaho Falls gained early prominence in their respective cities by calling for sewage treatment systems.

By the spring of 1954, sportsmen's groups around the state demanded action. At its annual Jamboree in February 1954, the Bonneville County Sportsmen's Association listened to a keynote address by Robert Harris of the U.S. Public Health Service, who stressed the need to clean up Idaho's streams. In March, State Senator John Rasor warned the Idaho Outdoor Association in Coeur d'Alene: "pollution is a cancer that comes with" population growth. "We must," he concluded, "bring water pollution under control."[100] The National Wildlife Week in March 1954 featured the theme of "Clean Waters for All America," and many Idaho newspapers carried editorials urging local attention to water pollution. There was a need, according to the St. Maries *Gazette-Record*, for "Facing Up to the Unpleasant Fact." The newspaper pledged its cooperation in keeping the theme in the public's mind.[101] The Twin Falls *Times-News* agreed that "it is high time we were doing something about it."[102] The Salmon *Recorder-Herald* hoped "the conservationists will keep hammering the theme for months and years ahead."[103]

State public health officials, unlike those concerned with dredge controls, worked persistently to bring localities along in responding to the rising chorus protesting sewage pollution. Also in notable contrast to dredge control, the legislature gave the State Board of Public Health wide-sweeping enforcement powers. In February 1955, after virtually no debate, the Senate passed by a vote of 34-9, the House by 53-6, a bill to consolidate state health programs under a new nine-member Board of Public Health. In the long list of its powers, the board was charged to set standards to limit water pollution, including "the effluent of sewerage systems, sewage treatment plants and discharges upon the land or into the surface and ground waters."[104] Gently but firmly, the board's staff used these powers to overcome local reluctance to pass bonds and build sewage treatment facilities.

Developments in Lewiston typified how Idaho towns and cities implemented sewage treatment systems. Although its residents had heard warnings from Dr. Jacobs and other authorities for several years, the city did little until the spring of 1954. The Pacific Northwest Control Council came to town in late March and made it very clear that officials had to do something about sewage. "Lewiston has been treating the Snake River shamefully," the *Morning Tribune* conceded; "something will have to be done about it soon."[105] Hearing H.C. Clare of the state Health Department express concern about the river's pollution level, D.K. Worden confessed that "as mayor of Lewiston and a physician, I am embarrassed by the situation here."[106] Nudged along by Clare's return visits, the Lewiston City Council scheduled for June 11, 1956, a $600,000 sewage disposal bond issue. (Not everyone thought this necessary. Robert Dale, a member of the Nez Perce County Planning Commission, argued that "there are many other things we need a lot worse."[107]) Although supported by Dr. Jacobs, the League of Women Voters, and local editorials, the bond missed the required two-thirds majority by 144 votes. Facing threat of a lawsuit from Clarkston (Lewiston's downstream neighbor in Washington), the city council scheduled another bond election in February 1957, which won handily with 74 percent in favor.

The task remained of bringing suburban areas along. Lewiston Orchards had its own bond election in November 1956, which gained a remarkable turnout of 50 percent of the voters, but failed passage by thirty-two votes. The suburb tried again in January 1957, and the margin of defeat increased to 223. The Lewiston *Morning Tribune* lamented that this probably doomed a sewage disposal plan in the Orchards "for years to come."[108] Proponents tried once more in September 1959, again missing the two-thirds majority, this time by only thirty-seven votes. Finally in November 1961, 82 percent of voters favored a sewage system bond of $1.1 million.

The story repeated itself in other communities along the Clearwater River. In 1950 all dumped raw sewage into the river. With the dedication of Orofino's plant by Governor Smylie in May 1962, all treated their sewage. "This is real progress," Smylie declared, "toward our long term goal of having waters once again as pure as they possibly can be."[109]

Equal progress was seen elsewhere in the state. Bonds passed in Idaho Falls in 1957, Pocatello and suburban Boise Bench in 1958 (Boise itself had led the way among larger Idaho cities by passing its bond in 1947), and Twin Falls in 1960. Between 1958 and 1963, the portion of the state's population served by sewage treatment facilities increased from 40 to 93 percent. Other than a portion of suburban Boise, every community larger than Post Falls (with a population of 1,983) had either a system in place or under construction by 1963.

Equivalent progress, however, was missing in abating industrial wastes from going into Idaho's rivers. Mobilizing public opinion, so effective in ending sewage pollution, had little impact on industrial waste disposal practices. The sharp discrepancy between Idaho's citizenry rising to the occasion, and the reluctance of the state's industries' to follow suit (as described in Chapter XI) would spell grave trouble for those companies—such as for ASARCO, which asked for the public trust in their future performance in environmentally sensitive areas.

ENDNOTES

1. "Idaho Dredge Petition Said 'Grassroots' Plan," Idaho Falls *Post-Register* (November 7, 1954): p. 2.
2. "One of Lemhi County's Important Industries," Salmon *Idaho Recorder* (October 17, 1912): p. 1.
3. "Monster Dredge Will Take $30,000 Worth of Pay Dirt Monthly from Feather River," Boise *Statesman* (August 27, 1922): Sec. 2, p. 1.
4. "Large-Scale Dredging for Gem State Gold Startling Possibility, Dean Reveals," Twin Falls *Times-News* (October 22, 1933): p. 5.
5. "Pollution Bill," editorial in Coeur d'Alene *Press* (January 16, 1939): p. 4.
6. "No Damage on Coeur d'Alene," Boise *Statesman* (June 8, 1905): p. 3.
7. "Farmers Lose Tailings Case," Coeur d'Alene *Press* (August 14, 1906): pp. 1, 3.
8. "Mine Pollution of River to Be Meeting Topic," Coeur d'Alene *Press* (August 9, 1930): p. 1.
9. "Would Stop Pollution," Coeur d'Alene *Press* (August 19, 1930): pp. 1, 2.
10. John Knox Coe, "Another Report Suits Mine People," editorial in Coeur d'Alene *Press* (January 10, 1931): p. 1.
11. "Report on Pollution," Coeur d'Alene *Press* (December 20, 1932): p. 1.
12. "Pollution Report Most Convincing," editorial in Coeur d'Alene *Press* (December 21, 1932): p. 1.
13. "Pollution Bill Is Voted Down," Coeur d'Alene *Press* (February 14, 1933): p. 1.
14. "Sewage Bill Is Defeated," Idaho Falls *Post-Register* (February 19, 1939): pp. 1, 8.
15. "Valley Sportsmen to Take Stand Against Pollution of Streams," Cascade *News* (May 24, 1940): p. 1.
16. Dick d'Easum, "Idaho Out O'Doors," Boise *Statesman* (November 2, 1940): p. 5.
17. "Sportsmen Air Game Troubles," Boise *Statesman* (January 13, 1941): pp. 1, 2.
18. "Wildlife Body for Pollution Study in Idaho," Coeur d'Alene *Press* (January 14, 1941): p. 6.
19. "Sportsmen Oppose New Dredge Plan," Boise *Capitol News* (December 5, 1941): p. 2.
20. "Bed Rock Flume," Boise *Statesman* (February 19, 1888): p. 3.
21. "Not All Roily Water Comes from Dredge," Challis *Messenger* (April 30, 1941): p. 1.
22. "Dredges Denied on South Fork of Clearwater," Lewiston *Morning Tribune* (March 2, 1948): p. 5.
23. Elvis Fisher, "Elk City Correspondent Upholds Gold Mining by Dredge in South Fork," Grangeville *Idaho County Free Press* (November 25, 1948): p. 3.
24. "Dredging Permit Denied," editorial in Twin Falls *Times-News* (August 27, 1950): p. 4.
25. "Opposes Use of Idaho Waters," Idaho Falls *Post* (January 21, 1927): p. 1.
26 Chapter 2, *1927 Session Laws*.
27. "Conserving Idaho's Resources," editorial in Idaho Falls *Times-Register* (February 9, 1926): p. 6.
28. "Grab for Snake River Power," editorial in Pocatello *Tribune* (October 22, 1941): p. 4.
29. "Sen. Thomas Warns of Water Resource Peril," Twin Falls *Times* (September 13, 1941): pp. 1, 8.
30. "A Thousand Times No," editorial in Arco *Advertiser* (August 22, 1941): p. 4.
31. John Knox Cox, "Waters of Idaho May Be Preserved," editorial in Coeur d'Alene *Press* (December 23, 1930): p. 1.
32. "State Chamber Opposes Creation of Columbia River Authority," Boise *Statesman* (August 11, 1941): p. 10.

33. "Columbian Octopus," Boise *Statesman* (August 12, 1941): p. 4.
34. "Power, Navigation Development of Area Envisioned at Hearing," Lewiston *Morning Tribune* (September 1, 1943): p. 10.
35. "Wonderland Created by Northwest Rivers Seen in Power," Lewiston *Morning Tribune* (June 2, 1944): pp. 1, 3.
36. "Bottolfsen in N. Idaho; Balk Federal Grab," Coeur d'Alene *Press* (April 27, 1944): p. 2.
37. "Shortsighted Stand," editorial in Lewiston *Morning Tribune* (October 29, 1944): p. 4.
38. "CVA Bad for Idaho," editorial in Idaho Falls *Post-Register* (March 7, 1945): p. 4.
39. "Eastern Idaho Waterusers Balk at CVA," Boise *Statesman* (June 20, 1945): p. 2.
40. "CVA Proposal Draws Fire of Mining Speaker," Lewiston *Morning Tribune* (June 23, 1945): p. 10.
41. "Idaho to Lose Its Water Rights under a River Valley Authority," Coeur d'Alene *Press* (September 28, 1945): p. 5.
42. "Let's Make Up Our Minds," editorial in Boise *Statesman* (September 24, 1945): p. 4.
43. "Mitchell's CVA Bill Opposed by Chamber Board," Lewiston *Morning Tribune* (October 9, 1945): p. 12.
44. "Taylor Replies to CVA Foes," Boise *Statesman* (August 22, 1945): pp. 1, 2.
45. "Davidson Lauds TVA in Address," Boise *Statesman* (September 16, 1945): p. 3.
46. "Davidson Asks CVA Support," Boise *Statesman* (September 23, 1945): p. 9.
47. "N. Idaho's CC on Record Against CVA," Coeur d'Alene *Press* (October 20, 1945): pp. 1, 5.
48. "CVA Official Urges Welsh to Offer Plan," Boise *Statesman* (November 8, 1945): p. 6.
49. "CVA and Education," editorial in Lewiston *Morning Tribune* (November 20, 1946): p. 4.
50. "On State Development," editorial in Boise *Statesman* (November 15, 1946): p. 4.
51. John Corlett, "Boiseans Hear President Urge Support for CVA," Boise *Statesman* (May 11, 1950): pp. 1, 5.
52. "TVA's Good Example," editorial in Lewiston *Morning Tribune* (January 15, 1949): p. 4.
53. "We Can Be 'Ignored,'" editorial in Twin Falls *Times-News* (January 28, 1949): p. 4.
54. "Hear 81st Congress to Shun CVA," Coeur d'Alene *Press* (March 25, 1949): p. 1.
55. Tom Aden, "State Must Insist Development of Idaho's Water Resources Be from Headwaters Down—Smylie," Coeur d'Alene *Press* (February 15, 1955): p. 2.
56. "Wildlife and the Rivers," editorial in Lewiston *Morning Tribune* (December 18, 1949): p. 4.
57. "Plan for CVA Is Denounced by Sportsmen," Twin Falls *Times-News* (November 27, 1949): pp. 1, 2.
58. Theo H. Wegener, "CVA Purpose to Change Our Form of Government," St. Maries *Gazette-Record* (July 7, 1949): p. 8.
59. "Wildlife Group, Conservationists Oppose Gold Dredging Projects," Lewiston *Morning Tribune* (September 11, 1950): p. 6.
60. "Cattleman Burstedt Eyes School Laws," Boise *Statesman* (January 16, 1949): p. 6.
61. "Yankee Fork Promises to Be Hot Issue in Dredge-Sportsmen Fight," Twin Falls *Times-News* (May 23, 1954): p. 10.
62. *Ibid.*
63. "Plant in Boise to Mill Idaho Monazite Sand," Boise *Statesman* (November 26, 1950): p. 8.
64. "Senate Blocks Bill to Set Dredging Rule," Boise *Statesman* (March 8, 1951): p. 5.
65. "Sportsmen, Stockmen Oppose Lease for Dredging," Coeur d'Alene *Press* (August 4, 1951): p. 2.
66. "Don't Let 'Em Dredge," editorial in Twin Falls *Times-News* (August 7, 1951): p. 4.
67. "Land Board Vetoes Plan to Dredge Salmon River," Pocatello *Idaho State Journal* (August 17, 1951): p. 1.
68. "Dredging on Idaho Rivers," editorial in Boise *Statesman* (August 23, 1951): p. 4.
69. "The Dredgers Are at It Again," editorial in Salmon *Recorder-Herald* (August 30, 1951): p. 4.
70. "Wildlife Men Modify License Fee Proposals, Hit Dredges," Lewiston *Morning Tribune* (December 10, 1951): p. 8.
71. "Rehabilitation Planned where Areas Dredged," Coeur d'Alene *Press* (February 1, 1952): p. 1.
72. "Dredge Bill Requires Smoothing Out Land," Lewiston *Morning Tribune* (February 11, 1953): p. 3.
73. "Burstedt Says Dredging Bill 'Right Step,'" Boise *Statesman* (February 20, 1953): p. 6.
74. "Operators Say Dredging Bill Is Too Tough," Boise *Statesman* (February 20, 1953): p. 32.

75. "Burstedt to Back New Dredge Bill," Idaho Falls *Post-Register* (February 25, 1953): p. 2.
76. "Dredging Control Proposal Blasted," Boise *Evening Statesman* (February 27, 1953): p. 11.
77. "Idaho Legislators Spar over 'Hot Potato' Dredging Bill," Cascade *News* (February 27, 1953): pp. 1, 4.
78. "Discussion of Dredging Bills Set for Sportsmen's Meeting," Boise *Statesman* (March 1, 1953): p. 3.
79. "House Passes Two Conflicting Bills to Regulate Dredging," Boise *Statesman* (March 5, 1953): p. 2; "Senate Passes Dredge Mining Control Bill," Boise *Statesman* (March 4, 1953): p. 3.
80. "McDowell Says Idahoans Comply with Dredge Law," Boise *Statesman* (July 14, 1953): p. 3.
81. "Idaho Can't Afford to Neglect Its Streams," editorial in Lewiston *Morning Tribune* (November 3, 1953): p. 4.
82. "Wildlife Federation Opens Drive for Dredge Control," Boise *Statesman* (March 21, 1954): p. 12.
83. "Dredge Operators Fight Move of Sportsmen to Tighten Idaho Laws," Coeur d'Alene *Press* (May 13, 1954): p. 8.
84. Forest Williams, "Appeals for Dredges," Boise *Statesman* (May 2, 1954): p. 5.
85. "The Dredge Initiative," editorial in Wallace *Miner* (October 28, 1954): p. 2.
86. "Four of Five Initiatives Fail to Make the Ballot," Boise *Statesman* (July 11, 1954): p. 4.
87. "Dredge Mining Control Act Initiative Explained by Sponsoring Organization," St. Maries *Gazette-Record* (October 14, 1954): p. 6.
88. Pierre Pulling, "Woods and Waters," Pocatello *Idaho State Journal* (May 16, 1954): p. 8.
89. "Dredging Firms to Confer on Mine Control Law," Coeur d'Alene *Press* (March 9, 1955): p. 2.
90. "Dredge Control Bill to Be Implemented," Lewiston *Morning Tribune* (March 9, 1955): p. 3.
91. "State Admits Dredging Laws Are Puzzling," Grangeville *Idaho County Free Press* (September 15, 1955): p. 1.
92. "State Engineer Tells Wildlife Club Dredges Can't Be Closed Arbitrarily," Lewiston *Morning Tribune* (September 27, 1955): p. 8.
93. Arthur Wilson to Clearwater Dredging Co., May 19, 1955, in "Dredge Hearing—Permit—Finch File," Idaho Department of Lands, Boise. Hereinafter referred to as "Finch File."
94. Entry in Minutes, September 23, 1955: Dredges in South Fork of Clearwater River. Report by O.T. Hansen, in "Finch File."
95. "Dredging Law Enforcement Is Demanded," Grangeville *Idaho County Free Press* (September 29, 1955): p. 10.
96. "Dismissal Sought in Dredge Hearing," Lewiston *Morning Tribune* (March 6, 1956): p. 8.
97. O.T. Hansen, "Dredge Hearing and Experimentation," ca. March 15, 1956, in "Finch File."
98. O.T. Hansen to Vernon B. Finch, August 8, 1956, in "Finch File."
99. "Snake Called 'Filthy Sewer,'" Lewiston *Morning Tribune* (October 12, 1949): p. 14.
100. "Lack of Education Blocking Anti-Pollution Laws, Convention Told," Coeur d'Alene *Press* (March 13, 1954): pp. 1, 7.
101. "Facing Up to the Unpleasant Fact," editorial in St. Maries *Gazette-Record* (March 25, 1954): Sec. 2, p. 2.
102. "Water Pollution," Twin Falls *Time-News* (March 21, 1954): p. 4.
103. "Facing an Unpleasant Fact," editorial in Salmon *Recorder-Herald* (March 25, 1954): p. 4.
104. Chapter 57, *1955 Session Laws.*
105. "Pollution Control Council to Meet Here; City Leaders Warned to 'Act,'" Lewiston *Morning Tribune* (March 23, 1954): p. 12.
106. "Water Pollution Here Must Be Stopped, or Federal Government May Step In," Lewiston *Morning Tribune* (March 26, 1954): pp. 10, 5.
107. "Sewage Plant Not Needed, Dole Tells Council," Lewiston *Morning Tribune* (May 29, 1956): p. 12.
108. "A Crushing Defeat for Sewage Disposal," editorial in Lewiston *Morning Tribune* (January 11, 1957): p. 4.
109. "Smylie Lauds Work toward Clean Rivers," Lewiston *Morning Tribune* (May 4, 1962): pp. 16, 5.

VIII

The Value of Wildness

U NLIKE THE VALUE OF WATER, which was basic and undebatable for almost everyone in Idaho, few people had much reason to consider the value of wildness. The Idaho, Selway, and Sawtooth primitive areas were designated in the 1930s with almost no public debate; administrating those areas rarely generated any widespread discussion for more than twenty years thereafter. Not until environmental activists prodded Congress into considering some sort of legislation to create a national wilderness system did Idahoans have to confront the questions: what is the value of wildness? And how should it be used?

The eight-year debate over the Wilderness Act from 1956, when the first version was introduced, until 1964, with its signage into law, had the most unusual characteristic of engaging a full-scale public debate without any immediate, practical consequence. As Senator Frank Church, the bill's floor leader in September 1961, repeatedly assured gatherings around the state, "the wilderness can be reserved without taking one dollar from anyone's pocket."[1] The wilderness system could be established "with no adverse effect on anyone"[2] because primitive areas already existed. The act "won't even create one acre of new wilderness" in Idaho.[3]

Church's opponents insisted there was no danger, at least in Idaho, of losing wild areas. As Arthur Roberts, McCall's mayor, put it in a statement for the Idaho State Chamber of Commerce, "there is no evidence that the wilderness type areas are being invaded by commercial forces or that such action is imminent."[4] Besides, the notion that wilderness areas were fast disappearing was only "Megapolitan Myopia," according to the Boise *Statesman* quoting the New York *Times*. "In the nature of things it's going to be a long, long while before this country ever runs short of wilderness."[5]

Nor were any immediate political consequences forthcoming. Many commentators thought it would be a big issue in Church's 1962 campaign for reelection. The Twin Falls *Times-News* suspected that even though Church seemed unbeatable, opposition to his support for the Wilderness Bill might be enough to defeat him. "Idahoans must fight the Wilderness bill like they would the plague," thundered the Boise *Statesman*, which warned Church that he would see that fight at the next election.[6] Church's supporters countered by applauding his political courage. The Lewiston *Morning Tribune* commended him for choosing "to stand on the toughest ground."[7]

As it turned out, the issue never amounted to much in the 1962 senatorial campaign. Jack Hawley, the Republican nominee, occasionally attempted to stir up opposition, claiming that "the push-it-down-your-throat philosophy against the best interests of the state cannot be tolerated."[8] But Church blithely denied that it was a question of politics. Typically, he told a group in Lewiston, "my basic reason for supporting [the bill] has nothing to do with economics. It has to do with philosophy… It is our moral responsibility that some of the heritage we have had as westerners is protected for future generations."[9]

Whether or not Idahoans favored such a high-minded stance, political lines had not yet been drawn over wilderness preservation. Don Samuelson was a supporter at the time, writing Church on Idaho Wildlife Federation stationery, urging his support for the Wilderness Bill, "because I believe that this is good legislation and that we should take steps now to make sure that these Areas are kept intact and managed in the best interests of the people."[10] Cecil Andrus, a young senator from Orofino, had yet to develop his conservationist position. When the legislature passed a memorial to Congress opposing any more wilderness areas in Idaho, Andrus spoke on its behalf: "we are not arguing whether wilderness areas be created by executive order or by Congress. We just don't want any more added in Idaho."[11]

Nevertheless, a great deal was at stake in the Wilderness Bill debate. John Corlett, political editor for the *Statesman*, whose "Politically Speaking" column appeared regularly in several Idaho newspapers, perceptively summed up the matter in October 1961:

> Church makes a good case for the raw provisions of the bill. But the fight is not so much against the bill. The fight is against the philosophy behind the bill. The fight is between those who view the public domain as usable in its many facets and those who would lock out what they call the "exploiters."

Furthermore, public domain users "firmly believe that once established, the wildlifers, exuberant over their first big victory, will move to wipe them off the other portions of the public domain."[12] No longer could a few prominent sportsmen get together with the governor and a handful of Forest Service officials and decide to strengthen game preserve regulations by designating the Idaho Primitive Area. A stark confrontation grew between two different visions of how to treat Idaho's undeveloped backcountry.

The Wilderness Bill's proponents used quite another language than that of primitive area advocates in the 1930s. Only rarely did one hear about the last frontier. Philip Fairbanks of Nampa wrote a letter to the editor in

February 1962, arguing that "the last frontier should be preserved for future generations,"[13] but his was an isolated exception. Although the Idaho Wildlife Federation consistently supported wilderness preservation, its leaders did not focus on wild game concerns. Art Manley, president of the Coeur d'Alene Wildlife Federation, wrote Church expressing disappointment with amendments Church had proposed to mollify industrial opponents: "looking to the future, we think we can see the time when our wilderness areas in Idaho will be among our greatest tourist attractions—and tourism already is one of Idaho's most important industries. That is, if we are not so shortsighted that we let these few remaining wilderness areas be gradually whittled away and destroyed to satisfy industry's demand for a quick dollar."[14]

Practical matters, such as tourism's value, often surfaced only to be passed by in favor of far less tangible, but much more passionately held concerns. Introducing the Wilderness Bill to the U.S. Senate in September 1961, Church began by observing that wilderness areas "will become mighty magnets for the tourist trade." However, that did not seem to really drive him. Instead, his core concern was revealed by a declaration that "without wilderness the country will become a cage." "The great purpose of the wilderness bill," according to Church, "is to set aside a reasonable part of the vanishing wilderness, to make certain that generations of Americans yet unborn will know what it is to experience life on undeveloped, unoccupied land in the same form and character as the Creator fashioned it." Unlike the 1930s, when primitive areas were seen as open-air museums, wilderness areas were by the 1960s becoming open-air temples. Church ended his Senate speech urging wilderness preservation for "all those who find, in high and lonely places, a refreshment of the spirit, and life's closest communion with God."[15] This peroration seemed to catch Idahoans' imagination, for it was reprinted in newspapers throughout the state.

Responding to opponents' arguments that wilderness areas would have few visitors and, therefore, fail to serve most people, Wilderness Bill advocates commonly insisted that the value of wildness had no necessary connection with how many people used it. "These wilderness values are to be compared with libraries and art galleries," College of Idaho biology professor Lyle Stanford wrote Church, "which we do not destroy because only a minority use them."[16] Nell Tobias, a longtime conservationist in McCall, invoked another analogy: "we have within our state a laboratory of untold value to mankind, as time allows science to relate man to the big picture of ecology."[17] Ted Trueblood combined the images of libraries and laboratories in his testimony at a congressional hearing in McCall in October 1961: "our remaining undisturbed wild areas are museums of nature. They are the libraries of God's works…a library of reference for the scientists of the future."[18]

Although the ecological viewpoint that saw humankind as an integral part of nature was only beginning to gain a following in Idaho, some Wilderness Act proponents did reflect that frame of mind. Franklin Jones of Boise, later an Idaho Wildlife Federation president, concluded his long letter to the *Statesman* by affirming that "a new spirit is abroad as both scientists and laymen realize that man and the rest of nature are united and indivisible."[19] One could argue that focusing largely on visitation counts only reflected outmoded thinking; the value of wildness continued even if no one visited it.

Ladd Hamilton noted in a Lewiston *Morning Tribune* editorial:

> The wilderness serves a therapeutic function simply by being there, and it salves the nerves of millions of people who will never see it but who can draw comfort from the reflection that there is a place where the highway ends, where no telephone rings, no bill falls due, no outboard motor shatters the buzzing dusk.[20]

But, proponents insisted, time was running out. If the Wilderness Act were not passed, America's wild places would soon disappear. Stuart Brandborg, who grew up in Lewiston and Grangeville and served on the Wilderness Society staff, warned the North Idaho Citizens for Wilderness that "selfish interests" aimed to ruin the land: "powerful lumber and mining interests are conducting an all-out fight to kill the wilderness bill. They want to take over our last remaining areas of wilderness for commercial purposes."[21] It didn't take somebody visiting from the nation's capital to make this argument. Many prominent Idaho conservationists were saying the same thing. Ted Trueblood lambasted the "Don Quixotes of lumber and mining and grazing whose only fear is that they might, somehow, be denied the privilege of making a dollar at the expense of the public."[22]

Such talk seemed not only unfair but also almost demented to many Idahoans who worked in natural resource-based industries. The "appeal for wilderness quickly leaves the realm of reason," stated Charles Schwab, president of the Bunker Hill Company, one of the largest firms in the Coeur d'Alene mining district, "and mounts into the heavy atmosphere of mysticism, emotion, and, I regret to say, sheer demagoguery."[23] Grangeville's *Idaho County Free Press* denied that some esoteric, aesthetic inspiration might be inherent in wildness. "There is no beauty in primitive wilderness unless man makes use of it and can work and play without depriving a fellowman the right to perform honest endeavors."[24] Al Teske, secretary of the Idaho Mining Association, castigated the Wilderness Bill's sacrificing industry to "bird-watching and organized idleness."[25] This contradicted the basic destiny of human beings in the opinion of the Challis *Messenger* editor. Are we on earth, he asked rhetorically, merely to observe or with a "purpose and a destiny that can only find fruit in enjoying ALL resources available for our population?" He had no doubts about his readers' response when he asked: "would you like to watch the water fall over a bluff or would you rather have electric lights?"[26] A.M. Derr, who ran against Church in 1962 for the Democratic nomination for U.S. senator, fumed at the "silly, romantic idealists" advocating the Wilderness Bill for wanting to "return back in history beyond the horse and buggy age. We do not need, we cannot afford a museum dedicating so much wealth to a single purpose, for a few."[27]

Many Idahoans failed to grasp the intellectual and spiritual values of wilderness exemplified in Church's Senate speech. Their opposition to the Wilderness Bill might have, in some cases, reflected a desire to exploit natural resources without restraint, but frequently it arose from a conservationist ethic that emphasized use rather than preservation. R.J. Bruning, editor of the Wallace *North Idaho News*, whose "Stream of Thought" column appeared in several Idaho papers including the *Statesman*, hammered away repeatedly on the theme that "true conservation means use of all resources. Neglect, or misuse, or non-use of any resource is not conservation, it is waste."[28]

Neither Bruning nor many of his readers could see any merit in what they saw as the Wilderness Society's abandonment of forests to fires and insect infestation. Traditionally, conservation meant managing the forests for sustained yield by minimizing losses from fire and disease. Now told that such an orientation was wrong, that it destroyed the pristine character of wildness, brought incredulity like that seen in a *Statesman* editorial titled "Nature in the Raw."[29] Reacting to a recently published Sierra Club book, *In Wilderness Is the Preservation of the World*, the editorial writer focused on a photograph of a caterpillar. "It calls for a considerable stretch of the imagination," in the editorialist's opinion, "to envision a nature lover with the sympathy so broad as to encompass this fuzzy worm, or a boll weevil, or a pine beetle." The writer found the caterpillar symbolic of what happens in wilderness areas where there is no chance to control "the anarchistic operation of nature's forces."

Unable to believe that most wilderness proponents were really caterpillar lovers, opponents cast about for some more-plausible explanation for the wilderness preservation movement. Some, including Governor Robert Smylie, saw it as a plot to overwhelm state's rights in favor of an ever-expanding web of federal controls. The Wilderness Bill, he warned in 1958, would create "a federal octopus whose tentacles would choke natural development and harvest of Idaho's resources."[30] In 1961 he called the bill "a betrayal of Idaho's future. There is no choice for Idahoans but to fight this monstrous proposal."[31] The *Statesman* published numerous editorials on the same theme, and John Corlett, its political editor, harped on it in his syndicated column. Other papers occasionally echoed the claim that the Wilderness Bill was only an "Opening Door," as the Twin Falls *Times-News* put it, for "eventual inclusion of whatever areas [might] be coveted."[32]

The most common explanation attributed the bill to the machinations of a wealthy and self-serving elite that wanted to set aside wilderness areas for their own private use. Arthur Wilson, state land commissioner, told a congressional hearing in Salt Lake City that he could not support "locking up millions of acres of land for the monopolistic use of a very select group of individuals."[33] Senator Henry Dworshak saw this as "class legislation," setting aside vast amounts of land for the "exclusive use of a small minority of well-endowed citizens," while excluding most people who did not have the stamina or wealth for "arduous, expensive pack trips."[34] What Idaho needed, according to R.J. Bruning, was not primitive areas, but the development of outdoor recreation opportunities for "the ordinary family on a weekend."[35] The Cascade *News* complained that wilderness areas represented a "totally negative approach," excluding "99 percent of American outdoor vacationers" and setting aside millions of acres without study to see "how much is needed for wilderness and how much would be better for other uses."[36]

Most of these people favored multiple use. Although formally sanctioned by Congress only in 1960 with the Multiple Use Sustained Yield Act, it "has long been accepted in Idaho and other western states," stated Senator Dworshak, and it constituted the "fundamental issue involved in the wilderness bill."[37] The North Idaho Chamber of Commerce resolved at a May 1961 meeting in Salmon that it supported "the sound conservation principles of multiple use of public lands."[38] Numerous local chambers of commerce concurred. (Arco's may have been unique in the state in its support of the Wilderness Bill, sending Church a copy of its letter to the Idaho State Chamber of Commerce stating it could not "support the short sighted policy" of opposing legislation for "preservation of unspoiled areas."[39])

Much more commonly, multiple-use proponents argued that Idaho had plenty of space to accommodate everyone. Idaho County itself had sufficient room, according to the Grangeville paper, "for all the mountain climbers, canoe paddlers, hikers, as well as big game hunters and fishermen," and still serve "professional foresters and natural resource students who find deep satisfaction in growing new trees, building adequate trails…and conserving and properly using the water supply for which the area is famous."[40] After all, the Idaho Falls *Post-Register* counseled, "the forests are not a ship in a bottle." Implementing better mining controls could mollify sportsmen angry about the havoc wreaked by dredging. There could be other uses "and still preserve the backwoods quality."[41]

With the "present very satisfactory and normal administration of our natural resources," the Idaho Legislature could see no reason to go off in new directions that would "irreparably damage" resource-based industries.[42] The legislature's language was most revealing. Legislators, like many of their constituents, opposed the Wilderness Bill by praising the status quo and insisting that the Forest Service was doing such an outstanding job that no change was needed. The editor of the St. Anthony *Chronicle-News* voiced a common sentiment: "we like what the Forest Service does. Trees, after all, grow. So do grasses… Foresters are careful that no more is used than is produced, so the forest is maintained."[43] In administering primitive areas, the Forest Service showed that it could deal with such ambiguities as scattered in-holdings and the use of machinery as needed. The Wilderness Bill, on the other hand, threatened to "get rid of the natives," as Frances Zaunmiller wailed in a *Idaho County Free Press* column, written from her home at Campbell's Ferry in the Idaho Primitive Area, where she had lived for twenty-one years. As for the "nostalgic drivel" spouted by those dreaming about an area "untainted by chain saws," the Forest Service knew that chain saws were necessary to clear trails.[44]

The Forest Service's reputation, in short, had come full circle. From the time of Senator Heyburn, when it seemed like a horrendous and alien intruder, it now was held up by stand-pat conservatives as the exemplar of all that was normal and healthy in managing Idaho's wildlands.

National Forest Service officials found this latter-day view no more agreeable than the earlier one. Neither attitude supported the service's commitment to a balance between use and preservation, where logging, mining, and grazing fit within a system also giving room for active and passive recreation as well as scenic preservation. Major Fenn and other early leaders pacified, or at least outlasted, Senator Heyburn and his supporters. Fenn's successors in the 1960s found it much harder to distance the NFS sufficiently from resource-based industrialists and gain the support of Senator Church and environmentalists.

Two incidents during the time of the Wilderness Bill debate illustrate the growing difficulty the Forest Service faced in attempting to balance the demands of the development-minded and the expectations of environmentalists. The first involved a controversy over a proposed power line to the backcountry village of Elk City (several dozen miles east of Grangeville). Washington Water Power wished to run the line along the road (now designated Idaho 14), but the Forest Service objected: WWP's proposal would mar the scenery by repeatedly switching across one side of the road to the other. Since the road was built with Forest Service funds, and the federal agency owned the forested lands along both sides, the power company had to obtain easements from the Forest Service, but it argued that the route recommended by the NFS was intolerably expensive.

This power line controversy brought a flurry of letters to the editor of the Lewiston *Morning Tribune*. Some found the Forest Service unreasonable. "Few people will be noticing such a commonplace as a power pole," wrote Alice Ullmer of Pierce, "but rather will be seeing the wild roaring river, the beauty of the untouched majestic mountains and the awe-inspiring stretches of sheer rock bluffs."[45] Others spoke up for the Forest Service. Betty Roberts of Moscow thought it a "deadly pastime of attacking the Forest Service for alleged acts of high-handed bureaucracy, when in actuality the Forest Service is only attempting to carry out the mandates of Congress and protect public property."[46] The letters were in response to a *Morning Tribune* editorial that concluded: "to preserve beauty and open space is almost impossible against the great crush of what is convenient or practical or profitable."[47]

The controversy also brought a rapid response from the governor and the legislature, which had little sympathy for the Forest Service's position. On January 30, 1961, Governor Smylie suggested that the Senate Forestry and Public Lands Committee have a hearing on the subject. Dispensing with such niceties, the committee declared that the Forest Service should modify its policies to permit the line's construction. "Whatever aesthetic beauty that might be involved," it said, "should be subservient to the public welfare."[48] The governor soon convened a meeting with WWP and Forest Service officials, and they agreed to a compromise route in early March.

At no time during this controversy did the Idaho Wildlife Federation, the Wilderness Society, or any other wilderness-minded group apparently make any public comment on it. The message seemed to be that while they would not support the Forest Service's critics on this issue, the Forest Service would have to fight its own battle without any help from those most concerned about the "aesthetic beauty" legislators found so easy to dismiss.

By the early 1960s, a breach emerged between Forest Service officials and environmentalists, as is clearly evident in the second incident, a Forest Service proposal to reclassify the Selway-Bitterroot Primitive Area into a wilderness. In July 1957, Ralph Space, supervisor of the Clearwater National Forest, announced the proposal at a Lewiston sportsmen's gathering. He noted that some of the existing primitive area would be omitted from the new wilderness area because roads "which negate the wilderness concept" ran through those portions. Space also conceded an ambiguity that would become a major issue in wilderness area management during the 1960s. "In the truest sense, a wilderness area should have no airplanes," he admitted, "but we have to accept conditions as they exist at the time the area is instituted."[49] The Wilderness Society argued that, by the same token, the presence of a few roads should not cause an otherwise-pristine area to be excluded. It feared that such exclusions would lead to timber harvesting, destroying all of the area's appeal.

The Forest Service proceeded with the Selway Wilderness Area proposal in characteristic fashion by holding informal meetings with various interest group representatives, eventually followed by public hearings, and, only after an extended period of time (five and a half years in this case), reaching a final decision. The NFS had found that such a process generally, at least in times past, resulted in a consensus among all interested parties, and avoided litigation or recourse to congressional action.

It soon became clear that the process no longer worked to achieve consensus. Major players did not accept the value of consensus. Space called a two-day meeting at the Fenn Ranger Station in October 1957, which immediately revealed the polarization of positions. On one side, George Rauch, logging manager for Potlatch Forests, Inc., insisted that "the need for land and its products and the payrolls created from the use of these products will not permit profligate or wasteful use of land by any group."[50] On the other side, Howard Zahniser, head of the Wilderness Society, argued that in wilderness areas, timber should be left unharvested and unprotected from disease or fire "as it has been in nature." He believed that "the emotional values of the isolated block of land are worth more than the combined physical values although only a few of the people of the nation will ever have a chance to use the region."[51]

Given this stark face-off between the voices of use versus preservation, the fight over boundaries became the central issue in the Selway Wilderness proposal. For Rauch, everything inside the area was lost to use, while for Zahniser, any portions placed outside the boundaries were doomed to destruction by loggers. Not all environmentalists agreed about the boundaries. The Idaho Wildlife Federation suggested that the Meadow Creek area along the Lewis-Clark Highway (U.S. Route 12) be included, but Grangeville sportsmen disagreed, noting that the Forest Service had already sold timber in that drainage. The Wilderness Society condemned the exclusion of the Magruder Corridor (to be discussed in Chapter IX), but not all northern Idaho sportsmen shared this position.

Nevertheless, everyone who supported wilderness preservation ardently opposed loggers' views as represented by Royce Cox, Potlatch Forest Industries chief forester and chairman of the Inland Empire Multiple Use Committee. Cox recommended reducing the wilderness area to 862,110 acres, barely half of the existing primitive area. This reinforced preservationists' fears that the Forest Service sympathized entirely too much with loggers. As Morton Brigham, a leading wilderness advocate in Lewiston, put it, "the proposal is clearly a scheme to cut down most of the trees on the Selway and Lochsa areas."[52] He wrote Frank Church, lamenting that "the matchless Selway would become a muddy river because of erosion on the steep slopes,"[53] and this only confirmed his conviction that loggers and miners believed "that nothing whatever should be kept a wilderness unless it is completely useless for anything else."[54]

Wilderness advocates took strong exception to the boundaries finally settled on by the Forest Service. The Wilderness Society mourned the new wilderness area's sharply reduced size, noting in its periodical, *Living Wilderness*, that it could be one of only two in the whole national forest system comprising more than a million acres.

Aside from boundaries, environmentalists began distrusting the Forest Service, regardless of what it did. Church reported to Bruce Bowler that Howard Zahniser thought, "any language drafted by the Forest Service was necessarily suspect, simply because of its source."[55] He and those who shared the Wilderness Society viewpoint were inclined to believe that the NFS was ready to compromise the core values of wildness. "A little bit of logging and road building in this country," Brigham wrote Church, "is like a little bit of cancer—it keeps spreading."[56] Paul Keeton, a Lewiston attorney, declared "there is no compromise with virginity… To tear this country to pieces with logging and mining and then to state under the doctrine of multiple use that it is still a recreation area is ludicrous." In his mind, the Forest Service action on the Selway clearly proved that without the Wilderness Bill, within twenty-five years "most of the beautiful country which we have left in the west would be obliterated as far as its primeval state is concerned."[57]

Church shared this distrust of the Forest Service, but did not condemn its search for compromises and repeatedly reminded his supporters that they had to allow him some room to maneuver. "If I am to be effective as a Senator," he wrote Bill Duff, the Idaho Wildlife Federation president at the time, "I must deal with realities," and wilderness advocates had "to recognize that some give and take is necessary."[58] In fact, Church was untroubled by eliminating certain portions of existing primitive areas. "Unquestionably, large parts of them are in fact suitable for multiple use."[59] But he adamantly opposed the Forest Service deciding the issue. "I believe that decisions to withdraw public lands for special use should always be made in the Congress, and not by appointed officials."[60]

Church honestly believed that defending the prerogatives of Congress was vital to democracy's continuance in America. "One of the most dangerous trends in our federal government," he told a dinner party in Grangeville, "is the concentration of power in administrative agencies." He told the same audience, "it seems to me that every time I have had an Idaho problem to discuss with" Forest Service officials, "I've had to go with hat in hand and say, 'I represent the people of Idaho, you have all the powers,' and they could do as they pleased."[61]

However, his animus toward the Forest Service also arose from a fundamental difference of philosophy. Although Church worked for politically acceptable compromises, he always shared the environmentalists' passion for wildness, and it was entirely appropriate that Idaho's largest wilderness area was later named in his honor. He was fully aware that the Forest Service, on the other hand, had a long institutional commitment to use-oriented conservation, where wilderness preservation was only one and not necessarily the most important value in the blend of multiple uses. Church believed that such an approach could and sometimes did lead to tolerance for wildland exploitative destruction. "The same interests," he argued, "which for years blocked legislation to remedy the dredge mining situation now are opposing the wilderness bill."[62] And he did not doubt that they were using the Forest Service as their cat's paw.

It is true that the NFS only belatedly and halfheartedly supported the Wilderness Bill. When the bill was first introduced, Dwight Eisenhower was in the White House, and he and his cabinet officers commonly favored production-oriented resource industries over environmentalists' claims. The Forest Service could safely oppose the Wilderness Bill and did so. Its Chief, Richard McArdle, told the Senate Public Lands Subcommittee in June 1957, "we see no need for the establishment of a national wilderness preservation system."[63] The implications of such a position were reflected at a meeting in Twin Falls in June 1959, when supervisors of the Boise, Challis, and Sawtooth national forests considered plans for the Sawtooth Mountains area. "The over-all plan," according to the Hailey *Times*, "will be programmed in a way to capture the fullest use of the resources within the area for the greatest number of people."[64] Wilderness preservation was not mentioned.

With the Kennedy administration, which was much more receptive to environmental concerns, Forest Service leaders began to support the Wilderness Bill, but this was viewed as nothing more than the baldest opportunism by many critics in Idaho. John Corlett, for example, dubbed it as a "good example of the true bureaucrat, who changes with each administrative change in the government."[65] In any case, men out in the field did not always hide their preference for the older approach. In October 1963, R.J. Bruning approvingly quoted Boyd Rasmussen, regional forester in Missoula, who found multiple use preferable to wilderness areas, which precluded all development when demands for camp and picnic areas were heavy.

Wilderness Bill opponents, such as Corlett and Bruning, took heart from such comments as Rasmussen's. They reinforced the notion that the Forest Service had developed working relationships with various forest users over the years and saw no reason to make any basic changes in the way forests were managed. The Idaho Falls *Post-Register* concluded its 1963 editorial, "On Using the Forests," by applauding the Forest Service's "shining record of full usage and integration without conflict."[66] The Twin Falls *Times-News* agreed that "present regulations have been more than adequate in dealing with the resources available."[67] With the Selway's reclassification, the Boise *Statesman* shook its editorial head: "now we can't help wondering what all the fuss has been about" the Wilderness Bill. If a wilderness area could be designated "with the stroke of a pen" by a cabinet officer, perhaps the bill was "a moot issue."[68]

Hearing the reactions around Idaho to the Wilderness Act's final passage by the U.S. Congress in 1964, one might be tempted to agree that far too much was made of the differences between those supporting and opposing it. Enthusiasm over the new law was notably lacking. Leon Weeks, Idaho Cattlemens's Association president, reflected the prevailing opinion on both sides: "we don't like it too well but we can live with it."[69] It would be several years before the act's implementation brought out the significance of diverging views between old-line conservationists and environmentalists on the value of wildness.

ENDNOTES

1. "Idahoans Rap Political Fight over Wilderness Legislation," Pocatello *Idaho State Journal* (October 20, 1961): p. 5.
2. "Wilderness Bill Delay Rejected," Idaho Falls *Post-Register* (September 5, 1961): pp. 1, 16.
3. "Wilderness Bill Helps, Not Harms Idaho, Says Sen. Church to C. of C.," Salmon *Recorder-Herald* (November 30, 1961): p. 1.
4. Statement of Arthur M. Roberts for Idaho State Chamber of Commerce, February 28, 1961, in Church Papers, Box 152, Folder 2.
5. "Megalopolis and Wilderness," editorial in Boise *Statesman* (September 13, 1961): p. 4.
6. "Senator Church Persists in Wilderness Bill Support; Idaho Will Give Him a Definite Answer Next Election," editorial in Boise *Statesman* (August 27, 1961): p. 4.
7. "Church Picks a Tough Battle Ground," editorial in Lewiston *Morning Tribune* (September 12, 1961): p. 4.
8. "Wilderness Not Dead Issue, Hawley Says in Statement," Boise *Statesman* (October 24, 1962): p. 18.
9. "Church Says His Support of Wilderness Bill Has Moral, Not Political, Reasons," Lewiston *Morning Tribune* (December 16, 1961): p. 12.
10. Don Samuelson to Frank Church, February 29, 1960, in Church Papers, Box 92, Folder 20.
11. "Senate OKs Memorial on Wilderness Bills," Boise *Statesman* (January 25, 1963): p. 6.
12. John Corlett, "Politically Speaking," Boise *Statesman* (October 29, 1961): p. 9.
13. Letter to the editor by Philip Fairbanks in Boise *Statesman* (February 25, 1962): p. 5.
14. Art Manley to Frank Church, June 22, 1961, in Church Papers, Box 152, Folder 4.
15. The full text of Church's speech to the Senate may be found in the Boise *Statesman* (September 6, 1961): p. 16.
16. Lyle M. Stanford to Frank Church, March 26, 1959, in Church Papers, Box 151, Folder 14.
17. Nell Tobias to Frank Church, January 22, 1963, in Church Papers, Box 152, Folder 13.
18. John Corlett, "House Group Hears Foes, Backers Battle over Wilderness Bill," Boise *Statesman* (October 31, 1961): pp. 1, 13.
19. "Franklin Jones Discusses Wilderness Legislation," Boise *Statesman* (May 3, 1962): p. 26.
20. L.H., "The Wilderness Works for All Just by Being There," editorial in Lewiston *Morning Tribune* (June 21, 1957): p. 4.
21. "Wilderness Bill Is Protection, Brandborg Says," Lewiston *Morning Tribune* (October 28, 1961): p. 12.
22. Letter to the editor by Ted Trueblood, Boise *Statesman* (September 3, 1961): Sec. 4, p. 4.
23. "Wilderness Legislation Discussion Features All-Idaho Congress Session," Boise *Statesman* (November 7, 1961): p. 9.
24. "In the Hands of the People," editorial in Grangeville *Idaho County Free Press* (August 11, 1960): Sec. 2, p. 2.
25. "Idahoan Attacks Wilderness Bill, Offers Alternative Plan," Boise *Statesman* (March 1, 1961): p. 3.
26. "The Wilderness Bill Would Hit Idaho," editorial in Challis *Messenger* (November 20, 1958): pp. 1, 4.

27. "Derr Fires Stiff Criticism against Wilderness Bill," Boise *Statesman* (August 10, 1961): p. 21.

28. RJB, "Stream of Thought," Coeur d'Alene *Press* (July 18, 1961): p. 2.

29. "Nature in the Raw," editorial in Boise *Statesman* (September 24, 1962): p. 4

30. "Smylie Fights Wilderness Bill," Pocatello *Idaho State Journal* (November 7, 1958): p. 1.

31. "Smylie Calls Wilderness Bill 'Monstrous' in Talk," Twin Falls *Time-News* (September 26, 1961): p. 1.

32. "Opening Door," editorial in Twin Falls *Times-News* (August 12, 1962): p. 4.

33. "Timber Protective Group Urges Defeat of U.S. Wilderness Bill," Pocatello *Idaho State Journal* (November 13, 1958): p. 24.

34. "Sen. Dworshak Opposes Pending Wilderness Bill," Salmon *Recorder-Herald* (September 21, 1961): p. 3.

35. RJB, "Stream of Thought," Coeur d'Alene *Press* (February 9, 1962): p. 2.

36. "Negative Approach," Cascade *News* (August 18, 1961): p. 2.

37. "Solon Blasts Demos on Wilderness Bill," Twin Falls *Times-News* (October 20, 1961): pp. 1, 2.

38. "Wilderness Bill in Present Form Opposed by North Idaho Chamber," Coeur d'Alene *Press* (May 27, 1961): p. 1.

39. Floyd Henderson, Acting President, Arco Chamber of Commerce to Idaho Chamber of Commerce, copy in Church Papers, Box 152, Folder 4.

40. "Is There an Answer?" editorial in Grangeville *Idaho County Free Press* (May 4, 1961): Sec. 2, p. 2.

41. "The Wilderness Bill," editorial in Idaho Falls *Post-Register* (October 11, 1959): p. 4.

42. "Public Lands, Forestry Asks Bill's Defeat," Boise *Statesman* (February 7, 1959): p. 5.

43. "Wilderness Bill Makes Poor Sense," editorial in St. Anthony *Chronicle-News* (December 14, 1961), in Church Papers, Box 152, Folder 12.

44. Frances Zaunmiller, "Frances Opposes Wilderness Bill, Tells Why," Grangeville *Idaho County Free Press* (April 6, 1961): Sec. 2, p. 5.

45. Alice Ullmer, letter to the editor, Lewiston *Morning Tribune* (February 13, 1961): p. 4.

46. Betty Roberts, letter to the editor, Lewiston *Morning Tribune* (February 6, 1961): p. 4.

47. "The Forest Service Is Not All Wrong," editorial in Lewiston *Morning Tribune* (January 23, 1961): p. 4.

48. "This 'Hearing' Didn't Provide Much Data," editorial in Lewiston *Morning Tribune* (February 3, 1961): p. 4.

49. "Forest Service Plans to Revise Boundaries of Wilderness," Lewiston *Morning Tribune* (July 11, 1957): p. 8.

50. "Foresters Eye Proposed Cut in Wilderness," Lewiston *Morning Tribune* (October 13, 1957): p. 12.

51. "Foresters Concur in Smaller Sized Primitive Region," Orofino *Clearwater Tribune* (October 17, 1957): p. 1.

52. Morton Brigham, letter to the editor in Lewiston *Morning Tribune* (June 5, 1962): p. 4.

53. Morton Brigham to Frank Church, February 24, 1961, in Church Papers, Box 152, Folder 4.

54. Morton Brigham to Frank Church, March 22, 1961, in Church Papers, Box 152, Folder 4.

55. Frank Church to Bruce Bowler, June 15, 1961, in Church Papers, Box 152, Folder 5.

56. Morton Brigham to Frank Church, January 19, 1969, in Church Papers, Box 152, Folder 17.

57. Paul C. Keeton to Frank Church, December 26, 1962, in Church Papers, Box 152, Folder 15.

58. Frank Church to Bill Duff, June 6, 1961, in Church Papers, Box 152, Folder 2.

59. Frank Church to W.G. Brassey, August 24, 1961, in Church Papers, Box 152, Folder 1.

60. Frank Church to T.J. Welch, February 1, 1962, in Church Papers, Box 152, Folder 12.

61. "Wilderness Bill Best for Idaho, Church Says," Grangeville *Idaho County Free Press* (November 9, 1961): p. 1.

62. "'Tour' Convinces Solon People Favor Wilds Bill," Idaho Falls *Post-Register* (November 12, 1961): p. 1.

63. "Wilderness Preservation Plan Is Considered by Senate Unit," Boise *Statesman* (June 20, 1957): p. 1.

64. "Forest Service Leaders Confer on Policy to Guide Plans," Hailey *Times* (June 4, 1959): p. 4.

65. John Corlett, "Politically Speaking," Boise *Statesman* (September 25, 1961): p. 8.

66. "On Using the Forests," Idaho Falls *Post-Register* (September 15, 1963): p. 4.

67. "Fight Pending," editorial in Twin Falls *Times-News* (August 30, 1961): p. 4.
68. "Now the Biggest Wilderness," editorial in Boise *Statesman* (January 14, 1963): p. 4.
69. Ken Robison, "Congress Votes to Preserve 9.2 Million Acre Wilderness," Boise *Statesman* (August 21, 1964): pp. 1, 13.

IX

Managing Wildness

A N INESCAPABLE PARADOX results in trying to protect wilderness areas. There seems to be no way to save wildness from human intrusion without establishing and enforcing rules and regulations that are themselves intrusions on what, by definition, are meant to be areas outside humanity's control.

The trick is to make those intrusions as inconspicuous as possible. The Wilderness Act of 1964 implicitly acknowledged this balancing act by defining wilderness as an area:

> retaining its primeval character and influence…which is protected and managed
> so as to preserve its natural conditions and which (1) generally appears to have
> been affected primarily by the forces of nature, with the impact of man's work
> substantially unnoticeable.[1]

Obviously, the "impact of man's work" would be controlled, or the wilderness would be overrun. As William Worf of the Forest Service's Missoula regional office warned people in Salmon, "the more a wilderness is used, the less it is wilderness."[2] Therefore, use had to be limited to maintain at least the appearance of wildness.

The Forest Service tended to deal with this paradox pragmatically. Since roads would quickly lead to overuse, they generally were not allowed in wilderness areas. When all-terrain vehicles appeared in the 1950s, the Forest Service banned their use in designated wilderness. Yet the NFS never attempted to ban all motorized access. As explained in Chapter VI, aviation remained an approved way for people to enjoy wilderness areas without devoting much time and energy hiking or packing in them. The Forest Service continued to assist in building and improving landing strips in the primitive areas well into the 1950s. Some—such as the Indian Creek field on the Middle Fork of the Salmon River—had been used by fire crews since 1920. But others existed primarily to serve backcountry resorts. The field at Moose Creek Ranch in the Selway country, for example, was nearly tripled in length in 1957, with 44 percent of funds provided by the Forest Service.

Chet Moulton, long-time director of the Idaho Department of Aeronautics, had enthusiastically supported the construction and enlargement of primitive area airfields. He adamantly opposed the Wilderness Bill, fearing it would force closure of those strips: "loss of the backcountry dude and guest ranches, ultimate denial of air use…and inability to properly harvest big game herds…does not seem realistic or progressive to a country developed under the American 'way-of-life' system."[3]

Nevertheless, it became increasingly clear that the volume of air traffic into the primitive areas threatened to banish the serenity supposedly characteristic of those localities. Pete Hill, manager of the Idaho Aviation Center in Idaho Falls, estimated in 1955 that thirty fields were located in the Salmon area alone. Some were surprisingly close together. The member-owned Flying B Ranch on the Salmon's Middle Fork had a landing strip only a mile downstream from one that served the Forest Service's Bernard Guard Station. Furthermore, the number of planes using these strips was rapidly escalating. Moose Creek received 569 landings in 1956. By 1968 that number was equaled even before the heaviest use during the fall hunting season. By 1969, 2,000 planes a year used Indian Creek, with fifty to sixty landings a day during hunting season. Chamberlain Basin saw seventy to eighty planes a day during the season's height.

Banning motorized trail bikes and ATVs while allowing aircraft traffic seemed patently unjust to many people. If the rich can fly in, Richard Penstrom of Caldwell argued in a letter to the Boise *Statesman*, an ordinary guy ought to be able to use his "$150 Tote Goat on the trail."[4] Others contacted Senator Church; "Air strips that are available in the Middle Fork area," Eldon Stokes of Salmon wrote in 1961, "allow anyone with money to land the most unPRIMITIVE craft; while we are barred from any roads that would give the average Idaho person anywhere near this type of access."[5]

Church never took these objections to heart. "I personally feel," he replied to Mr. and Mrs. Virgil Bush of Mountain Home, "that, on balance, the present bill as written, presents the most realistic approach to the problem."[6] The task remained to avoid "excess access," and here Church and the Forest Service agreed, even in the face of the argument that, as the St. Maries *Gazette-Record* put it, "if the public, through its government, is going to set aside a good portion of public land for preservation and public use, it should be in a manner that all the public has equal opportunity to use it."[7]

On occasion, the Forest Service appeared to respond to such complaints. In 1966 it spent $209,000 to buy the 755-acre Moose Creek Ranch, then thoroughly demolished it, burning the structures, breaking up and burying all the concrete, and leaving the site to "give the appearance," the Grangeville *Idaho County Free Press* reported in 1968, "of a large natural meadow."[8] Nevertheless, the Forest Service had no intention of foregoing aviation for management and fire control in wilderness areas, nor did it make any consistent effort to minimize aviation use in the wilderness in those years.

The fight over the Magruder Corridor sharply illustrated the problems that arose from allowing roads into wild areas. Contrary to its usual policy, the Forest Service allowed the Civilian Conservation Corps in the 1930s to build a road, presumably for fire-control access, through the Selway-Bitterroot Primitive Area, stretching for well over one hundred miles from Elk City, Idaho, to Darby, Montana. The route basically followed the high divide between the Selway drainage on the north, and the Salmon watershed to the south. When the agency studied the area's redesignation to wilderness, it concluded that 400,000 acres along that route should be excluded because the presence of roads was incompatible with wilderness. The excluded acreage, known as the Magruder Corridor, would be available for commercial logging, according to Forest Service plans. Timber interests in north central Idaho applauded the plan; conservationists howled in protest. The controversy gained national attention, foreshadowing the issues and policy dilemmas of the White Clouds debate.

At first glance, it seemed yet one more fight "in the old conflict over wilderness versus multiple use," according to Ferris Weddle in a full-page feature story in the Lewiston *Morning Tribune*. Of all the wild rivers then being considered for protection by Congress, Weddle thought the Selway was "the jewel…a wildlife paradise…a sportsmen's dream."[9] "Logging this area," wildlifer Ernest Day fumed, "would be trying to exact an ecological pound of flesh without drawing a drop of ecological blood."[10]

Nonsense, responded those eager to see the corridor's timber harvested. "If commercial activity has been prevalent in the Magruder Corridor, then how," the *Statesman* asked, "can the principle of a true wilderness concept be applied now?"[11] Gordon Crupper of the Intermountain Lumber Company in Salmon estimated annual production of twelve million board feet from the corridor, the same as that allowable for the whole Bitterroot National Forest. As for stream sedimentation feared by conservationists, the Priest River *Times* retorted: "road building causes no more stream sedimentation than the huge landslides or forest fires that have occurred historically through natural causes, and all of these had only temporary effect."[12] Furthermore, the Grangeville *Idaho County Free Press* concluded, "we don't need more vast areas in Idaho classified as 'wilderness.' There is plenty of the Gem State that will never be anything other than wilderness, whether classified or not."[13]

However, the issue entailed more than simply use versus preservation. Those opposing wilderness designation for the Magruder Corridor claimed that logging would actually have a positive effect on recreational use. The Grangeville Chamber of Commerce predicted that logging operations would provide end-of-road camping facilities and points of embarkation "to vast portions of the wilderness, which would otherwise be almost entirely out of reach."[14] The *Statesman* found the Grangeville argument to be "most valid."[15]

Jim Parsons, whose column was published in several northern Idaho papers, reassured his readers that "the public interest requires that some lands be developed for more intensive forms of recreational and other uses."[16] J. Everett Sanderson, supervisor of the Nez Perce National Forest, reiterated the idea that logging increased recreational opportunities: "after the logging is done, we find thousands of people visiting these scenic areas, which would not be possible without the logging road."[17]

In June 1967, Secretary of Agriculture Orville Freeman proposed to formulate a third alternative by setting up as a policy goal neither a pure wilderness nor an ordinary multiple-purpose forest, but a "wilderness under limited multiple-use," as the Grangeville paper termed it.[18] Freeman based his decision on the report of a special committee he appointed the previous fall to study the whole Magruder Corridor controversy. The committee, composed of several western educators, including Donald Obee, chairman of the Division of Life Sciences at Boise College (later Boise State University), held information-gathering public meetings in Boise, Grangeville, and Missoula. Since the Forest Service was not allowed to make any presentation, the Grangeville *Idaho County Free Press* complained that "wildlifers and tie-up groups were given clear sailing."[19]

The Idaho Alpine Club presentation at the Boise meeting typified conservationists' unwillingness to see the Elk City-Darby road as sufficient reason to exclude the Magruder Corridor from protection. The club's delegation from Idaho Falls stressed the growing number of visitors to wilderness areas and, therefore, the need for more such areas. It recommended banning any further road building in the Magruder Corridor, but allowing the road's continued existence in a "relatively primitive but passable state."[20] The Idaho Outfitters and Guides' Association concurred. Orville Freeman decided that the Forest Service should delay all area logging and draft a new management plan that would "maintain wild land conditions consistent with the primary values of the Corridor: watershed, fisheries, and historic and recreational resources."[21]

The Forest Service took three years to prepare its response to Freeman's instructions. Its recommendation, reported at public hearings in Grangeville, Lewiston, and Hamilton, Montana, in June 1970, was that more study was needed. The agency suggested a full-scale ecological study for at least five years before any kind of earthmoving be allowed in the Magruder Corridor. The Lewiston *Morning Tribune*, an unabashed proponent of wilderness preservation, called this recommendation "timely and wise." It thought that neither conservationists nor loggers would be completely satisfied, "but as a compromise it leans to the side of caution, and that is all to the good."[22] In fact, the only thing the conservationists did not get was a long-term commitment. For the next few years, loggers were denied any access, and wilderness preservation won at least a stay of execution. By the same token, "the third way" was deferred until some unspecified future date.

Forest Service temporizing might work with large, geographically contiguous wilderness areas, but management challenges could not be evaded when attention was turned to wild and scenic rivers. These long, narrow strips of legislatively protected wildness generated endless confrontations between preservationists and user-advocates whereby the Forest Service had many ways to lose and almost no way to win a consensus of support. In addition, unlike pressures for the Wilderness Act, which originated far from Idaho, the Wild and Scenic Rivers Act of 1968 came as much from state concerns as from those elsewhere in the nation.

From a national perspective, the act was the conservation component of President Lyndon Johnson's "Great Society" program. As early as 1961, at the suggestion of the National Park Service, a Senate Select Committee on Natural Water Resources recommended preserving the nation's remaining free-flowing streams. Although the departments of Agriculture and Interior had compiled a list of 650 possible candidates by 1963, not until Johnson's State of the Union Address in 1965, along with a separate presidential message on natural beauty, did the idea of protecting wild rivers really get on the national agenda. Later that year, Idaho Senator Frank Church introduced the Wild and Scenic Rivers bill in the Senate, which promptly approved it by a vote of 71-1 in January 1966. After suffering the delaying tactics of Congressman Aspinall, chairman of the House Interior Committee, the act also passed the House in September 1968, 267-7, and the bill became law on October 2, 1968.[23]

It was no accident that Church sponsored the bill, for it directly responded to ongoing Idaho issues, since the state had more than half the mileage included among the originally designated wild rivers. Its origin in Idaho came first from the apparent non-enforceability of the dredge-control law, resulting from the Idaho Supreme Court decision on the Finch case in September 1957, discussed in Chapter VII.

Adding to frustrations over dredging were fears about what continuing dam construction might do to anadromous fish. Dredging might destroy salmon and steelhead spawning beds, but returning fish might never even make it back to Idaho if the "mania for dam building" was not stopped. "Is the Salmon River Next?" asked the Salmon *Recorder-Herald* in March 1955. "Everyone will lose if legislation is not passed to protect this stream from undue industrial encroachment."[24]

A bill for that purpose, sponsored by the Idaho Wildlife Federation, was introduced in the 1955 legislative session, but it never left committee. Salmon River dam opponents continued to raise their voices against any new dams that might further obstruct salmon returning to spawn. Eventually that position merged into a broader one of scenic protection. Thus, fulminating against reports that Secretary of the Interior McKay might be considering damming the Salmon, the *Recorder-Herald* pleaded that "surely a state like Idaho is entitled to have at least one river unspoiled by dams and the great benefits of the industrial age." Revealingly, the editorial ended by affirming that "the song of a bird in the early morning is astronomically better than the monstrous hum of a generator."[25]

Meanwhile, there was possible recourse to federal administrative action. Federal lands bordered most of the Salmon River's headwaters. If the state would not stop the dredgers, then federal authorities might forestall them by withdrawing those lands from mining claims. In September 1955, Idaho's Fish and Game Department encouraged the National Fish and Wildlife Service to ask the U.S. Bureau of Land Management to withdraw some 31,000 acres in Bear Valley and Stanley Basin from mineral entry. The following April, Fish and Game urged "all sportsmen and other conservationists" to support this move because "preservation of these streams and channel beds in their natural condition is of vital importance to the existence of the salmon and steelhead fishery of the Salmon River."[26]

The Boise hearing in September 1957 to consider this proposed land withdrawal pointed toward wide public support for wild and scenic river protection in Idaho. As expected, the Idaho Mining Association protested the withdrawal. Its secretary, Harry Marsh, argued that the withdrawn lands contained one of the few American deposits of columbium and tantalum. George McDowell, the state mining inspector, called the withdrawal "an unreasonable demand" and criticized "overzealous sports groups," while William Wilcox, a miner from Salmon, declared that "I don't believe mining on the Salmon River would hurt the fishing industry one bit."[27] However, miners found little support, with the Boise Chamber of Commerce the only business group to back them.

On the other side were not only experts from state and federal wildlife agencies, but also leading conservationists, such as Ernest Day and Bruce Bowler, and business groups, such as the Twin Falls Chamber of Commerce. Their argument quickly went beyond the importance of preserving spawning beds to a resounding indictment of the scenic havoc left by dredgers. Samuel Hutchinson, a Fish and Wildlife assistant regional director, reminded listeners "of outstanding examples of early day wanton destruction," such as on the Yankee Fork, and called for preventing the area from "becoming a mute monument and reminder to man's thoughtlessness and waste."[28] Marshall Hunt of Twin Falls put it much more bluntly: "we've been raped once in that area and we can't tolerate any more of it."[29] Far better, Ernest Day testified, to focus on tourism than a devastating onetime use such as mining. In short, the "highest beneficial use" of the Salmon River headwaters, according to Bruce Bowler, was the maintenance of spawning beds and scenic preservation.[30]

Preservation of the "Wildest of the Wild," as the Twin Falls *Times-News* called the Salmon River,[31] aroused passionate public commitment, as revealed in numerous letters to Senator Church. For example, Mrs. Renice Carper wrote from Orofino: "I feel the free-flowing white waters of the famous Salmon River should *never* be obstructed *anywhere* at *anytime* in the future."[32] The Cottonwood Chamber of Commerce went on record favoring "the retention of the Salmon River as a fish sanctuary in perpetuity." Furthermore, "one river in the Northwest should be held in its primitive state for future generations to enjoy and in our opinion no stream would better serve the purpose than the fabled 'River of No Return.'"[33] Editorialists across the state agreed. The *Post-Register*, to cite only one example, claimed that "there is still wisdom" in preserving the Salmon "even beyond a 'satisfactory solution' to the fish problem" because "it drains this nation's most spectacular and untrammeled tumult of mountains."[34]

Church shared this mixture of motives, where pragmatic policy considerations ineluctably merged into emotional affirmations. When he first wrote in May 1959 for assistance from the Legislative Counsel in preparing a bill, his language was business-like: "I am interested in introducing legislation which will inhibit the licensing of hydroelectric or flood control structures in the Salmon River…which would have the effect of placing a barrier to the migration of salmon."[35] Within a few months, his focus had shifted from simply preserving salmon in Idaho to tourism prospects. In his newsletter, "Washington—On the Line," Church noted that "Idaho's potential as a summer playground has hardly more than been tapped." Idaho needed to "wisely conserve and utilize certain of our unique attractions." This led to the next topic: "SAVING THE SALMON RIVER"; "First among those to be protected is the Salmon River."[36]

By the time Church introduced the wild rivers bill, the task had become a question of protecting an essential part of Idaho's heritage:

> suddenly we have awakened to the realization that only a few rivers remain untamed, that part of our scenic and cultural heritage is threatened with destruction by the sheer thirst of our economic progress. Unless we take immediate steps the generations which wait at our threshold may never know the excitement of white water, fish in crystal clear rivers, or leisurely float down blue streams which meander between tree-covered banks.[37]

While many in Idaho applauded the inclusion of the Salmon and Clearwater in the first group of proposed wild rivers, some critics were unconvinced by Church's heady rhetoric. "As with the Wilderness concept there can't be much quarrel with the basic idea," the Cascade *News* conceded, but the question remained: would it be to the advantage of the majority of people? Perhaps in the future, the rivers would be "much more valuable for uses other than recreation."[38] Senator Len Jordan worried that there might be unfortunate side effects. By not using the water in those streams, would Idaho be sending an unwitting invitation for the water-hungry Southwest to capture them? Why should Idaho surrender control of two major rivers "when downstream interests seem determined to exploit our watershed and spawning beds. Is Idaho to be the voiceless, voteless, unrewarded member of the northwest?"[39] Jordan feared that by allowing wild-river designation of the Salmon and Clearwater, "we are playing our blue chips prematurely." Before going along with this idea, "we should explore and find out where the cash box is going to be to help reclaim millions of acres of land in Idaho."[40]

Initially, few people in Idaho seemed to share Jordan's worries. On the other hand, the various reasons why they supported the proposed wild rivers bill boded ill for those who would eventually have to develop management regulations once the bill became law. Many saw it as a means of preserving scenery. The *Statesman* took pride in Idaho for being one of the last states "which has the opportunity and courage to preserve an abundance of aesthetic qualities."[41] The *Idaho State Journal* harkened back to the last-frontier theme of the 1930s. Having developed much of the state's water resources, "we can pause to consider the means to retain some of those features which make Idaho the last frontier that it is."[42]

Others saw the bill as an outstanding opportunity to maximize the tourist trade. State Representative Herman McDevitt believed that wild rivers legislation "can make this state the Alps of the United States, and we will have a great tourist industry here."[43] Governor Robert Smylie warmly supported the wild rivers bill, in sharp contrast to his opposition to the Wilderness Act, but for rather mundane reasons. The "major result," as he saw it, would be "to restore to the Congress itself control over the rivers, which in general legislation has been delegated to the Federal Power Commission."[44] In addition to preserving Idaho's heritage, Church believed that it would protect the state's waters from any attempt to divert them for use in the Southwest.

Management questions surfaced immediately. Church chaired a Senate committee hearing in Boise on May 18, 1965, with 250 people attending and fifty-eight testifying. Most approved the bill's objectives, but many protested what they saw as its vague language, which left private-property rights in doubt. Church quickly assured them that there was no intention of permitting condemnation of private property. John Corlett got the impression from the hearing that "the 'wild rivers' were not to be closed off for the benefit of the few, but rather were to be made as accessible as possible to the public generally and still keep their freeflowing and scenic characteristics."[45] Church seemed to confirm this. On July 16, Bill Hall of the Lewiston *Morning Tribune* quoted him as saying, "ordinary multiple use would go on, and there would be no significant impairment whatever on the utilization of the land."[46] By early

August, Church was planning amendments to the bill. Although he hoped to add the Selway River and the Salmon River from Riggins to its confluence with the Snake, condemnation of private property would be prohibited, and mining, grazing, and logging would be allowed.

The Water Resources Board was not at all sure that Church was right; maybe wild-river designation would not adequately protect "unused" water from being transferred to the arid Southwest. George Crookham, board chairman, remained persuaded that "we are down to the point now on water resource development that it's use it or lose it."[47] Nor was he convinced that preservation could be termed as a beneficial use. Bill Hall spoke for the preservationists by affirming "the real value of a wild river is approximately the same as a wedding ring, a pair of baby shoes, or, perhaps, a fuzzy snapshot of a smiling man with a ten-pound steelhead."[48] Even the politically liberal *Idaho Observer* argued that "the hydroelectric power potential of the Salmon River has not been taken sufficiently into account in the current debate."[49] State Senator Cecil Andrus spoke against designation of either the Salmon or Clearwater. "Andrus has the right idea," Corlett wrote in his column. "Idaho needs to prepare for every eventuality and 'wild river' might not fit the pattern."[50]

The Water Resources Board held a hearing in Lewiston in late October 1965, where the two positions were summed up by an exchange between Herman McDevitt and Len Jordan. McDevitt blasted the board for "being used as a political tool" of Jordan. "Wild rivers have been adequately studied… The tourists show they are willing to come where the wild rivers are." "I want all the wild rivers Idaho can feasibly afford," Jordan responded.[51]

As it turned out, Jordan and the board won. To get Jordan's support for the wild rivers bill, Church had to agree to place the Salmon River's main stem in the "study category," with a five-year moratorium on all dams while its candidacy for wild-river status was given further consideration. Ironically, the Wild and Scenic Rivers Act of 1968 excluded the river that had largely precipitated the legislation in the first place, while it included the Middle Fork of the Salmon, already protected by being in the Idaho Primitive Area. Three other Idaho rivers made the original "wild" list: the Selway, Lochsa, and Middle Fork of the Clearwater. Four besides the Salmon were on the "study" list: the Moyie, Priest, and St. Joe in the Panhandle and the Bruneau in south central Idaho. The four wild rivers totaled 314.8 miles; the five to be studied amounted to 484.7 miles.

Over the next several years, the Forest Service would have to come up with management plans for each wild river. That would be no easy task since neither a clear statement of legislative purpose nor a readily discernible public consensus existed. Presumably the act indicated the nation's intent, as the *Morning Tribune* phrased it, to "keep some small portions of this great raw land in its natural state."[52] However, Frank Church denied that the act would create "corridors of wilderness." Rather, the aim was "to protect the rivers against dam construction and commercialization that conflicts with the scenic view."[53] On the other hand, Church ended his editorial for the Salmon *Recorder-Herald*, entitled "Let's Save Our Wild Rivers," by quoting Sigurd Olsen: "unless we preserve places where the endless spiritual needs of man can be fulfilled and nourished, we will destroy our culture and ourselves."[54] If that did not make the wild rivers "corridors of wilderness," it implied something much more in the way of control than simply banning petty commercialism.

It was easier, initially, to say what wild-river protection was not, than to define what it was. It was not, in Idaho at least, protection of the salmon fishery, which was first closed to sportsmen in 1965 by the Fish and Game Department because of rapidly waning fish populations. Some blamed this on the Columbia River dams, which blocked salmon from returning to spawning waters in Idaho. Others saw the problem in excessive downstream commercial fishing. In any case, Idaho officials could do nothing about it.

Neither did wild-river protection entail preservation of historical relics. In 1952, when the Salmon River country was proposed as the setting for filming *The River of No Return*, local people expected the Hollywood movie to encompass "the old prospector days...Indians, Chinamen and others who figured in the history of the country."[55] The movie ended up being shot elsewhere, but wild-river managers showed little interest in preserving early settlers' cabins, old mine heads, or anything reflecting "the history of the country."

The Forest Service's refusal to include history in its definition of natural heritage can best be demonstrated by the story of Thunder Mountain, site of Idaho's last major gold rush dating to the early twentieth century. The Thunder Mountain district (roughly halfway between Cascade and Salmon near the Middle Fork of the Salmon River) lay within the Idaho Primitive Area, although the Forest Service never acknowledged its existence in any of its area descriptions. The Thunder Mountain story was most unusual because the deserted boomtown of Roosevelt succumbed to a drainage-damming landslide that flooded the town under some forty feet of water in what became known as Roosevelt Lake. This caught the interest of famed Western novelist Zane Gray, who wrote *Thunder Mountain* in 1935, and of Hollywood, which released a movie version late the same year. Cascade began its annual observance of Thunder Mountain Days in 1938, but Forest Service officials consistently ignored that history, either as evidence of a "period of high excitement and golden hope," as the McCall paper put it,[56] or as an unusual example of extremely recent geological history.

In developing its management plans for wild rivers, the Forest Service tended to borrow from its manual on how to treat wilderness areas. It aimed to maintain "conditions of solitude, challenge, and primitive environment,"[57] which sounded fine to conservationists. In testifying on the Salmon's Middle

Fork management plan, Ernest Day affirmed that "nothing should be allowed that would impair the water—the gin-clear quality of the Middle Fork. It should be saved at all costs."[58]

Outfitters managing facilities for commercial river touring thought this unfair and indefensible. It meant they could only utilize temporary shelters that had to be shielded from view. Don Smith of North Fork began complaining in 1965 about such restrictions. In his thirty-five years on the river, he had spent thousands of dollars advertising his business, and now "the Forest Service wants us to hide behind a bush as the tourist goes by." Echoing ranchers' arguments for some security in their grazing rights, Smith asked for similar concerns for outfitters: "I think we are entitled to a piece of ground down there for a certain number of years so we can spend a certain amount of dollars and have a decent camp."[59]

In early 1970, Smith and his colleagues formed the Upper Salmon River Boatmen's Association to lobby for relaxation of Forest Service requirements, particularly those controlling campsites. "A cow receives more consideration than a human being," fumed Norman Guth, the association's vice president.[60] Boatmen insisted that they needed solid roofs and floors at their camps. "We can't feed 25 people without accommodations," Don Smith told the *Statesman*.[61] Governor Samuelson took the boatmen's side: "if they take out the facilities it will be an exclusive canyon for the millionaires."[62] John Emerson, supervisor of the Salmon National Forest, agreed to put off regulation enforcement for a year, but insisted that this was only to "enable all to work toward the wilderness objectives."[63]

The Forest Service took a similarly uncompromising position when it came to protecting the margins of wild rivers. According to Senator Jordan, the original intent was to include only about three hundred feet of land on each bank, while allowing grazing and other existing uses. But the plan for the Middle Fork of the Salmon pushed the margins out for more than a mile on each side, encompassing 32,000 acres, including eight privately owned parcels totaling 769 acres as well as 1,013 acres owned by state agencies. Similar inholdings existed along the Selway River. The Forest Service sought to buy out all private holdings. When Governor Samuelson castigated what he saw as a waste of taxpayers' money, the Missoula regional office responded that it was necessary to preserve a wilderness atmosphere: "development could easily be carried to such an extent that a trip down the Selway River or Moose Creek could hardly be considered a wilderness experience."[64]

Some people, particularly in Idaho County, adamantly opposed these policies. What they amounted to, cried Frances Zaunmiller of Campbell's Ferry and long-time columnist for the Grangeville *Idaho County Free Press*, was a "step-up in the Forest Service HATE PROGRAM toward the Natives of the Back Country."[65] The newspaper's editor replied, "perhaps we should close the roads and airways to the State of Idaho, and if we could keep all of the people out of the state, we would have no problems."[66]

Zaunmiller's shrill harangues drew little sympathy or even notice around the state, but the case of "Buckskin Billy" caught many newspaper writers' imagination. Sylvan Hart had resided since the mid-1930s on Little Five Mile Creek where it flows into the Salmon River. His colorful ways, including dressing in buckskin, had long since gained him his nickname. The *Idaho State Journal* saw Hart's carefree life as an example of how a person could "thumb your nose at the fast-paced city life."[67] He also had a way of dramatizing himself, making delicious copy for jaded journalists. In an interview with Hugh Mulligan, he gestured with his knife, then reassured the reporter: "don't worry about the knife. I only use it for carving up grizzly bears, Democrats and other varmints."[68] In early 1966, it looked like the Forest Service would try to remove Buckskin Billy as a squatter intruding on the wilderness. Newspaper readers around the state kept current on his effort to stay put. When it finally was determined that he resided on an old mining claim, the Forest Service gave him a non-transferable life interest in the property. The *Statesman* published an editorial celebrating the fact that "Buckskin Billy Will Stay,"[69]

Making peace with the state of Idaho proved to be much more difficult. Two issues troubled officials. The first was control of the waterways. There had been longstanding agreement that traffic on navigable streams fell within federal purview, while the state managed non-navigable streams. The Forest Service took the position that, until courts ruled otherwise, the Middle Fork of the Salmon was navigable, and, therefore, it could regulate boaters using it. This became an issue when it became clear that the rapidly escalating number of boaters would soon lead to limitations for sanitation reasons as well as to protect the wilderness experience. In 1969, 12,300 people visited the Middle Fork, with 1,620 taking float trips. Forest officials began talking about imposing limits on boaters. Secretary of State Pete Cennarusa objected. "I think the public should have the right to determine the extent of recreation"[70] in the area. Governor Samuelson feared that limitations would end up favoring visitors with the most money: "you can't just limit it to the millionaires or those who can afford $100 a day to hire an outfitter."[71]

This issue was still hypothetical in 1970; an enforced reservation system would not come for several more years. But the question of access to state lands in wilderness areas already had become a sore point, particularly for Attorney General Robert Robson. In December 1969, he warned the Land Board that the Forest Service was trying to grab complete control of Idaho's primitive areas through its administrative regulations. Robson declared that he intended to meet with Forest Service Chief Edward Cliff to negotiate an arrangement. Actually, Robson looked for a confrontation rather than a settlement: "I want to toss a little cold water on some of the proposed regulations of the wild river system."[72]

Demanding "reasonable ingress and egress to all state lands" within primitive areas and along wild rivers reflected Robson's belief that Forest Service regulations had no application on state lands, unless Idaho agreed to accept them.[73] Since less than 9,000 acres were involved, why not simply exchange them for lands outside primitive areas? Landing strips made up some of the acreage; Chet Moulton's "lifetime of work in building airports in the remote area could go down the drain."[74] And that marked only part of the threat that Robson saw in federal wilderness preservation policies. In declaring that he would fight to maintain Idaho's right to use wild riverbeds, including the granting of leases for dredging, he said he opposed the federal government "locking up" wild-river areas "so we can't use the assets."[75] As he saw it, the choice had become whether Idaho could develop its resources or be just a "huge recreational park." He was convinced that "Idaho can't become just a big playground. It can't afford this. As it is Idaho has a narrow tax base which is a real problem."[76]

Robson's aggressive stance evoked widespread alarm in Idaho. Senator Jordan urged the state to cooperate, expressing his hope that state and federal positions could be reconciled. Senator Church said the free flow of wild rivers "is most vital," that dredging them and rendering them "sterile as sluice boxes for generations to come would constitute a waste of resources."[77] Meanwhile, the Boise *Statesman* reminded everyone that the possibility of dredging had led to the wild rivers' designation by Congress. The Idaho Environmental Council condemned Robson for trying to sabotage the wild-river system. Gerald Jayne, the council's president, wrote to the Forest Service's Edward Cliff, urging him to give "this attempt the short shrift it deserves."[78] The Idaho Falls *Post-Register* took Robson's arguments as another example of the "many indications the past few years of the indifference of state government to the public's interest."[79]

Robson's fight with the Forest Service had, by the spring of 1970, merged into the much more wide-sweeping debate over conservation versus use, highlighted by the White Clouds controversy. When the *Statesman* editorialized in July that "We Don't Really Have a Choice," it referred to the White Clouds, but the point also applied to Robson. Idaho needed, so this argument went, both recreation and industrial development, and the challenge was to develop "proper zoning and pollution" policies to protect the state's "high quality environment."[80]

ENDNOTES

1. Section 2(c) as quoted in Craig W. Allin, *The Politics of Wilderness Preservation* (Westport, Conn.: Greenwood, 1982): p. 158.
2. "Forest Service Recreation Official Sees Problems in Future Administration of Nation's Wilderness," Boise *Statesman* (June 10, 1970): p. 15.
3. "Primitive or Wilderness—Which Shall It Be?" *Rudder Flutter* (November 1958): pp. 2–3. This was the house organ of the Idaho Department of Aeronautics.

4. Boise *Statesman* (October 29, 1961): p. 5.
5. Eldon Stokes to Frank Church, September 19, 1961, in Church Papers, Box 152, Folder 3.
6. Frank Church to Mr. and Mrs. Virgil Bush, October 3, 1961, in Church Papers, Box 152, Folder 3.
7. "Wilderness Objectives Contradictory," editorial in St. Maries *Gazette-Record* (May 1, 1969): p. 12.
8. "USFS Purchases Private Land in Wilderness Area," Grangeville *Idaho County Free Press* (November 21, 1968): p. 1.
9. Ferris Weddle, "Storm Clouds Swirl over Upper Selway," Lewiston *Morning Tribune* (May 23, 1965): Sec. 2, p. 1.
10. Bob Lorimer, "Rift Separates Loggers, Wildlifers at Magruder Corridor Discussion," Boise *Statesman* (December 17, 1966): p. 24.
11. "Conservationists' Arguments Do Not Convince as More Wilderness Proposed for Gem State," editorial in Boise *Statesman* (December 18, 1966): p. 4.
12. "Stand Fast on Magruder," editorial in Priest River *Times* (January 19, 1967): p. 2.
13. "Leave Magruder Corridor Open," editorial in Grangeville *Idaho County Free Press* (August 13, 1970): Sec. 2, p. 2.
14. "'Magruder Corridor' Resolution," Grangeville *Idaho County Free Press* (April 1, 1965): p. 1.
15. "More Wilderness Classification," editorial in Boise *Statesman* (April 6, 1965): p. 4.
16. Jim Parsons, "Wilderness Area Advocates Try Anew to Get Magruder Corridor," Sandpoint *News-Bulletin* (June 23, 1966): Sec. 2, p. 1.
17. Leo W. Jeffries, "Log the Upper Selway? Yes, Say Foresters," Lewiston *Morning Tribune* (July 10, 1966): Sec. 2, pp. 1, 2.
18. "Freeman Has Spoken," editorial in Grangeville *Idaho County Free Press* (June 8, 1967): Sec. 3, p. 2.
19. "One-sided Meetings," editorial in Grangeville *Idaho County Free Press* (December 22, 1966): Sec. 2, p. 2.
20. "Alpine Club Supports Selway Wilderness," Idaho Falls *Post-Register* (December 16, 1966): p. 14.
21. "New Magruder Corridor Plan Ordered by U.S.," Salmon *Recorder-Herald* (June 8, 1967): pp. 1, 12.
22. "The Hazards of Multiple Use," editorial in Lewiston *Morning Tribune* (November 10, 1970): p. 4.
23. A succinct history of the bill is provided by Allin, *The Politics of Wilderness Preservation*, pp. 172–74.
24. "Is the Salmon River Next?" editorial in Salmon *Recorder-Herald* (March 3, 1955): p. 6.
25. "McKay's Dam Foolishness," editorial in Salmon *Recorder-Herald* (June 9, 1955): p. 4.
26. "Fish, Game Department Asks Aid in Supporting Withdrawal Move," Twin Falls *Times-News* (April 22, 1956): p. 14.
27. Earle L. Jester, "Tourist Loss Is Seen in Mine Land Dispute," Boise *Statesman* (September 20, 1957): pp. 1, 12; Earle L. Jester, "Salmon Land Withdrawal Is Debated," Boise *Statesman* (September 20, 1957): pp. 1, 6.
28. "Hearings Started on Salmon Land Withdrawal," Twin Falls *Times-News* (September 19, 1957): pp. 1, 12; Earle L. Jester, "Salmon River Waters 'Vital,' Hearing Told," Idaho Falls *Post-Register* (September 19, 1957): pp. 1, 13.
29. Earle L. Jester, "Land Closure Hearing Ended after Two Days," Boise *Statesman* (September 21, 1957): pp. 1, 3.
30. "Hearings Started on Salmon River Land Withdrawal," Twin Falls *Times-News* (September 19, 1957): pp. 1, 2.
31. "Wildest of the Wild," editorial in Twin Falls *Times-News* (March 15, 1965): p. 4.
32. Mrs. Renice Carper to Frank Church, February 9, 1960, in Church Papers, Box 92, Folder 21.
33. George Kopczynski to Frank Church, December 14, 1960, in Church Papers, Box 155, Folder 22.
34. "Salmon River Set Apart," editorial in Idaho Falls *Post-Register* (February 5, 1961): p. 4.
35. Frank Church to Legislative Counsel, May 1, 1959, in Church Papers, Box 155, Folder 19.

36. Newsletter No. 862-1, in Church Papers, Box 92, Folder 19.
37. "Church Bill Asks River Protection," Salmon *Recorder-Herald* (March 18, 1965): p. 4. Newspapers throughout the state ran similar stories, relying on the press release issued by Church's office, a copy of which is in Church Papers, Box 156, Folder 5.
38. Untitled editorial in Cascade *News* (April 9, 1965): p. 2.
39. "Sen. Jordan Encourages Wild Study," Boise *Statesman* (August 18, 1965): p. 20.
40. John Corlett, "Jordan Inspires Ire of Idaho Legislator on Wild River Policy," Boise *Statesman* (October 27, 1965): pp. 1, 5.
41. "Wild Rivers Legislation," editorial in Boise *Statesman* (August 7, 1965): p. 4.
42. "Saving Our Wild Rivers," editorial in Pocatello *Idaho State Journal* (May 11, 1965): p. 4.
43. "Andrus Objects to Designation of Lower Salmon as Wild River," Lewiston *Morning Tribune* (May 19, 1965): pp. 18, 11.
44. "Smylie Asks Enactment of Wild Rivers Proposal," Boise *Evening Statesman* (April 22, 1965): p. C1.
45. John Corlett, "Politically Speaking," Boise *Statesman* (May 20, 1965): p. B8.
46. Bill Hall, "Church Says Wild Rivers Bill Doesn't Bar Multiple Use," Lewiston *Morning Tribune* (July 16, 1965): p. 16.
47. "Idaho's Stand on Wild Rivers Bill Imminent," Coeur d'Alene *Press* (September 21, 1965): p. 3.
48. B.H., "The Horse Is Back before the Cart," editorial in Lewiston *Morning Tribune* (September 19, 1965): p. 4.
49. Editorial note prefacing Ferris Weddle, "Will the Wild Rivers Stay Wild," Boise *Idaho Observer* (September 23, 1965): pp. 1, 2.
50. John Corlett, "Politically Speaking," Boise *Statesman* (April 25, 1965): p. 11.
51. John Corlett, "Jordan Inspires Ire of Idaho Lawmaker on Wild River Policy," Boise *Statesman* (October 27, 1965): pp. 1, 5.
52. "Congress Gives the Rivers Life," editorial in Lewiston *Morning Tribune* (October 3, 1968): p. 4.
53. "Sen. Church Calls for Protection of Idaho's Recreation Potential," Lewiston *Morning Tribune* (May 27, 1967): pp. 14, 3.
54. Frank Church, "Let's Save Our Wild Rivers," Salmon *Recorder-Herald* (October 14, 1965): p. 6.
55. "Motion Picture Company to Make Movie on Middle Fork," Salmon *Recorder-Herald* (September 11, 1952): p. 1.
56. "Thunder Mountain Strike Short Lived," McCall *Payette Lake Star* (July 30, 1939): p. 8.
57. "Outfitters Face Stricter Controls under Wilderness Act," Salmon *Recorder-Herald* (May 21, 1971): pp. 1, 7.
58. Bob Lorimer, "Several Concerned with Salmon Middle Fork Classification Agree on Little at Forest Service Sponsored Meeting in Boise," Boise *Statesman* (June 14, 1969): p. 15.
59. Bob Johnson, "Veteran of Salmon River Brandishes Protest on Campsite Regulation," Boise *Statesman* (December 10, 1965): p. D5.
60. "Boatmen Gain River Camp 'Status Quo,'" Salmon *Recorder-Herald* (June 11, 1970): pp. 1, 5.
61. "Boatmen Offer Plan for Primitive Area Use," Boise *Statesman* (March 22, 1970): p. C12.
62. Bob Johnson, "Outfitters Fear Wilderness Act," Idaho Falls *Post-Register* (June 1, 1970): p. 8.
63. "Salmon Boat Camps Set for Another Year," Boise *Statesman* (June 18, 1970): p. D1.
64. "Forest Service Defends Private Lands Purchase to Preserve Wild Status," Boise *Statesman* (January 9, 1969): p. B5.
65. Frances Z. Wisner, "Report Given on Wild Rivers Hearing," Grangeville *Idaho County Free Press* (July 3, 1969): Sec. 3, p. 6. Although Frances was recently married and used her married name, she was still widely known as Frances Zaunmiller.
66. "Why Not?" editorial in Grangeville *Idaho County Free Press* (July 30, 1970): Sec. 3, p. 2.
67. "Idaho's Salmon River Country Hides 'Most Admirable' Hermit," Pocatello *Idaho State Journal* (April 4, 1969): "Enjoy" section, p. 2.
68. Hugh A. Mulligan, "Securely Living in His Beloved Wild Salmon Canyon, Buckskin Billy Reads, Philosophizes, Avoids Ulcers," Boise *Statesman* (October 20, 1963): p. 13.
69. "Buckskin Billy Will Stay," editorial in Boise *Statesman* (February 7, 1966): p. 4.
70. "Wild Rivers Regulations Rouse Fears," Boise *Statesman* (October 24, 1969): p. C8
71. Bob Johnson, "Samuelson Informs Outfitters Idaho Needs 'Clean' Industry," Boise *Statesman* (May 17, 1970): p. D1.

72. Tom Ochiltree, "Robson Seeks Agreement on Wild Rivers Areas," Grangeville *Idaho County Free Press* (February 12, 1970): p. 1.

73. "Idaho Asks Access to Wild Areas, Possession of Navigable Streambeds," Boise *Statesman* (March 25, 1979): p. 15.

74. "Robson Poses Court Action over Wild River System," Lewiston *Morning Tribune* (December 24, 1969): p. 16.

75. "Attorney General Clarifies Remarks on Wild Rivers Bill," Boise *Statesman* (December 25, 1969): pp. D1, 5.

76. "What Is Idaho's Real Potential?" editorial in Boise *Statesman* (November 16, 1969): p. 4; Tom Ochiltree, "Robson Seeks Agreement with US on Use of Land in Wild Rivers Areas," Boise *Statesman* (February 6, 1970): p. 1.

77. "Senator Says Free Flow of Wild Rivers Is Most Vital," Twin Falls *Times-News* (January 9, 1970): p. 1.

78. "Robson Said 'Sabotaging' Gem Wild Rivers System," Boise *Statesman* (January 15, 1970): p. C4.

79. "Strange Worry on the Middle Fork," editorial in Idaho Falls *Post-Register* (January 3, 1970): p. 4.

80. "We Don't Really Have a Choice," editorial in Boise *Statesman* (July 2, 1970): p. 4.

X

Moving beyond Scenic Preservation

ONCERN FOR PROTECTING Idaho's "high quality environment" was moving beyond scenic preservation to broader environmental and ecological issues by the 1960s. This by no means indicated an indifference to the state's scenic highlights. Quite the contrary. Scenic preservation rarely generated statewide controversy because so few people wished to argue the matter.

The rapid expansion of state parks during the twelve years of the Smylie administration (ending in January 1967) evoked some criticism, but almost never did critics scoff at aesthetic concerns. Take, for example, Governor Robert Smylie's deal with the Harriman family in December 1961 to convert its 10,000-acre ranch on the Henry's Fork of the Snake River into a state park. Legislators argued over the requirement that Idaho initiate a professional state park service. Some fish and game enthusiasts, including the editor of the Idaho Falls *Post-Register*, thought the restrictions imposed to protect the ranch's flock of trumpeter swans rather excessive. Instead of a "cloistered zoo, a big game, bird and fish management principle should be incorporated into the gift document."[1] Nevertheless, no one objected to Smylie's belief that "it will doubtless become one of the outstanding state parks in the nation."[2]

While Don Samuelson changed many of his predecessor's policies, he did nothing to interfere with the creation of new state parks, apparently reflecting a widespread public support for scenic preservation, even for sites that had never previously gained much attention. The Bruneau Sand Dunes (a dozen miles southeast of Mountain Home) had rarely been mentioned by travel writers, even though they represented a striking geological oddity with million-year-old dunes—the tallest rising 425 feet above a new lake that appeared only a few years previously from the rising waters of C.J. Strike Dam on the Snake River. In 1964, Rodney Hawes, editor of the Marsing *Owyhee Nugget*, began a campaign advocating national park status for the area. While that idea never went far, the dunes did become a state park in 1967. Acquisition was easy enough, with the Bureau of Land Management selling 2,280 acres to the state for only $2.50 per acre. But development involved more than a trivial sum; the Parks Department allotted (without any negative public reaction) $810,756 for construction and maintenance over the next five years.

The Tubbs Hill story in northern Idaho epitomizes Idahoans' changing attitudes toward scenic preservation from the early years of the twentieth century to the 1960s. Covering about four hundred acres of Coeur d'Alene's lakeshore, Tubbs Hill had been a city park since 1968. With its natural brush and forest vegetation left largely undisturbed, it offered a dramatic contrast to the high-rise elegance of The Coeur D'Alene Resort immediately to the west.

How, a latter-day visitor might well ask, did Tubbs Hill escape the pressures for development and remain a tranquil, tree-covered retreat right next door to the downtown core? Certainly not because of some remarkable foresight of the city fathers in the first years of settlement. Its slopes remained untouched for many years probably for no better reason than that nearby level land was far easier to develop. Part of the hill had been platted for a subdivision by 1922 when the Coeur d'Alene *Press* printed a long feature story on its prospects as an upper-end suburb, but critics complained that it would be too long of a drive to downtown, so no development occurred. In 1939 the State Land Board mentioned it as a possible state park, and, in October 1941, the Fish and Game Commission designated Tubbs Hill as a game preserve to protect strollers and picnickers from hunters attracted to its growing population of Chinese pheasants. Even with the immense local pressure for housing that came with the creation of the Farragut naval training base, Tubbs Hill almost inexplicably escaped World War II unscathed.

Serious local debate over the best use of Tubbs Hill began shortly after the end of the war. Some argued that "picturesque and primitive Tubbs Hill is an invaluable asset to the city of Coeur d'Alene"[3] as a recreational area. That was the view of Harold Abbott of the Spokane Parks Board, who in 1947 was invited by local National Forest and Chamber of Commerce officials to view some of the region's scenic spots. Quite another view surfaced the following year, when the Kootenai County sheriff suggested building a road to the top of the hill and erecting a short-wave radio tower to serve local and state police. Mayor J.G. Adams replied that the city had no funds for road construction, but "we definitely are going to have something on the hill someday, we hope," and welcomed any start to development. As it stood, Tubbs Hill was nothing more than a neglected "rock pile."[4]

Nothing came of the radio tower idea, but periodically over the next two decades, development proposals met a similar mix of opinions, some arguing that Tubbs Hill was a fire hazard and hiding place for illicit activities, others defending its scenic merits as a bit of undisturbed landscape. Faced with a proposal for a plush resort hotel on top of the hill, in 1963 local residents expressed conflicting opinions in letters to the local paper. Mark Sinclair declared that the place needed cleaning up; if developers wanted to improve part of the Hill, "they should have our blessing" as long as they allowed public access.[5] Such attitudes brought a protesting moan from Tom Collier: "must the last vestiges of Nature be obliterated before man is satisfied?"[6]

Local officials were faced with a clear-cut choice by July 1963. A small group of hill property owners petitioned for rezoning forty acres on top for a "luxurious resort hotel beamed specifically to attract well-to-do tourists and conventions."[7] The newly organized Lakeshore Development Committee, led by Orrin Lee, pleaded that the zoning request be denied and Tubbs Hill be kept for public use. The committee had the advantage of numbers and eloquent spokesmen. When the city council held a public hearing on July 16, more than 250 attended, most of them for the hill's preservation, and they handed in a petition with 739 signatures. The preservationists included Art Manley, the Idaho Wildlife Federation president at the time, and Scott Reed, an attorney who within a few years played a leading role in statewide environmental concerns. Manley saw the resort proposal as "a big step toward the sure and inevitable loss of the entire hill to free public use."[8] "It would be more farsighted," Reed asserted, "for the city to protect the natural beauty of Tubbs Hill rather than to promote the process of commercialization by government subsidized speculators."[9]

Typical of many such confrontations, the preservationists lost the battle, but eventually won the war. Despite the opposition's strength at the hearing, the council voted to approve the rezone by the narrowest of margins, with the mayor casting the deciding vote. Nevertheless, after a series of maneuvers by the committee, developers, and city officials, the preservationists finally had their way. In February 1965, the Lakeshore Development Committee proposed that the city of Coeur d'Alene purchase the entire hill's privately owned land and develop it into a natural park, with improvements limited to some trails and a few picnic spots. The City Planning Commission unanimously approved the scheme. It took the council another three years to act, but in March 1968, it did approve $125,000 (half from federal Bureau of Outdoor Recreation matching funds) to acquire all remaining privately held land on the hill, giving the city title to about two-thirds of the hill. Art Manley applauded the move, hailing it as "living proof that we can have 'progress' without sacrificing natural beauty and destroying our environment."[10]

Sometimes outstanding scenic areas were preserved with surprising ease. Upper Priest Lake is a good case in point. This 1,700-acre lake in northwest Bonner County, about 75 miles north of Spokane, remained completely undeveloped into the 1960s, without roads or man-made structures to mar its pristine shoreline or even any visible evidence of logging on the forested slopes rising behind. Most of the surrounding area was encompassed in state and national forests, and Upper Priest Lake might have been taken by Wilderness

Act opponents as conclusive proof that wilderness preservation advocates were needlessly crying wolf about disappearing natural areas. Curiously enough, that argument did not surface. However, when several Spokane doctors, who owned about four hundred acres along the shoreline, suggested developing their properties, preservationists sprang into action in January 1963. During the winter meeting in Bonners Ferry of the Idaho Wildlife Federation's District 1, the Sandpoint Sportsmen's Club (with Don Samuelson taking an active part) introduced a resolution urging that Upper Priest Lake be set aside as a primitive area. All twenty-three clubs in the district voted in support of the resolution.

No one opposed the idea. The only issue seemed to be where to find the money to buy out the owners of about 4,400 feet of shoreline. When local funds were not forthcoming, the owners warned the preservationists that they needed closure, that they had to be bought out by spring 1964, or else they would subdivide and begin selling recreation property on the open market.

In February 1964, Bob Thomas of the Coeur d'Alene Wildlife Federation and Art Manley of the Idaho Wildlife Federation met with the Priest Lake Sportsmen's Association, reporting that Senator Church was preparing legislation to enable state and national forests to negotiate a purchase or exchange of the four hundred acres. The Senate Appropriations Committee voted in April to deny the $400,000 Church requested to purchase the land, but he remained optimistic. Speaking to three hundred people at the District 1 spring meeting, he pledged to continue his efforts to preserve Upper Priest Lake. Meanwhile, the Nature Conservancy stepped in with a short-term loan of $30,000 to forestall subdivision.

In August 1964, Church introduced a bill, cosponsored by Maurine Neuberger of Oregon, to save Upper Priest Lake by authorizing the purchase of the four hundred acres and their inclusion in Kaniksu National Forest. Upper Priest Lake, Church assured his colleagues, "is as wild and natural as God made it."[11] Senator Bible of Nevada brought his Interior subcommittee to have a look in October. The hearing at Hill's Resort on the main Priest Lake was a veritable love feast. The 125 attending overwhelmingly supported the proposal. State Senator Don Samuelson testified that "our people are almost unanimously in favor of retaining Upper Priest Lake in its natural state."[12] Governor Smylie issued a statement praising the upper lake: "its quiet beauty makes it a veritable jewel in the mountains." Preserving it "in its present unspoiled form will make it a national treasure of the first consequence in years to come."[13]

With such backing, the preservation of Upper Priest Lake was soon assured. Church's bill easily sailed through Congress. In June 1965, Governor Smylie and Regional Forester Neal Rahm signed a preservation agreement. The following summer, the Bureau of Land Management designated it "scenic," thereby protecting the area from mining entry and construction of roads, cabins, or mills. In 1968, state and federal authorities agreed that Kaniksu National Forest would administer the 6,000-acre scenic area. Diamond International (which owned some of the forested land visible from Upper Priest Lake) also ratified the management policy statement in September 1969. To this day, Upper Priest Lake remains undeveloped, accessible only by boat from the main lake or by trails through the forests.

Why, then, was there such prolonged controversy over preservation of the Sawtooths and Hells Canyon? Of all the scenic attractions in Idaho, those two were surely the most significant, biggest, and eye-catching. And yet, it took more than a decade of debate, moves, and countermoves before the Sawtooth and Hells Canyon national recreation areas were finally established.

The answer is that in neither case was scenic preservation really at issue. It would be hard to find anyone, then or now, willing to argue against the Sawtooth's scenic merits. Senator Frank Church, who renewed the campaign for their designation as a national park, believed "there is no scenic grandeur anywhere in the United States that excels the jagged peaks of the Sawtooth Mountains."[14]

"Seldom has there been so much yodeling about mountains in Idaho," the Grangeville *Idaho County Free Press* joked. "Senator Church is at his yodeling best, too" with his park proposal. But what was the point? "If you want to see the Sawtooth wilderness, do it."[15] John Corlett approvingly quoted David Ainsworth, manager of radio station KSRA in Salmon: "the beauty of the Sawtooths will not be enhanced one bit by the fact that they are in a national park."[16]

Initially, Church would not have disagreed with the argument that the Sawtooths' scenic integrity faced no threat. "While your reasons for the park sound persuasive on the surface," the Custer County Commissioners wrote him in January 1960, "there is absolutely no basis in fact for these arguments on closer analysis. This primitive area is being preserved and the recreational portion of it is being improved steadily by the Forest Service."[17] But in Church's opinion, Forest Service managers did not maximize the economic benefits that Idaho might derive from the tourist industry. "Whether we like it or not," he wrote the Stanley Basin Chamber of Commerce, "the National Park Service has been able to get more money for recreation and related activities than has the Forest Service."[18] Prestige also came with national park status. In August 1963, Church explained his thinking in a letter to the Idaho Motel Association: "the comparative prestige of a national park designation, and the ability of the National Park Service to concentrate its funds and efforts on a few specific developments across the country, seem to me to be persuasive reasons for favoring this change in the management of the Sawtooth area."[19]

The same forces that had successfully opposed a Sawtooth National Park in earlier decades immediately spoke up against this latest effort. National Forest officials fended off the suggestion that, somehow, the National Park Service would do a better job managing the area. They reminded local residents how comfortable they had found NFS administration, based as it was on the now-long-accepted principle of multiple use. J.L. Sevy, supervisor of the Sawtooth National Forest, told the *Times-News*, "we must be concerned about 'feeding our children,' not just 'preserving for our children.'"[20] William Rozack of the Boise National Forest spoke to a group in McCall. He avoided giving his own opinion about the national park idea, but he "wondered whether the proposal would provide something not already provided for."[21]

Church's files are filled with letters from constituents defending the Forest Service's record. In addition to its responsiveness to various local economic interests, its employees were seen as skillful in ironing out differences, while National Park officials, according to Lynn Crandall of Idaho Falls, "are an arbitrary group with no talent for adjusting differences of opinion."[22] In addition to the miners and stockmen who always spoke against the restrictions implied by NPS administration, a new group, Northside Communities, Inc., now also lobbied against the park proposal. It wrote Church, protesting that a national park "would seriously affect the economy of communities which depend upon resources" in the national forests.[23]

National park proponents gave little heed to these arguments. The *Intermountain*, a weekly published in Pocatello, claimed that "the pretense that such a park would retard Idaho's progress is a pose by self-seeking rascals."[24] Not want a national park in Idaho?, the Lewiston *Morning Tribune* rhetorically asked. "It is all right to be eccentric, but let's not be silly."[25]

Far more serious, however, was the case made by a number of conservationists and wildlifers. The *Post-Register* noted that Church's proposal was opposed by wilderness advocates as well as livestock and mining interests, arguing that "the spats and polish of the U.S. Park Service would only bring an undesirable formality to this untrammeled scenic retreat."[26] Bill Reynolds, the Idaho Wildlife Federation president in 1963, complained, "it seems that everything unique they're trying to commercialize on." In his opinion, "the beauty of the primitive areas is as a primitive area. As soon as you establish roads and such you ruin some of the beauty."[27] One of the most-pungent wildlifer critiques came in a letter to Church from Roger Williams of Wendell:

> As a native of the state of Idaho I think we need it, like we need a sore thumb. All it will do is wreck our hunting and fishing, something we've been proud of for a long time & sure don't want to lose.[28]

Church worked diligently to build support for his park proposal. He mounted a postcard poll that showed heavy majorities throughout the state favoring a feasibility study. This helped to disarm critics. Governor Smylie, for example, conceded, "I don't see how anybody can be against being informed."[29]

Church reassured sportsmen that he thought "it would be perfectly feasible to make provision for harvesting game in controlled hunts."[30] He stressed that his idea of a "wilderness national park" would leave the existing Sawtooth Primitive Area undisturbed, while most visitors would cluster at nearby lakes. "My own feeling," he explained in a letter to Robert Wing of Lewiston, "is that the principal attraction, to the great multitude of visitors, will be the magnificent profile of the Sawtooths as seen from the adjacent lakelands, and the sense of *proximity* to Wilderness. Few will venture beyond a short 'nature walk' of some kind into the edges of the Wilderness itself."[31] This seemed a sensible approach to many, even those, as the St. Maries *Gazette-Record* put it, who found that "wilderness area" and "national park" "automatically raises the bile."[32]

By 1965, when the feasibility study was being completed, Church had won a strong following for his plan. Both congressmen from Idaho, Compton White and Ralph Harding, vigorously supported the bill in the U.S. House of Representatives. Idaho Wildlife Federation leaders had been won over, and the Boise *Statesman*, which roundly condemned the whole idea five years before, now affirmed that "Idaho needs a national park," and Church's proposal "should meet with general approval among Idahoans."[33]

Nevertheless, it continued to face powerful partisan opposition. State Auditor Joe R. Williams, a Democrat, agreed that "I think the time has come to act,"[34] but Republican Governor Smylie found it "ill-advised," and Republican Len Jordan, Idaho's other senator, remained unwilling to lend his support. "It would seem the use of the word 'wilderness' in connection with a National Park is incompatible and confusing," he wrote Church, explaining why he would not cosponsor the bill. Besides, "I am sure most of the area will always be wilderness as God made it, but I would prefer that parts of it be opened by roads for greater enjoyment by more people."[35]

The issue seemed to be deadlocked, but it was dramatically redefined by the January 1966 report of the Sawtooth Mountain Study Team. Contrary to those who argued that major changes were not needed, the report found "intrusive and seemingly destructive developments" to be "the greatest immediate threat to the scenic integrity of valley lands and their enjoyment by visitors." New homesites, subdivisions, and power lines were listed as "inharmonious structures" threatening the Sawtooth Valley's aesthetic integrity.[36] Futhermore, the primitive area's present use already neared capacity. Without clearly offering a recommendation, the report seemed to favor national recreation area status over a national park. By continuing multiple-use management by the Forest Service, a Sawtooth National Recreation Area would minimize negative impacts on the local economy.

The task, in other words, was no longer to encourage tourist use of the area, but to control its impact. Even before the report's official release, Church had begun to refocus his concern for the Sawtooths. In mid-December 1965, he took the occasion of the annual Kiwanis Farm City Banquet in Twin Falls to "deplore the defacing of the landscape with 'helter-skelter' subdivision developments, which are spoiling the area." He warned, "only establishment of a park or a recreation area can possibly save this last beautiful area in the nation."[37]

The issue had evolved to land-use planning. Unless zoning controls were put in place, so the argument ran, the "old Western scene" of Sawtooth Valley would be replaced by a scattering of vacation homes uncoordinated by any regional plan. County zoning was becoming common in Idaho's more-urban counties by the mid-1960s, but Custer County had thus far shown no inclination to follow suit.

Support for such controls tended to increase with one's distance from the Sawtooth Valley village of Stanley. Nearby it was seen as, to quote the attorney for a local dude ranch, "an unwarranted threat to the security of the people in the ownership of these lands."[38] In Twin Falls, the closest large city, rapid and unplanned growth of summer homes was conceded, but "they won't detract that much from the magnificent Sawtooths."[39]

By the time one reached Boise, however, Church's view was strongly supported. "He is right," the Boise *Statesman* declared.[40] "I don't think anybody wants to create a rural slum," Governor Smylie told the Land Board.[41] Art Manley of Coeur d'Alene, testifying at the Senate hearing in Sun Valley in June 1966, said he was "shocked at the uncontrollable growth of real estate developments" in Stanley Basin.[42]

On the other hand, both the Custer County Commissioners and the Salmon Chamber of Commerce submitted resolutions to the hearing favoring the NRA, but asking for the elimination of "any and all provisions relative to local zoning."[43] John Corlett blandly reported that "only a few wilderness holdouts argued for the park" at the hearing, but the zoning section would probably be cut from the bill by the Senate Interior Committee.[44]

All four members of Idaho's congressional delegation concluded that the Sun Valley hearing demonstrated strong support for the proposed Sawtooth National Recreation Area. Accordingly, they introduced in both houses a bill to create the NRA in the spring of 1967. "On the valley lands," according to Len Jordan, "we believe grazing, typical ranching facilities and appropriately located and designed business structures and homes can be harmonized with national recreation area objectives."[45]

With this legislation, preservation eventually would go far beyond just merely saving notable natural highlights from destruction; it focused as well on protecting and managing the social, administrative, economic, and visual fabric of the Sawtooth locality. As Len Jordan put it, "I think we are breaking new ground with this concept."[46] It attempted to avoid "a subdivision look" in the Sawtooth Valley, "which cannot help but seriously detract from the frontier ranching and wilderness quality" that the NRA bill "seeks to preserve." The *Post Register*, however, feared the bill did not "prescribe standards for zoning and use of private land" that were essential to maintaining the old-time look many wanted to preserve.[47]

Avoiding such controversial topics, the bill's proponents preferred to emphasize that traditional activities could continue as long as they did not damage the area's "natural or historic values." Representative Orval Hansen told people in Salmon, "ranching and home-building activities in the Stanley Basin will not be deterred" by the NRA.[48] This was disingenuous at best. By 1968, according to the *Times-News*, "the thing most people didn't want to happen, is happening… Much property is changing hands without regard to any concrete plan." Nearly 1,600 subdivision lots were located in the area, with about one-third already having been sold.[49]

The consensus that the congressional delegation thought it had seen at the 1966 Sun Valley hearing soon proved illusory. Property owners in the proposed NRA found the zoning controls excessive, but more environmentalists complained that they were dangerously weak. Boyd Norton of Idaho Falls, an Idaho Alpine Club founder, condemned the NRA as "a mere caricature of a national park, which purports to protect the area but which would ultimately wreck it."[50] "We are not assured the valley floor will remain meadow instead of subdivision," Mr. and Mrs. Richard Miller wrote the *Post-Register*, "or that the mountain scene will not be lit by neon, or crowded by 'alpine hotels' and summer homes."[51]

Like-minded people soon formed the Greater Sawtooth Preservation Council, led by environmentalists in Pocatello and Idaho Falls. The council campaigned for a national park, arguing that the NRA provided "no effective safeguards against the neon signs, the subdivisions, the motorcycles and the high-pitched noisy, urban environment that people seek to forget on vacation."[52] By the spring of 1970, the council had formulated a combination national park and recreation area covering 1.3 million acres (two-and-a-half times larger than the proposed Sawtooth NRA) including the White Cloud, Boulder, and Pioneer mountain ranges.

This expanded proposal polarized the debate, with only the most-avid environmentalists supporting it (who formed local council chapters in Ketchum, Boise, and Moscow), while other environmentalist had doubts about it. Speaking against the Greater Sawtooth Preservation Council's expanded proposal, the *Post-Register* insisted that "the time bomb is in Sawtooth Valley now, not the White Clouds, Boulders or Pioneers." While it would probably take years to sort out the arguments for and against mining in the White Clouds and to develop appropriate new legislation, the ongoing, unplanned, suburban-type development in the Sawtooth Valley was "the most critical challenge."[53] The *Statesman* agreed with the *Post-Register* that there was "no good reason for delay on the Sawtooth bill, with or without the White Clouds."[54] Nevertheless, the Idaho congressional delegation announced in August 1970 that it would sponsor a park-recreation area bill, with a national park similar to that advocated by the council, but with priority placed on an NRA to control growth in Sawtooth Valley. A hearing was scheduled for August 26, 1970, in Sun Valley.

If sponsors hoped that this latest Sawtooth bill would meet general approval, they soon were disabused of that notion. Nor did people wait until the hearing to express their opinions. Some agreed with the Pocatello *Idaho State Journal* that the bill represented "an excellent solution to a complex problem."[55] But Governor Samuelson made no bones about his disapproval. "I want no part of a national park… They would just…lock up a piece of ground and let it sit there and die, and this is not good management."[56] The Lewiston *Morning Tribune* retorted that such a position was "laughable," that a national park's economic impact "is, as everyone knows, beneficial."[57] Former Governor Smylie snipped that "there was a time when the Governor was an honest conservationist," but "something awfully funny must have happened to Don Samuelson on the way to the Governor's office."[58]

The scene at the Sun Valley hearing was anything but a love feast, as had occurred at Priest Lake in 1964. Nearly five hundred people attended, with far too little time in a single day for all to be heard. Even Samuelson's representative was gaveled into insulted silence by the chairman, North Carolina Senator Roy Taylor, for overrunning his allotted time. Eventually, the subcommittee broke into two sections to allow at least one minute each for 365 witnesses. "It was just too much in too little time," the *Times-News* observed.[59] The press could not make sense out of it, other than to quote some of the testimony more or less randomly. Many journalists' suspected that the senators holding the hearing left with no clear sense of local opinion. Idahoans obviously had very strong opinions on the subject, but they differed to such an extent that a disinterested observer would have been justified to leave the whole matter alone until something more like a consensus emerged.

Consequently, another two years passed before Congress finally approved the Sawtooth National Recreation Area, while the adjoining national park never materialized. As finally drafted, the NRA did not give the Forest Service strong zoning powers. Instead, the act permitted the acquisition of scenic easements, which was far less controversial, of course, but increasingly expensive and therefore sharply limited in applicability. The fight to "save Sawtooth Valley" has continued into the twenty-first century, with no resolution yet in sight.

Hells Canyon gained NRA status less than four years after the Sawtooths, but the story of how that came to be is almost entirely different. The Sawtooths' scenic attractions had always been recognized and never seriously threatened. Hells Canyon's scenic merits, on the other hand, received only belated recognition, and it very nearly suffered the fate of Shoshone Falls.

From the time when frontiersmen named Hells Canyon for its "sinister splendor," or so the story goes,[60] most observers had difficulty assessing it aesthetically. It was obviously vast—surpassing even the Grand Canyon as the deepest gorge in North America—but it could only be appreciated from distant overlooks. Getting to such a vantage point in the Seven Devils Mountains bordering Hells Canyon in Idaho has never been easy, where the few, largely single-track, roads remain unpaved to this day. The roads on the high ridges of the Oregon side were difficult, too. But the view has always been considered impressive. As early as August 1900, the *Statesman* reported that a copper prospector looking down 5,000 feet to the Snake River declared, "it was grand." However, he (and most later viewers) focused not on the canyon itself, but rather "I was never before more impressed with the majesty of our mountains."[61] As late as the early 1960s, occasional proposals for designating a national park or scenic area concentrated more on the Seven Devils Mountains (or the Wallowa range on the Oregon side), than on Hells Canyon itself.

The trouble with Hells Canyon, seen up close, was that it lacked the "bright glory or magnificent mesas" of the Grand Canyon. Rather, its "gloomy battlements" rose above the Snake River, which surged "an angry white through much of the abyss."[62] Typically, a 1928 article describing "Idaho's Royal Gorge" emphasized the "somber tones and dark colors" of its canyon walls, which resembled "the chasmic pictures that accompany the deluxe editions of *Dante's Inferno*."[63] Furthermore, it lacked the great quantity of big game that attracted early white-water boaters on the Salmon River, while its rapids were so powerful that they seemed downright suicidal to white-water enthusiasts. The *Saturday Evening Post* published a "Farewell to Hells Canyon" in 1967, expecting its "stark beauty" to be buried forever with the construction of a new dam. Although the article included eight stunning color photographs, it began with somber reflection: "this is hard country where animals and machines and expectations wear out quickly." The author later returned to expand on the canyon's ominous character:

> It does not uplift the spirit, although its awesomeness occasionally softens to beauty. Its presence leans like a wind against the weak spots in a man's fabric. Bones ache here, hopes fray.[64]

Little wonder, then, that any movement to preserve Hells Canyon came very late. If it was most appealing from thousands of feet above, why should anyone worry about dams, whose reservoirs would reduce the canyon's depth only a few hundred feet? Hells Canyon might be hard to admire at river level, but its potential for hydroelectric power development was tantalizingly obvious. The elevation between Weiser and Lewiston drops 1,400 feet. With the volume of water carried by the river, it had the theoretical energy of 2.85 million horsepower or 18 billion kilowatt-hours.

As early as 1922, Pacific Power and Light began to plan a dam at the Oxbow site, later used by Idaho Power. That early PP&L dam generated only a few hundred kilowatt-hours, however. Not until the 1950s did large-scale hydroelectric development come to the "Middle Snake"—the two hundred-mile stretch between Weiser and Lewiston (the mid-part of which was Hells Canyon). A bitter battle was fought between proponents of private and public power, waged in Congress and before the Federal Power Commission, as well as within the region. Private power interests eventually won. Idaho Power built its three "low dams" at Brownlee, Oxbow, and Hells Canyon, while the "high dam" favored by the public power advocates repeatedly failed to get the necessary administrative and budgetary support. The three "low dams" impacted a portion of the southern, or upstream, end of the Snake's long, great chasm, whereas a "high dam," farther north, would have directly affected the deepest and wildest portion of Hells Canyon.

Until 1967, however, the debate over dam construction almost always was phrased in terms of which ones to build, rather than whether the canyon ought to be preserved in its natural state. "On one thing everybody in the debate agrees," *Life* reported in November 1953, "the Snake must be tamed."[65] In the late 1930s, some had talked about the possibility of a national park, but those most warmly pushing the idea, J.D. Wood and some associates in Weiser, tied the proposal to a multimillion-dollar highway running through the canyon. The State Planning Board called for a committee to study the matter in August 1939, and the committee actually took a three-day area tour late the next month, but the proposal failed to gain any substantial public support. Arthur Campbell, state mine inspector and member of the State Planning Board, typified the thinking of the time when he told the *Morning Tribune* he opposed a national park "until its resources have been exploited, including the mineral, hydroelectric power and scenic attributes."[66]

The "scenic attributes," it seems clear in this context, meant overlooks from the Seven Devils. A few hardy souls might brave boating through the canyon itself, but that was more of an exotic kind of thrill-seeking than a scenic pleasure trip appealing to the general public. "Nature had certainly gone berserk when she made that country," wrote a woman who grew up in Lewiston, "tossing mountains hither and yon." Long a resident of Indianapolis, she fondly recalled it as "fascinating country," but most visitors preferred to observe it from a safe distance.[67]

And when the dams were built, so it seemed to many Idahoans, they would add rather than detract from the scenic effect. The Priest River *Times* saw Idaho Power's Hells Canyon Dam as a "spectacular show of modern engineering and construction staggering the imagination."[68] Better still in the eyes of many weekend recreationists, the raging white-water was now replaced by tranquil lakes above the dams. "This summer," the *Statesman* reported in May 1968, "the entire Idaho shoreline of the jewel-like lake" of Oxbow Reservoir "will become available for public use," with the opening of a road built by Idaho Power to provide access during the dam's construction.[69]

The Forest Service plan for a Hells Canyon/Seven Devils Scenic Area reportedly was first drafted in 1943, but not until 1958 did it begin to be publicized. Initially, it was a quite modest proposal, contemplating only a few new roads, campgrounds, and trails into the Seven Devils. This later provoked the wrath of Senator Church, but the only misgivings expressed by local residents at the time focussed on wilderness preservation. "There ought to be," argued Eli Rapaich, a Lewiston attorney, "a few places where a tree can die a natural death."[70] But the original plan had almost nothing to do with Hells Canyon. The road eventually built up to Heavens Gate in the Seven Devils, for example, offers remarkable views, and its fairly continuous 5 percent grade, climbing for more than twenty miles from the Salmon River at Riggins, passes through a wide spectrum of forest and meadow zones. But one catches only occasional, partial glimpses of Hells Canyon in the hazy distance.

In 1960 Roy Stockman, a well-known sportsman living in Grangeville, wrote Church: "I think this Seven Devils area bordering Hells Canyon has far more to offer" than the Sawtooths. "I think your suggestion may have considerable merit," Church replied, "and if and when I get through the storm my Sawtooth proposal has created, I shall look into it carefully."[71]

When Church did look into it in 1962, he lambasted the Forest Service for its "unbridled bureaucratic license."[72] This may have been provoked by Church's distrust of the agency. Or it may have been that, since he was running for reelection that year, he was irritated by his Republican opponent's citing the scenic area as being "in line with the traditional multiple use concept,"[73] as opposed to the Wilderness Bill that Church backed. If Church's critique had anything to do with Hells Canyon itself (which is hard to determine, since his otherwise-voluminous papers contain nothing on Hells Canyon for this whole period), it might have been because the Forest Service had expanded its scenic area plan to include various improvements along the Snake, including twelve boating sites. Since Church was, at the time, a strong advocate of a high dam in Hells Canyon, which would have flooded the valley floor, he could not have been pleased with the complications implicit in the Forest Service's expressed intention that "most of the area will remain wild."[74] In any case, the expanded version of the scenic area never got beyond the planning stage.

Hells Canyon as a public-policy issue took a completely new turn in June 1967. After hearing an appeal revolving around the question of the canyon's public versus private power development, the U.S. Supreme Court stunned everyone by remanding the case to the Federal Power Commission with instructions to explore "all the issues relevant to the public interest," including preservation of wildlife and migratory fish, and even wild river designation.[75] In case anyone missed the point, Justice William O. Douglas, who wrote the court's opinion for this case, quoted Justice Oliver Wendell Holmes: "a river is more than an amenity, it is a treasure."[76]

The press took some time to grasp the decision's implications. The Lewiston *Morning Tribune*, for example, blithely reaffirmed its conviction that the High Mountain Sheep Dam in Hells Canyon "can and will be built ... These other problems probably will not prove to be overriding; they have been hashed over long since."[77]

But it took less than two months for the Hells Canyon Preservation Council to be formed by a group of environmentalists in Pocatello and Idaho Falls. Press pundits saw this as hopeless. "It is a well-intentioned crusade," the *Morning Tribune* editorialized, "but it has come too late." Idaho Power's dams already had taken the Snake captive, so it "probably should be written off by the conservationists as a lost cause."[78]

The fact that the movement to preserve Hells Canyon centered in eastern Idaho is less puzzling then it might seem. Several founders of the Hells Canyon Preservation Council were young scientists at the National Reactor Testing Station, who were convinced that the potential of atomic power made hydro-electric dams expensive anachronisms. Those same scientists also shared a great love for challenging outdoor sports and the lure of wilderness. Boyd Norton, for example, helped to start the Idaho Alpine Club and later moved to Denver as the Wilderness Society's regional representative. He and Pete Henault liked to show off Hells Canyon to important potential supporters, not by power boating up from Lewiston, but by white-water rafting downstream.

The council held its organizational meeting in Pocatello on July 18, 1967. In explaining its purposes, Norton mentioned Douglas's Supreme Court decision and the "Farewell to Hells Canyon" article published just two weeks before in the *Saturday Evening Post*. The council knew it wanted to preserve Hells Canyon, but its spokesmen had no ready-made answer to those who asked why. Norton said the article described the canyon's "incomparable beauty and ruggedness,"[79] but that sounded less than compelling. Nine months later in a panel discussion at Idaho Falls, Cyril Slansky urged that Hells Canyon be left "unchanged as a monument to progress and common sense,"[80] but it remained unclear what the progress was toward.

The council's rationale for preserving Hells Canyon finally achieved clarity in September 1968. Leading its delegation to the Federal Power Commission hearing in Lewiston, Norton started by affirming that "the primary values that I speak of are those of esthetics [and] wild river experiences." But he then went on to suggest a full-fledged environmental justification:

There is a growing worry among people, both scientific and non-scientific, in Idaho and across the nation, about the things we are doing to our environment without proper regard for the consequences. One of the most important things we've learned in our consultation with biologists and ecologists is the fact that we don't have answers to some of the questions raised on the effects of more dams.[81]

This was moving beyond traditional rhetorical flourishes and toward an ecological approach to preservation. No longer did one need to phrase the issue in words such as Oregon Senator Packwood's: "the area symbolizes the West. It is rugged and real. It bridges the past and the present."[82] Instead, "Hells Canyon is needed," as council member Jim Campbell put it, "as an ecological benchmark where the unusual and unique combination of plants and animals are protected."[83] Gerald Jayne, another council member, saw the canyon as "a unique ecological and geological system," where "all of the life zones in the United States can be walked through in one or two days."[84] In short, "we're not just trying to save some fish," the Associated Press quoted Arthur Solman of Northwest Steelheaders. "We're trying to save the total environment and stop pollution."[85]

The council soon found nationally prominent allies. Radio-TV personality Arthur Godfrey took a tour and was so impressed that he said nothing should be done without consulting ecologists. He also prevailed upon Walter Hickel, secretary of the interior, to come have a look. Accompanied by singer Burl Ives (another nationally recognized celebrity), Hickel and Godfrey's trip through Hells Canyon gained intense press coverage. Regardless of how one might have felt about Hells Canyon, such national attention had to be reckoned with. The Boise *Statesman* seemed to agree with those who believed that even with another dam, "there'd be a lot of canyon left," but Godfrey "thinks the canyon is worth preserving as it is," and "the views of people of that persuasion will have to be considered."[86]

Many of the most prominent visitors to Hells Canyon in the later 1960s traveled in a powerboat operated by Floyd Harvey of Lewiston. He had launched his own one-man campaign to save the canyon years before, but until the environmentalists took up his cause, he was dismissed as something of a crank by most of his neighbors.[87] Even in the last years of the 1960s, Harvey was given little public credit for the importance of his zealous efforts to give tours to influential people. In May 1968, he took a group into the canyon that included representatives from the New York *Times, Audubon Magazine, National Geographic, Sports Afield, Cascade* magazine, and the National Park Service. Though reported in the *Morning Tribune,* it came at the end of a long article focusing on the preservationist position of the Lewiston Chamber of Commerce's Fish and Game Committee.

IDAHO, early 1970s

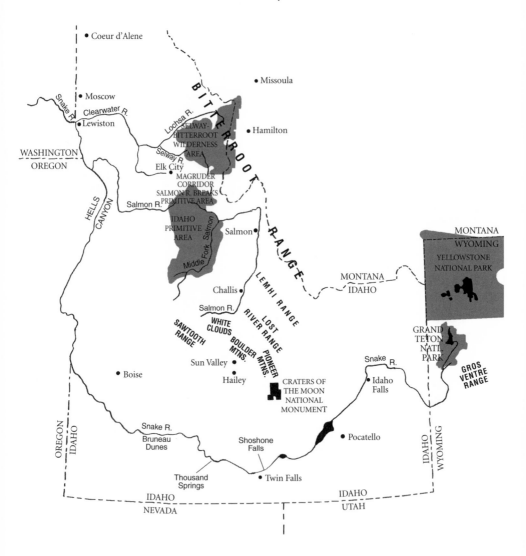

Nevertheless, by mid-1968 the combined efforts of the Hells Canyon Preservation Council and Floyd Harvey had built broad nationwide support for a ten-year moratorium on any further dams on the middle Snake. Initially conceived by Senator Len Jordan, the moratorium soon gained Frank Church's support and that of a growing number of interest groups in the Pacific Northwest. The Boise *Statesman* thought it the "Best Answer for the Middle Snake," taking the editorial position that if any new dam were to be built, it should offer "considerably more than power" than could be generated by steam or nuclear energy.[88]

The Lewiston *Morning Tribune*, which had strongly supported dams at Asotin, Washington, and in the canyon for more than a decade, now conceded that "the case for a moratorium is strong."[89] Within another week, the Lewiston paper's conversion to a preservationist position was complete. On September 4, 1968, the day the Federal Power Commission started its hearing where Boyd Norton made his statement, Bill Hall's editorial declared, "it is not necessary for this generation of inadequately informed experts in their monumental conceit, to assume the decision must be made in this year or even in their lifetimes."[90]

Across the state in Idaho Falls, the *Post-Register* called the moratorium "no less than inspired revelation in action."[91] Even Governor Samuelson, frequently an unabashed development supporter, told the FPC that he could see the merits of the preservationists as well as those favoring another dam.

The battle lines had been completely reversed. Prior to the Supreme Court decision in June 1967, only a few isolated visionaries, such as Floyd Harvey, had even dreamt of keeping the Snake a free-flowing river through Hells Canyon. Fifteen months later, developers faced an opposition overwhelming in its numbers and nationwide scope. A coalition of environmental groups, including the Hells Canyon Preservation Council, advocated the designation of a Hells Canyon-Snake National River, encompassing 625,000 acres. A growing number, who had a horrific vision of what more development might look like, supported them. The next reservoir, Arthur Godfrey lamented, would be a sorry sight, indeed: "a deep sluggish polluted lake full of hordes of faint-hearted outboard motor nuts spewing one-third of their fuel—unburned—into the waters along with their beer cans and other people-droppings."[92] Without going so far as to enact national river status, by late 1968 Congress was moving toward passage of the ten-year moratorium on dam-building sponsored by Jordan and Church.

The tables had not just been turned on developers who heedlessly pushed ahead regardless of environmental consequences, but in saving Hells Canyon, preservationists had helped to bring into public view a whole new attitude toward the environment. The *Morning Tribune* ruefully reflected on the fact that the fight over Hells Canyon had depended on the "tenacity of a few natives" and "a handful of knowledgeable outsiders":

Isn't it odd that those of us who have lived here could look at that stretch of river and at that monstrous wound and not fully grasp that there was something as valuable as the Grand Canyon and the redwoods which instinctively we knew must be saved?[93]

By January 1970, even the Idaho Water Resources Board, one of the most-zealous dam backers, had begun to see things differently. "Ideally," Robert Lee, its director, testified, "it would be good to have a moratorium on all developments until a master plan for future water use had been worked out."[94]

The battle over the Snake River continued for another five years before Congress designated the Hells Canyon National Recreation Area, but only the most-hidebound dam proponents would have denied that the odds against their succeeding had, by 1970, become almost insurmountable. Not only did they face a flood tide of opinion favoring the canyon's preservation, but they also discovered that this tide rose from a fundamental change during the 1960s in American attitudes toward conservation and the way humans should relate to their surroundings. Idahoans fully participated in that change, as will be seen in the next chapter.

Endnotes

1. "Conversations on Harriman State Park," editorial in Idaho Falls *Post-Register* (May 13, 1963): p. 4.
2. "Railroad Ranch Idaho Gift," Idaho Falls *Post-Register* (December 22, 1961): pp. 1, 11.
3. "Primitive Tubbs Hill Hailed as a Distinct Asset to Coeur d'Alene," Coeur d'Alene *Press* (May 22, 1947): p. 1.
4. "Road Will Be Blazed to Tubbs Hill Peak—Signal for Development," Coeur d'Alene *Press* (October 19, 1948): p. 2.
5. Coeur d'Alene *Press* (April 30, 1963): p. 3.
6. Coeur d'Alene *Press* (April 23, 1963): p. 2.
7. "Hearing Set on Tubbs Project," Coeur d'Alene *Press* (April 15, 1963): p. 1.
8. Letter to the editor, in Coeur d'Alene *Press* (July 12, 1963): p. 2.
9. Letter to the editor, in Coeur d'Alene *Press* (July 13, 1963): p. 2.
10. Letter to the editor, in Coeur d'Alene *Press* (March 8, 1968): p. 4.
11. "Legislation Introduced to Save Upper Priest Lake Area," Lewiston *Morning Tribune* (August 4, 1964): p. 10.
12. "Strong Backing for Upper Priest Lake," Sandpoint *News-Bulletin* (October 15, 1964): Sec. 2, p. 1.
13. "Smylie OKs Lake Land Acquisition," Boise *Statesman* (October 8, 1964): p. 2.
14. "Senator Sees No Detriment in Park Plan," Twin Falls *Times-News* (January 14, 1960): p. 1. See also Douglas W. Dodd, "Preserving Multiple-Use Management: The U.S. Forest Service, the National Park Service, and the Struggle for Idaho's Sawtooth Mountain Country, 1911–1972" (Ann Arbor, Mich.: UMI Dissertation Services, 2002): pp. 175–222.
15. "Sawtooth Yodel," editorial in Grangeville *Idaho County Free Press* (February 25, 1960): Sec. 2, p. 2.
16. John Corlett, "Politically Speaking," Boise *Statesman* (February 19, 1960): p. 7.
17. Custer County Commissioners to Frank Church, January 22, 1960, in Church Papers, Box 92, Folder 20.
18. Frank Church to Joe Williams, Secretary of the Stanley Basin Chamber of Commerce, March 9, 1960, in Church Papers, Box 92, Folder 23.
19. Frank Church to N.E. Van Sant, Executive Secretary of the Idaho Motel Association, August 27, 1963, in Church Papers, Box 93, Folder 7.
20. "Definition of Issues over Proposed Sawtooth Park Urged by Forest Official," Twin Falls *Times-News* (January 20, 1960): pp. 1, 2.

21. "National Parks, Forests Compared in Lunch Talk," McCall *Payette Lakes Star* (March 24, 1960): p. 1.
22. Lynn Crandall to Frank Church, February 12, 1960, in Church Papers, Box 92, Folder 22.
23. Jim Freeman, president, and Blanche Bungum, secretary, Northside Communities Inc., to Frank Church, December 14, 1959, in Church Papers, Box 92, Folder 18.
24. Untitled editorial, *Intermountain* (January 29, 1960) in Church Papers, Box 92, Folder 19.
25. "A National Park Study within Idaho?" editorial in Lewiston *Morning Tribune* (January 31, 1960): p. 4.
26. "Spats for Stanley Basin," editorial in Idaho Falls *Post-Register* (January 24, 1960): p. 4.
27. "Harding to Offer Bill on Sawtooths," Pocatello *Idaho State Journal* (August 25, 1963): p. 21.
28. Roger Williams to Frank Church, February 10, 1960, in Church Papers, Box 92, Folder 21.
29. "Smylie Prefers Study of Sawtooth Proposal," Boise *Statesman* (September 6, 1963): p. 6.
30. Frank Church to Milton Richard, February 17, 1960, in Church Papers, Box 92, Folder 21.
31. Frank Church to Robert Wing, October 9, 1963, in Church Papers, Box 93, Folder 8.
32. "Don't Jump at the Dirty Words," editorial in St. Maries *Gazette-Record* (February 11, 1960): p. 8.
33. "At Last, a National Park," editorial in Boise *Statesman* (February 3, 1965): p. 4.
34. "Democrats on Land Board Voice Support of Proposal on Sawtooth Park Status," Boise *Statesman* (September 13, 1963): p. 12.
35. Len B. Jordan to Frank Church, March 23, 1963, in Len B. Jordan Papers (Boise State University Library Special Collections), Box 130, Folder 12.
36. "Copies of Sawtooth Study Report Arrive," Twin Falls *Times-News* (January 25, 1966): pp. 1, 2.
37. O.A. (Gus) Kelker, "Senator Says Agencies Can't Agree on Sawtooths," Twin Falls *Times-News* (December 17, 1965): pp. 1, 2.
38. "Recreation Area Backed," Idaho Falls *Post-Register* (June 14, 1966): pp. 1, 13.
39. "Under Control," editorial in Twin Falls *Times-News* (December 26, 1965): p. 4.
40. "Idahoans Disappointed over Lack of Action, Delay in Deciding Fate of Sawtooth Region," editorial in Boise *Statesman* (December 26, 1965): p. 4.
41. "Board Favors Holding Stanley Land," Boise *Statesman* (June 17, 1966): pp. 1, 5.
42. "Gov. Smylie Backs Recreation Area Plan for Stanley Basin," Boise *Statesman* (June 13, 1966): pp. 1, 3.
43. "Sawtooth Valley Association Hears Reports On Recreation Area," Challis *Messenger* (May 26, 1966): p. 1; "Recreation Area Status Favored for Sawtooth," Salmon *Recorder-Herald* (June 16, 1966): p. 7.
44. John Corlett, "'National Park' Seems Extinct," Boise *Statesman* (June 17, 1966): p. 8.
45. "Bill Introduced to Create Sawtooth Recreation Area," Twin Falls *Times-News* (March 14, 1967): p. 1.
46. Tom Ochiltree, "Senate Interior Panel Nods to Bill for Sawtooth Recreation Area," Boise *Statesman* (June 17, 1967): p. 1.
47. "Sawtooth Bill Needs Changes," editorial in Idaho Falls *Post-Register* (April 17, 1967): p. 4.
48. "National Recreation Area Favored for Stanley Basin," Idaho Falls *Post-Register* (February 2, 1968): p. 5.
49. O.A. (Gus) Kelker, "National Recreation Area Plan for Sawtooth-Stanley Section of Idaho May Die in Committee," Twin Falls *Times-News* (September 8, 1968): pp. A1, 3.
50. "New Teton Wilderness, Proposed Sawtooth Plan Opposed by Leader," Idaho Falls *Post-Register* (November 29, 1967): p. 17.
51. Letter to the editor, Idaho Falls *Post-Register* (February 6, 1969): p. 9.
52. "Not Two Sawtooth Formulas at Once," editorial in Idaho Falls *Post-Register* (June 2, 1969): p. 4.
53. "New Thinking for the Sawtooths," editorial in Idaho Falls *Post-Register* (April 3, 1970): p. 4.
54. "Action Needed Now on Sawtooths," editorial in Boise *Statesman* (July 19, 1970): p. 4
55. "Agreement on Sawtooths," editorial in Pocatello *Idaho State Journal* (August 12, 1970): p. 4.
56. John Corlett, "Gov. Samuelson Balks at Sawtooth Park Plan," Boise *Statesman* (August 20, 1970): p. D1.
57. B.H., "Is a National Park Bad for Idaho?" editorial in Lewiston *Morning Tribune* (August 21, 1970): p. 4.

58. Robert E. Smylie, "Governor Dynamites the Sawtooth Park," Boise *Intermountain Observer* (August 22, 1970): p. 16.
59. "A Better Way?" editorial in Twin Falls *Times-News* (September 1, 1970): p. 4.
60. Richard L. Neuberger, "Hell's Canyon, the Biggest of All," *Harpers Magazine* (April 1939): p. 587.
61. "In Seven Devils," Boise *Statesman* (August 3, 1900): p. 4.
62. Neuberger, *op. cit.*
63. "Idaho's Royal Gorge," Boise *Statesman* (August 26, 1928): p. 2.
64. John Skow, "Farewell to Hells Canyon," *Saturday Evening Post* (July 1, 1967): pp. 76–83.
65. "The Issue: U.S. or Private Dams," *Life* (November 9, 1953): p. 30.
66. "Exploitation of Canyon Favored," Lewiston *Morning Tribune* (October 12, 1939): p. 14.
67. Grace Ketenbach Pfaffin, "Matchless Hells Canyon—Its Past and Present History," Lewiston *Morning Tribune* (October 17, 1948): Sect. 2, pp. 1, 8.
68. "Idaho Power Company Tames the Snake River—Hells Canyon, North America's Deepest Gorge," Priest River *Times* (May 5, 1966): p. 4.
69. "Lake Developed at Hells Canyon," Boise *Statesman* (May 6, 1968 Afternoon Edition): p. 17.
70. "Access Roads to Wilderness Spark Debate," Lewiston *Morning Tribune* (September 29, 1958): pp. 10, 5.
71. Roy Stockman to Frank Church, February 15, 1960, in Church Papers, Box 92, Folder 23; Church to Stockman, March 1, 1960, in *Ibid.*
72. "Church Statement Critical of 'Bureaucratic License' in Scenic Area's Creation," Boise *Statesman* (June 14, 1962): p. 22.
73. "Designation of Scenic Area Gains Hawley Support," Boise *Statesman* (June 15, 1962): p. 21.
74. "USFS Tells Plans for Scenic Area in Devils-Hells Canyon," Grangeville *Idaho County Free Press* (March 28, 1963): p. 1. This article summarizes a booklet issued by the Forest Service with "detailed plans" for the area.
75. "Court Stalls Snake Dam for Review," Boise *Statesman* (June 6, 1967): pp. 1, 2.
76. "Delay Seen for Mountain Sheep," editorial in Boise *Statesman* (June 7, 1967): p. 4.
77. "A Delay for an Important Decision" editorial in Lewiston *Morning Tribune* (June 6, 1967): p. 4.
78. "It's Too Late to Save the Snake," editorial in Lewiston *Morning Tribune* (February 6, 1968): p. 4.
79. "Group Forms to 'Protect' Hells Canyon," Boise *Statesman* (July 20, 1967): p. 25.
80. "Mountain Sheep Dam Panel Ends Jamboree Clinic," Idaho Falls *Post-Register* (March 17, 1968): pp. 1, 15.
81. "Hells Canyon Spokesman Argues against New Dams," Idaho Falls *Post-Register* (September 8, 1968): p. 20.
82. Tom Ochiltree, "Senatorial Actions Seek to Save Snake from More Dams," Boise *Statesman* (January 24, 1970): p. 18.
83. "Hells Canyon Council Protests River Project," Idaho Falls *Post-Register* (January 29, 1970): p. 7.
84. "Field Hearings Desired on Hells Canyon Proposal," Idaho Falls *Post-Register* (March 18, 1970): p. 30.
85. "Outdoor Groups Seek to Halt Snake River Dams Construction," Idaho Falls *Post-Register* (March 12, 1970): p. 13.
86. "More Than a Regional Battle," editorial in Boise *Statesman* (August 10, 1969): p. 4.
87. William Ashworth, *Hells Canyon: The Deepest Gorge on Earth* (New York: Hawthorn, 1977): pp. 144–48, 161–64, 189–90.
88. "Best Answer for the Middle Snake," editorial in Boise *Statesman* (August 25, 1968): p. 4.
89. "A Respite on the Middle Snake," editorial in Lewiston *Morning Tribune* (August 28, 1968): p. 4.
90. Bill Hall, "The Conceit in Deciding Right Now," editorial in Lewiston *Morning Tribune* (September 4, 1968): p. 4.
91. "Time, a Solution on Mid-Snake," editorial in Idaho Falls *Post-Register* (September 6, 1968): p. 4.
92. "Godfrey Urges Hickel to Save Snake; Developers Offended," Lewiston *Morning Tribune* (August 4, 1969): p. 14.
93. Bill Hall, "Some National Aid on Hells Canyon," editorial in Lewiston *Morning Tribune* (August 23, 1969): p. 4.
94. Tom Ochiltree, "Idaho May Oppose Middle Snake Dam," Boise *Statesman* (January 7, 1970): pp. 1, 2.

XI

From *Silent Spring* to Earth Day in Idaho

T HE PUBLICATION OF Rachel Carson's *Silent Spring* in 1962 went virtually un-
noticed in Idaho. Unlike the situation in many other states, where pesticide
proponents initially published heated refutations of Carson,[1] the Idaho press
generally ignored her somber warnings. The Boise *Evening Statesman* took
editorial note in December that the "Pesticide Furor" "continues unabated,"[2]
but neither it nor any other paper in Idaho gave any extended coverage of
the issue. As seen in Chapter V, most Idahoans continued to hold a strictly
utilitarian view of conservation in the early 1960s, where even predator poisoning drew only scattered and ineffective opposition. Few could grasp the
ecological arguments against DDT use.

It seemed like a godsend when the pesticide first became available shortly
after World War II. "Boy, will the bugs take a beating!" the Twin Falls *Times-
News* chortled in July 1945. "And what a cinch this business of insect-control
will be."[3] So it still appeared, despite Carson's concerns. "Certainly we're not
about to turn back the clock," the Boise *Statesman* assured its readers in May
1963, "and abandon the use of pesticides with their practical values."[4] Noting
the controls used in aerial spraying in Targhee National Forest to minimize
damage to wildlife and fish, the Idaho Falls *Post-Register* concluded, "this
makes good sense in the absence of a final evaluation of pesticides." When
"the final verdict" comes in, it will probably find fault with excessive use, "not
the pesticide itself."[5]

Consequently, it came as an unwelcome surprise when a few women in
Salmon began to noisily protest the Forest Service's plans in 1964 to spray
500,000 acres in the Salmon and Challis national forests, reportedly the largest treatment in the nation against spruce budworm. The Challis *Messenger*
expostulated in May that "with full awareness of the national concern over
pesticide use, the Forest Service has drawn on its 15 years of experience in
aerial spraying to produce this year its most thoroughly planned and carefully
screened control program."[6]

Nevertheless, a Committee Against Mass Poisoning (quickly shortened
to CAMP) formed a few weeks later. Louise Nelson, who spearheaded the

movement, explained her thinking in a letter to the editor of the Salmon *Recorder-Herald*. She may have made her home on Fourth of July Creek outside of Salmon (a distant 120 miles from Idaho Falls), but she had been doing some reading. "Sprays are more dangerous than radioactive fallout, claim some authorities," so we should "work with nature by using biological controls and natural predators, rather than poisoning our environment." She urged the people of Salmon to "rise up against this monstrous evil that is being perpetrated upon us, however well-meaning are the officials who administer this program."[7]

Unimpressed by her arguments, the local chamber of commerce unanimously approved the program, blandly observing that the amount of chemicals used "is small compared with that applied in private use such as crops."[8] Reflecting the prevailing lack of ecological awareness, newspapers elsewhere in the state summarized CAMP protests as arising simply from fears for the welfare of fish in the streams running through the area to be sprayed, and concluded that "surely the timber must be saved."[9]

The confrontation between CAMP and those favoring aerial spraying was anything but a fair fight. Louise Nelson and her friends called several meetings in Salmon, but the only outside allies came from the Western Montana Fish and Game Association. CAMP gathered five hundred signatures on petitions it sent to the Idaho congressional delegation and various federal officials. An overwhelming consensus held that CAMP had it wrong, typified by the response to the petition from Orville Freeman, secretary of agriculture: "observations over the years have not indicated serious side effects that would warrant discontinuance."[10] One might concede, to quote the Twin Falls *Times-News*, that "in the past 100 years particularly, American civilization has raised hob with Nature's balance," and yet conclude pesticide use was "better than letting insects and pests decimate forests and farmlands unchecked."[11] Roger Guernsey, the state forester, defended spraying against "a lot of hysteria and misinformation on the use of insecticides."[12] Salmon's newspaper editor agreed that criticism of pesticide use "has reached unjustified dimensions."[13]

In May 1965, a conference of experts at Sun Valley came up with mixed assessments of insecticide impacts on public health, but the *Times-News* typified prevailing reactions in an editorial entitled "No Silent Spring?" It suggested that "the pesticides might be here to stay and may even increase in variety and effectiveness."[14]

Ironically, despite the weight of opposing expert opinion, CAMP's view of how nature works was sustained by the way things turned out. The Forest Service proceeded with its spraying program during the summer of 1965, but suspended the planned spraying for 1966 because the budworms did not develop sufficiently to warrant treatment. It wasn't clear why. Some argued that the budworms only appeared cyclically; others attributed the budworm decline to unusual frosts in the fall of 1965 and spring of 1966. In any case, the budworm infestation ended because of natural forces, not insecticide use.

A few years later, considerably more people in Idaho began sharing CAMP's fear of pesticides. In January 1969, the Lewiston *Morning Tribune* took editorial note of the growing evidence against DDT and concluded that unless it was banned soon, "the world may yet experience that 'Silent Spring' that Rachel Carson warned us of."[15] In July the Boise *Statesman* began an editorial urging the banning of DDT by asserting its use "is something like Russian roulette."[16] The following January, it praised the Boise City Council decision not to use DDT, with the affirmation that "protection of the environment is not a frill but a necessity."[17] Though Idaho's overall environmental learning curve may have been different from other parts of the country, in regard to attitudes toward DDT and pesticides, at least, the state exemplified the dramatic change in national awareness and concern that occurred by the end of the 1960s.

As described in Chapter VII, the fight against water pollution in Idaho had achieved substantial victories during the 1950s. But despite all the emotional valence that water protection had for Idahoans and with the irrefutable and widely understood dangers that water pollution posed for public health, major battles were still to be fought in the 1960s. It was not simply a matter of getting the small, relatively remote villages to install sewage treatment systems. Even Boise's northwest portion, including the affluent Highlands, did not approve a sewer system until February 1968. This came about only after the release of numerous alerts banning swimming in the Boise River, below the city's western edge, because of seepage from hundreds of septic tanks serving that part of suburban Boise. Meanwhile, industrial pollution, particularly from potato-processing plants, caused massive and repeated fish kills well into the 1960s. (In 1970 it would remain debatable whether or not the problems of water pollution had yet peaked.)

What happened when environmental health hazards were less obvious to the public such as in the case of foul air? Like almost all forms of pollution, Idahoans initially showed little concern for polluted air. To some extent, it was only after World War II that most Idahoans began to confront anything like the pollution problems commonly found in more populous and industrialized parts of the country. Earlier in the century, population densities had been too light for auto emissions to be a serious problem, and only in the Coeur d'Alene mining district did heavy industry emit large quantities of pollutants into the sky. The phosphate plants at Pocatello and Soda Springs and the paper mill in Lewiston were not even constructed until after 1945.

Nevertheless, even where air pollution existed, the public tended either to ignore it or temporize without any evident commitment to end the problem. Noxious gases from the Coeur d'Alene district smelters, laden with lead and other heavy metals, were clearly visible from the early 1900s, and the deadly impact on the forests bordering the Silver Valley could be seen by all. However, unlike water pollution that was protested from an early day, no really effective campaign against air pollution developed in northern Idaho until the 1960s.

Since at least the 1920s, smog was a problem in Boise, particularly during winter months. In November 1923, the *Capital News* editorialized about "The Smoke Nuisance," complaining that "the city is buried under a pall of smoke the greater part of the day."[18] "The problem CAN be solved," the *Statesman* insisted fifteen years later, "and it's high time that we recognize the facts and do something."[19] Although the city council held meetings on the subject from time to time, brought experts to town to discuss smoke abatement, and eventually appointed a committee, no serious effort was made to end it until the 1960s.

With such prevailing attitudes, there was little reason to expect a quick public response when air pollution problems became significantly more widespread in the 1950s. The case of Lewiston's paper mill is indicative. Local boosters had worked for decades to get the mill, charmed by the large and steady payrolls that it would bring to the community. In June 1949, the Lewiston *Morning Tribune* enthusiastically welcomed the announcement that Potlatch Forests Incorporated (PFI) planned to erect the large facility. The newspaper also noted that some smell would be involved, but assured its readers, "mechanical and natural processes" would minimize it.[20] In October, William Davis, PFI's president, admitted "there will be some odor, but it should not be too objectionable." He was confident that "people will rapidly get used to it and seldom notice it."[21] In December 1950, when the pulp mill went into production, the *Morning Tribune* claimed the smell "was scarcely noticed."[22]

Within days, the pall of sulfurous smoke brought cries of outrage. Joseph Ford of Clarkston, Washington (Lewiston's sister city across the Snake River), protested that he had moved from Los Angeles to enjoy clean air and demanded that the Lewiston City Council do something, "or I'm moving out." Although they took no action, several council members agreed with Ford that "the smell was indeed bad." Hearing that petitions were circulating, Councilman John Barlow said, "I'll sign every one of them."[23]

Lewiston's leaders, however, showed no signs of rushing to force PFI to reduce its air pollution. The *Morning Tribune* probably reflected local business opinion when it urged those who complained to remember that the company had warned about the smells. Besides, "the disagreeable and obvious should not obscure that which is good and far-reaching."[24] Albert Wilson, editor of *Pulp and Paper* magazine, visiting Lewiston in January 1951, reported that the industry was spending millions every year trying to eliminate the odors. In his opinion, the PFI mill was state of the art in emission controls.

PFI saw no reason to respond to the protests. Answering a query from the Lewiston City Council, the company's president sent the council a letter saying "in effect, that Lewiston must put up with the odor" or lose the industry.[25] At the end of January 1951, fifty people gathered to organize a committee to force PFI to "abate this public nuisance," but at their initial meeting, they were cautioned by H.C. Clare of the Idaho Department of Public Health: "I am inclined to agree that it will be impossible to eliminate odors from sulphate plants."[26] Ten days later, PFI brought Willis Van Horne of the Institute of Paper Chemistry to speak at a Lewiston dinner meeting and reassure the community, "your odor problem in Lewiston isn't as acute as it is in many kraft mill communities. The odor here," he concluded, "is not as intense or as all-pervading as many are."[27]

If a jury finding is a fair indication of community views, then it can be said that public opinion in the Lewiston area sustained the position taken by its local leaders. This occurred when a case arose based on the belief that existing law could be used to force PFI to curtail air pollution. At the initial meeting of the People's Association of the Lewiston-Clarkston Valley on March 8, Henry Felton, a local attorney, declared "any 100 of us can stop the pulp plant at Lewiston under provisions of Idaho law."[28] Nevertheless, more than four years elapsed before the first test case went to court. In April 1955, Clarkston attorney S. Dean Arnold brought suit against PFI in Asotin County court, alleging that fumes from its plant had blackened the paint on his house and caused he and his wife headaches and nausea. It took two and a half months to form a jury, but finally in mid-June the case was heard.

Speaking for his company, William Davis assured the court, "I never find any objectionable or disagreeable odors at the mill."[29] His defense attorney felt certain that chemical analyses would demonstrate "we have done everything humanly possible to eliminate the contention it is a nuisance."[30] The jury deliberated for four hours and awarded Arnold $7.50, based on the conclusion that PFI fumes accounted for only 1 percent of the total damage ($750 to repaint his house). The jury tacitly agreed with the defense—there was no evidence that the air pollution posed any hazard to public health.

The state only grudgingly moved to deal with growing air pollution problems brought by new factories in Lewiston, Pocatello, and Soda Springs. During its meeting in McCall in December 1956, the Idaho Wildlife Federation voted to propose to the 1957 legislature a bill to regulate air and stream pollution. The legislature did approve a three-person study committee, but it was only mandated "to see if all practical steps were being taken" toward abatement. Even then, industrial spokesmen "refuse[d] to allow the state to inspect their plants to prove it."[31]

The study committee recommended to the 1959 legislature that an Idaho Air Pollution Control Commission be set up under the Board of Health, but reactions to the proposal boded ill for the commission's effectiveness. On the one hand, PFI welcomed it, expecting it to "reduce the possibility of false fears and apprehensiveness." So said Robert Bundy, PFI's president, who went on to claim, "there has never been an indication of any accumulation of contaminants…around a pulp mill, which could even approach a condition harmful to health."[32] Senator Grant Young hoped the commission would "eliminate the causes of bad feeling and…bring together the people and the interests involved."[33]

On the other hand, Dan Emery, a member of Lewiston's anti-smog committee, castigated the enabling legislation as "a lovely little monstrosity—the work of a stacked committee" providing far too few enforcement powers.[34] And Terrell Carver, director of the Health Board, found it "cumbersome and unwieldy," wishing it had more representation from the public at large.[35] According to C.J. Hopkins, PFI secretary (and soon to be appointed to the commission), "it all depends on who is determining what is reasonable. That's like trying to determine how high is up."[36]

The Air Pollution Control Commission was, at best, a weak compromise. Speaking for conservationists, Sam Day conceded in the *Morning Tribune*, "it may not solve the problems of air pollution, but it will mark a start."[37] Representative Carl Moore of Lewiston expressed relief that "it will not frighten our industries out of the state or others from coming in."[38]

The commission turned out to be little more than a puppet of the industries it was supposed to control. Part of the problem was lack of funding. The legislature's Joint Finance and Appropriations Committee recommended an initial budget of $49,000, finally slashed to $6,000. In 1961 the commission received no state funding at all. Worse still, in the minds of some critics, such as Representative William Webster from the Coeur d'Alene area, the commission was "too weak and had no teeth."[39] Its members tended to combine an understandable caution, wanting to gather as many facts as possible before making judgments, with a supercilious attitude toward public impatience. When the commission held its first meeting in Lewiston in December 1959, local activists asked that PFI be recognized as "the chief source of air contamination in this valley," creating, in Henry Felton's words, a "stinking mess."[40] In response, J. Blaine Anderson of Blackfoot, the commission chairman, insisted that its first task was solely to learn about air pollution problems throughout the state.

In June 1961, when citizens kept pressing for action, M.L. Jackson, professor of chemical engineering at the University of Idaho and acting commission chairman, haughtily wrote the *Morning Tribune*: "I think most of the people don't know what they're talking about."[41]

The commission, during its meeting in Pocatello in March 1960, had proved no more responsive to public concerns in eastern Idaho. The Georgetown

Village Board complained that the Central Farmers Fertilizer Company plant near their community emitted noxious fumes and odors. Although the board had met with the company on several occasions and were assured that something would be done, nothing changed. In response, company spokesmen said they had installed the most modern equipment and continued to work on the problem. What that work amounted to remained unclear, but neither Central Farmers nor most other Idaho industrialists at the time were willing to spend the significant amounts of cash needed to control pollution. Typically, at the same meeting, Wyman Zachary, representing Brown Tie and Lumber Company of McCall, admitted that its sawmill emitted some burning sawdust, but protested that adequate precipitation facilities to end the problem would cost $200,000, which he insisted was far beyond the company's means.

Consequently, little happened over the years. In January 1967, the Pocatello *Idaho State Journal* published an article focusing on the commission's accomplishments, and found that after seven years, "air pollution control in this state is non-existent." Attempting to explain why, Dr. Ray Swanson claimed that the state did not have the resources to develop standards and would have to rely on the federal government to do it, predicting that it would be "a long, long time before any standards are set up in Idaho."[42]

Despite Swanson's prognostications and the commission's open hostility, the federal government already had stepped in to enforce pollution abatement in the Lewiston area. Frustrated with the failure of PFI and local Idaho authorities to take complaints seriously, Clarkston mayor Bill Courtney called for federal intervention on the grounds that this was an interstate issue. Two air pollution specialists from the U.S. Public Health Service (PHS) arrived for an initial survey in June 1961. PFI had cause to worry. Although PHS planned an extensive study before deciding on any abatement orders, it began with the assumption that "there is no air pollution that can't be controlled... if you spend the money."[43] In July 1963, the Public Health Service issued a preliminary report, running to 404 pages, with the bottom line summarized in a Lewiston *Morning Tribune* headline: "Valley Air Polluted; PFI Pulp Mill Named Main Source."[44]

Typical of Idahoan readiness to resent federal "interference," state officials expressed reservations about the preliminary report. Governor Robert E. Smylie doubted any need for enforcement proceedings, emphasizing that "PFI is a leader in the field of developing effective mechanisms for control of the problem."[45]

When the final report appeared in December 1963, it found no welcome at the state capitol. The Idaho Air Pollution Control Commission angrily rejected the PHS findings. Its chairman, Boise attorney Jess Hawley, claimed "various parts of the report are full of innuendo, conjecture, [and] unwarranted conclusions unsupported by the facts." The completeness of the commission's denial is indicated in the comment by commission member Frank Hendrickson of Soda Springs: "just because there is something in the air, we can't say there is an air-pollution problem."[46] Dr. Terrell Carver, director of the State Board of Health, announced that the health issue was moot: "the question of whether there is pollution depends a lot on what your definition of air pollution is."[47]

Undeterred by the hostility of officials in Boise, the Public Health Service moved ahead. Although the Lewiston City Council initially refused to participate in a regional air-pollution control commission as recommended by the PHS, the federal Clean Air Act of 1965 gave the PHS authority to enforce its abatement orders. It gained strong local support from the *Morning Tribune*, which had reversed its previous position and began a vigorous campaign for effective air pollution controls. An editorial by Bill Hall in December 1965 noted increasing problems in Pocatello and Soda Springs, as well as in Lewiston. Hall conceded, "the air cannot be cleaned overnight," but he concluded, "the dangers are such that it can't wait forever."[48] After holding a series of hearings in Lewiston and Clarkston, the PHS issued its abatement recommendations in March 1967, which included requiring PFI to implement "stringent methods" for controlling emissions by the year's end and stopping all open burning in the area within six months.[49]

Meanwhile, pressures elsewhere in Idaho built to the point where the legislature had to act. During the 1967 session, it heard compelling testimony about the seriousness of air pollution in southeastern Idaho, particularly regarding phosphate plants. "I'm concerned about the health of my family," said Richard Torgeson, a Caribou County farmer. "I have been out when you couldn't drive, you couldn't turn the heater or the defroster on. If you did, you would choke."[50] Soda Springs mayor Chris Phelps warned, "if something isn't done our county cannot exist as it does today."[51] Recognizing the implications of the federal Clean Air Act, the legislature realized that if it didn't do something, "this is a case where the federal government does come in and step on our toes," as Representative Edward Williams of Lewiston put it.[52] Consequently, the legislature passed a bill reforming the Idaho Air Pollution Control Commission, putting it under the Board of Health's direction and giving it a much larger budget and significantly stronger enforcement powers.

The spring of 1967 also marked a major change in the way Idaho dealt with water pollution. In March, Idaho's Board of Health began a series of meetings around the state to gain public input regarding water quality standards. According to the federal Water Quality Act of 1965, those standards had to be established for interstate streams by July 1, 1967. Anyone under the illusion that effective water pollution control was already implemented in Idaho would have found the testimony at those meetings very disheartening. In May the board received a petition, signed by 1,179 Blackfoot area residents, protesting that the Snake River downstream from Idaho Falls "looks and smells like a gigantic sewer."[53] Quite clearly, "Idaho Still Has Water Pollution," to quote the title of an editorial published by the Idaho Falls *Post-Register* in September.[54]

What happened? What became of the progress in sewage treatment during the 1950s? The answer, which Idahoans did not really begin to cope with until the mid-1960s, was that the primary treatment plants built during the 1950s by communities around the state did not, by themselves, end water pollution. Primary treatment, which relied on settling ponds, sharply reduced solid matter in sewage, but did almost nothing to remove organic substances dissolved in the water. Until secondary treatment was added, the E. coli and other bacteria in "treated sewage" continued to pose public health hazards, while fish kills demonstrated that organic wastes were dangerous to river life.

In addition, a growing body of evidence proved that other water pollution abatement efforts had to be coordinated with municipal sewage treatment if the state hoped to attain an acceptable level of purity in its waters. Industrialization in southern Idaho involved far more than phosphate plants. Potato processors dumped huge quantities of waste into rivers. Slaughterhouses and canneries added effluents. Then there was the previously unrecognized effect of phosphates in household detergents, which rivers churned into foaming suds, sometimes rising three or four feet high and running for miles downstream. Farmers had to confront the dangers of fertilizers in irrigation water, while ranchers began to hear of water pollution caused by feedlots. Finally, pollution from motorboats and untreated sewage from lakeside cabins threatened Idaho's large lakes.

In the early 1960s, state authorities struggled to deal with water pollution from all these sources primarily through public education and moral suasion. Hearing of the growing contamination of Lake Coeur d'Alene, the Board of Health suggested in August 1961 that the three counties directly involved work jointly to control the problem. Later that year, the *Times-News* concluded its editorial on a conference regarding stream pollution in the Twin Falls area by asking for a "good, enforceable law."[55] Seeing no response to that call, the editor feared it would take "some sort of epidemic, originating with the river, that would result in a number of deaths" to stimulate public demand for laws requiring water pollution abatement.[56]

Without tougher enforcement measures, the Board of Health formed a watchdog panel of volunteers to keep up the pressure on communities and industries to reduce water pollution. Thus the board appointed the Water Pollution Control Advisory Council in June 1962 to study pollution problems and make recommendations to the Board of Health. Its membership clearly meant to take its mission seriously. In addition to prominent businessmen, the original nine members included the perennial conservationist, Bruce Bowler, as well as Robert Salter, assistant director of the Fish and Game Department, and Herbert Derrick, city manager of Twin Falls and a vocal pollution control advocate. But the prevailing stance was anything but punitive. "A firm attitude for pollution control is the only one," as the Idaho Falls *Post-Register* put it, "but the complexity of the problem invites understanding."[57] The response of the Health Board in May 1965 to an appeal from PFI for patience illustrated this. William Gray, vice president for pulp and paper, stated his confidence that "we will eventually have the technology to eliminate virtually all air and water pollution." Dr. Paul Ellis, the Health Board chairman, replied, "I'm satisfied they're doing everything they can as fast as they can."[58]

Three months later at an advisory council meeting in Coeur d'Alene, Herb Derrick responded to queries about the council's achievements: "we have done about what we set out to do and this is quite a lot."[59] More than $27 million was spent in Idaho since 1948 to reduce water pollution. By 1965, the council reported to the governor, 93 percent of Idaho towns and cities had sewage treatment plants, up from 3 percent in 1935. The potato industry spent about $2.5 million in primary treatment, with a 55 percent reduction of pollutants dumped into streams.

Nevertheless, as the Lewiston *Morning Tribune* justifiably concluded in an October 1965 editorial, "it is becoming increasingly clear that it will take nothing less than the full force of the federal government to control water pollution in the United States," because "pollution is increasing faster than the ability of either states or commissions to control it."[60] Two years later, motivated by provisions of the Water Quality Act, Idaho was one of the first ten states to have its water pollution abatement plan approved by the U.S. Department of the Interior. The plan was ambitious indeed, aiming to build over the next six years secondary treatment plants for all municipal sewage and "a comparable degree of treatment for industrial wastes."[61]

The attitudinal changes toward air and water pollution becoming evident in 1967 were not merely submissive responses to federal legislation and administrative policies. The laws certainly had an impact, and several federal departments were applying whatever pressure they could to bring about pollution abatement in Idaho. In late 1967, for example, the Department of Housing and Urban Development informed Ada County it would receive no more grants until sewer service was completed for Boise's suburbs. But Idahoans were growing concerned about pollution problems even when there was no federal pushing.

This increasing awareness felt by many Idahoans was clearly evident when the issue of dredging cropped up again in early 1968. After the Finch case in 1957 (discussed in Chapter VII), little was heard about dredgers for more than a decade, presumably because the market for gold and uranium fell off to the point where dredging was uneconomical. But in January 1968, conservationists faced a new threat from a dredging proposal, this time on the upper reaches of the St. Joe River east of St. Maries. When the Land Board received a request for a dredging permit from the Idaho Mining Company of Missoula, the board scheduled a hearing in Wallace for February 1.

Times assuredly had changed. In the mid-1950s, the press tended to ignore the anti-dredge initiative, and business groups frequently were disinclined to support wildlifers. In 1968, on the other hand, the prospect of dredging the St. Joe prompted press coverage throughout the state and vociferous opposition from business associations. The Coeur d'Alene Chamber of Commerce, for example, voted its disapproval of the dredging proposal and authorized a delegation to attend the Wallace hearing. Roger Carlson, its president, explained, "the St. Joe is one of the most beautiful rivers in America and is a haven for fishermen and an ever-increasing number of outdoor people. We hope to keep it that way."[62] The Boise *Statesman* declared that the Land Board "will be acting against the will of the people and in violation of its trust over Idaho streams if it approves" this proposal.[63] By early February, the *Statesman* and the *Post-Register* were calling for much stronger controls on all dredging in the state.

In the 1950s, dredging opponents fought for terrain restoration after the dredgers were done. Now, they questioned whether it should be permitted at all. "We doubt," the *Statesman* declared, "that it is possible to restore a stream, once dredged, to anything approaching its original state."[64] "Only the most overriding national interest in the most selected places would warrant consideration of dredge mining" stated the *Post-Register*.[65]

Idaho lawmakers had an unusual opportunity to respond quickly to the demand for revisions in the dredge control law. Although the legislature usually met just in odd-numbered years, the governor already had called a special session for early February 1968. Responding to the public outcry, Governor Don Samuelson amended the special session's agenda to include dredge mining. The House quickly passed amendments so restrictive that it was questionable whether any dredging could meet the new requirements. In the Senate, however, Sam Kaufman, a Republican senator from Boise (and an attorney who represented the Idaho Mining Association) persuaded his colleagues to restrict the law to public land. When Democrats voted the bill down on the grounds that it would emasculate all dredge controls in Idaho, Samuelson blamed the Democrats for disappointing public expectations. Cy Chase, former state senator from St. Maries, struck back, calling the governor "reckless and irresponsible" in his comments.[66] That exchange was only the beginning of what became a crucial development in Idaho politics, eventually leading to the White Clouds dispute.

The dredge issue gained considerable attention from the press over the next year. An initiative to tighten dredge regulations was drafted by Scott Reed of Coeur d'Alene and circulated statewide by wildlifers and a sponsoring organization led by Robert Hammes, publisher of the St. Maries paper. Secretary of State Pete Cenarussa refused to place the initiative on the ballot because the state constitution allowed initiatives only in years when a governor was being elected, and this was an off year. When appealed, the state supreme court sustained Cenarussa's decision. In early 1969, the legislature hammered out an amended dredge control law that Art Manley of the IWF assured conservationists responded to their concerns. The struggle revealed for the first time a growing chasm between Governor Samuelson, an active wildlifer for many years, and the state's conservationists, who increasingly saw him as a willing tool of those determined to exploit natural resources regardless of environmental degradation.

Ironically, the polarization that developed between Samuelson and his erstwhile IWF friends was not inevitable. Initially, it was the legislature, not the governor, that took the heat from those angry about the special session's lack of action. The failure to pass a tougher dredge control law "reflects a strange detachment from the temper of public feeling," stated the Idaho Falls *Post-Register*.[67] And while some state officials, particularly Mining Inspector O.T. Hansen, were publicly unsympathetic to the environmentalist viewpoint, Samuelson might have distanced himself from such a position. But he did not.

Samuelson allowed himself to be portrayed as the villain in the eyes of an increasingly conservation-minded public. "Bluntly put," Robert Hammes angrily ended a St. Maries *Gazette-Record* editorial, "Governor Samuelson is either dumb or dishonest" in the matter of why the special session failed to act.[68] At the Idaho Wildlife Federation annual convention in Lewiston in April 1968, Scott Reed ended a speech on the anti-dredge movement's history by claiming Samuelson "has practically adopted the language" of O.T. Hansen.[69] Several newspapers took up the refrain in November when the Governor's Conference on Natural Resources concluded that dredging should be "encouraged and stimulated."[70] The *Statesman* dismissed as "unacceptable" the conference's aim to limit restrictions only to mining company assurances that they would strive for "reasonable reclamation and water clarity."[71] The proper test of a dredge mining law "is not whether the law is satisfactory to the mining companies," the *Morning Tribune* argued, but "whether it will do the job."[72]

The polarization had become almost unbridgeable by the time the legislature took up dredge control in February 1969. Pierre Pulling, an ardent environmentalist, called all dredgers spoilers and their business "a disgrace [that] ought to be wiped out." On the other side, Mining Inspector Hansen defended dredge mining, asserting that tourism produced no "tangible, taxable good," while dredges did.[73] To which, the *Morning-Tribune*'s Bill Hall retorted, "you can look at a mountain for a long time without wearing it out."[74] The Pocatello *Idaho State Journal* encapsulated the situation with two quotations.

The first was from Tony Park, who had represented the initiative's backers: "I don't think any bill [the lawmakers] will pass will satisfy the mining interests." The second came from Eugene Anderson, who drafted the bill favored by the Idaho Mining Association: "there are a lot of people who want to prohibit dredge or placer mining. Nothing can satisfy them."[75]

Samuelson did little or nothing to counter the idea that Hansen spoke for his administration. In fact, as will be seen in Chapter XII, he made a growing number of speeches seeming to confirm that, faced with a choice between supporting mining or conservationists, he backed miners. By July 1970, things evolved to where the *Statesman* even questioned the governor's right to participate in Land Board decisions regarding dredging questions: "both the governor and the attorney general are too closely allied to mining interests to represent the people of Idaho on dredge mining questions. They are too inclined to see streams as fodder for a dredger, rather than as natural assets worth protecting for public use."[76] Why Samuelson drifted so far away from wildlifers remains a mystery, perhaps only answerable by some future biographer. Certainly his own autobiography[77] sheds no light on the question.

Meanwhile, the Senate's Cecil Andrus took this opportunity to make his move toward winning the backing of conservationists. Up to the beginning of 1970, Andrus had no particular standing with them. On several important issues in the past, he had even been on the opposite side—he opposed the Wilderness Bill in the early 1960s; he backed power development proponents in Hells Canyon; and he opposed wild-river status for the Salmon River's main stem. But in January 1970, he introduced a bill in the Idaho Senate that would ban dredging on all designated wild rivers.

The bill passed the Senate 18-15 over the protests of such Republicans as Warren Brown of McCall, who insisted that "the state must have industries that use our natural resources. This state cannot survive on the income from the tourist alone."[78] "When it comes to a showdown," the *Statesman* grumbled, "almost all the GOP senators obediently line up with the mining lobby."[79] After a series of parliamentary maneuvers, the House finally passed Andrus's bill, "which gave conservationists one of the few victories [to] emerge from this legislative session."[80]

While dredging was an issue in Idaho without noticeable federal input, worry over the safety of radioactive wastes at the National Reactor Testing Station (NRTS) between Arco and Idaho Falls was one that the Atomic Energy Commission (AEC) did everything it could to dismiss. The NRTS was located at the former naval gunnery range in 1949 because the lava plains seemed otherwise useless. For the same reason, no significant protests emerged as the station's boundaries greatly expanded in the subsequent decade. Business leaders welcomed the massive revenue that came with the NRTS, eventually involving several thousand highly paid employees and billions of dollars in capital expenditures. To this day, it is by far the largest employer in eastern Idaho.

The Atomic Energy Commission repeatedly reassured Idahoans that radioactivity posed no threat to anyone outside the station's bounds. Highly trained specialists with impressive technical credentials detailed all the safety precautions taken, including the site's very extensive boundaries. Waste disposal was "relatively no more complicated than ordinary sewage disposal," two AEC engineers told a Boise conference in 1956. "There is no problem," they assured listeners, "that cannot be solved."[81] Although AEC officials conceded they did not yet know how to handle all long-term aspects of radioactive waste, they suggested that disposal was no more than a "pesky chore," that "time and testing, in Idaho and elsewhere, is the formula that scientists are confident will provide the answer."[82]

For twenty years, the AEC succeeded in efforts to allay public fears. No one sounded any alarm when it announced in May 1960 that the Idaho site was one of two selected for interim burial of wastes from AEC licensees. As late as September 1969, William Ginkel, NRTS manager, dismissed questions from reporters about the dangers of buried wastes: "we have substantial, technical experience. There's no real or potential basis for alarm—ever."[83]

Those questions were provoked by the allegations of Robert Erkins that the waste material posed a grave threat to the Snake River aquifer, which lay beneath the site. After learning that large quantities of nuclear waste were being received from the Rocky Flats facility in Colorado, Erkins wrote the governor expressing his concern. A Hagerman trout farmer, Erkins lived more than a hundred miles away from the NRTS, but he feared that radioactive material would seep into the aquifer, run underground, and resurface at Hagerman's Thousand Springs.

Michael Christie, head of Idaho Health Department's radiological section, reflected the prevailing view among specialists: "the only danger would be if the stuff ever got away. I'm sure it is not going to do that."[84] But what if it did, the uninformed public asked? A *Statesman* editorial's answer expressed the opinion of many readers: "if there is a chance of a rainstorm even once in 100 years that would wash the solid wastes into the aquifer, it would be too much of a chance to take."[85]

Many were beginning to share Erkins' skepticism. "I have learned through sad experience in recent years that much of the 'scientific statements' are in the end at best only 'wishful hopes,'" stated Gus Kelker in the Twin Falls *Times-News*.[86] Fearing that, if Erkins was correct, and the Twin Falls water supply would be endangered, the *Times-News* urged, "Let's Move Now."[87] Governor Samuelson appointed a special task force to study the question, while Senator Frank Church asked that the site's waste disposal be studied by four federal agencies, including the Water Pollution Control Administration.

Skepticism turned to distrust in March 1970 with the release, at Church's insistence, of a report completed in 1966 by a National Academy of Science special committee. The reason the AEC previously had refused to release the report was immediately obvious. Although the committee found no immediate hazard from atomic waste burial in the Idaho desert, it concluded that the practice would eventually lead to "serious fouling of the environment."[88] The AEC insisted that the report was acted upon, just not published. But even the Idaho Falls *Post-Register*, which had always tried to put the best possible light on NRTS actions, responded in an editorial tellingly titled "Mobile Graveyard" that "the late, late disclosure of the report is all too characteristic of the AEC and its public information policies."[89]

The story of how Idaho dealt with this newly discovered pollution challenge warrants a whole separate study, but initial reactions reflected a major change in how Idahoans thought about pollution. Until the mid-1960s, the focus almost always had been on particular kinds of pollution—air, water, and so on. And the fight to control it frequently met a flood of technical jargon from the involved economic interests, justifying prevailing practices, but also implying that critics did not know enough to make meaningful comments.

By 1967, however, there was a growing tendency to take a broader view—to talk about the combined impact of various kinds of pollution. When the *Morning Tribune* considered a proposal to locate an aluminum plant nearby, it noted that the Lewiston valley was "pollution-prone because of its geography and air currents."[90] The following year, the Idaho Falls *Post-Register* pointed to "a curious complexity in how irrigation will be affected" by water pollution standards.[91] An October 1968 article in the *Statesman* about the impact of burning wastes quoted Lyle Stanford, a College of Idaho biology professor: "we quite commonly do allow dissipation and misuse of whole segments and aggregations of environment." His solution? "A necessary, great new concept of environment must be to consider it as a public resource."[92]

Such a consideration came slowly. Governor Smylie spoke of it in May 1966, noting it was time to move beyond a "scattergun approach," and he called for "environmental conservation,"[93] but it would take another two or three years before most Idahoans were ready to respond to that call. In October 1968, the *Post-Register* found a "nagging defect" in the fight against air and water pollution because there was no combined view of "total resource management."[94] In April 1969, the *Statesman* reflected on a state-sponsored conference on the environment, concluding, "every community also faces a challenge in enhancing and protecting its environment."[95] That same month, Senator Church pleaded the case for a "new conservation" in a speech at Coeur d'Alene. The old conservation, he said, mainly focused on forests and soils. "Today we face the total task of achieving nothing less than a healthy and habitable environment."[96]

By January 1970, "all of a sudden," the St. Maries *Gazette-Record* observed, "'environment' is a key word in political speeches."[97] And not just those of a more liberal stripe talked that way. The Idaho Environmental Council (founded in January 1969), of course, repeatedly took to task those who failed to show a full commitment to protecting the environment, and Scott Reed told Coeur d'Alene wildlifers that they needed to avoid leaving our children "in environmental bankruptcy."[98] But conservative Republicans also were saying much the same thing. James McClure, the U.S representative from Idaho's First District, told a GOP women's luncheon in Boise, "We need quiet, steadfast determination to correct the [environmental] problems in this country."[99]

Even leading industrialists began falling into line. Chairman L.J. Randall of the Hecla Mining Company, a major Silver Valley firm, told a University of Idaho audience in November 1969 that the days of fouling "our streams and polluting the air are past."[100] In January 1970, Jack Simplot announced "from now on, environmental control will receive top priority and every employee in the company will be encouraged to get involved."[101]

This did not suddenly spell the end of pollution problems in Idaho, but it ushered in a dramatically different attitude over how to proceed. In mid-April 1970, Simplot spoke with Highland High School students in Pocatello, candidly confessing, "we've known for 25 years that we have to do something about air pollution, but nobody made us do it."[102] Now someone was, namely Robert Robson, the state's attorney general. Though a conservative Republican and political cohort of Governor Samuelson's, Robson made it clear that he would, if necessary, take polluters to court. In August 1969, he met with city officials in the Silver Valley, focusing on the continued dumping of raw sewage into the South Fork of the Coeur d'Alene River. "I am in a position where I have to enforce the law," he warned listeners, "and it may mean shutting down this county industrially and domestically."[103] Robson took a similarly uncompromising stance toward Payette Lake's sewage pollution, and in July 1970 he sued the Amalgamated Sugar Company in Twin Falls for its unabated degradation of Rock Creek.

Although a judge dismissed the Amalgamated Sugar case on grounds that administrative remedies were yet to be exhausted, the fact remains that Idaho, by this time, had entered a new era where the public demanded strict enforcement of pollution control regulations. (Meanwhile, in the nation's capitol, the National Environmental Policy Act of 1969 was proceeding through the Congress, to be signed by President Richard Nixon on January 1, 1970.)

Symbolically, a special Idaho commission that was considering making revisions to the state constitution was encouraged to include an "environmental bill of rights." Proposed by the fledgling Idaho Environmental Council in October 1969, this "environmental bill of rights" would guarantee all Idahoans the right to clean air and water, freedom from excessive noise, plus a policy commitment to preserve the state's scenic beauty and historical heritage. Several newspapers around the state printed an Associated Press report on the proposal. Conceding that this might have been a radical idea in the past, the *Statesman* believed that the time had come when "the central idea that the people have a right to enjoy a decent environment should be acceptable."[104] Patricia McDermott, state representative from Pocatello, asked the commission to include the environmental bill of rights in its proposed changes.

Nothing came of the IEC's proposal, but its cries for environmental attention soon echoed throughout the state. The Pocatello *Idaho State Journal* quoted the IEC's view of impending crisis in December 1969: "our very survival depends largely on how well and how soon met are the problems of pollution, ecological disruption, depletion, overpopulation and loss of open space which plague the nation."[105] Such sentiments, of course, were standard fare in the nation's metropolitan centers, but now they also were being voiced in conservative, small-town Idaho. In March 1970, the *News-Bulletin* in Sandpoint (Samuelson's hometown) printed an editorial lamenting, "Idaho's natural environment has suffered tremendous damage for generations and the pace of that damage is constantly accelerating." The time was long past, the editorial went on, to merely sound the alarm. "We must recognize that we are not immune to the worldwide environmental threat," and must care for our land, water, and air "in a much more constructive manner than we have in the past."[106]

When Attorney General Robson warned the Silver Valley that he would go to court if it did not clean up the Coeur d'Alene River, he began with the accusation, "Shoshone County has not joined the State of Idaho." The state had now joined the nation in environmental awareness.

Conclusive proof came with the observance of the first Earth Day on April 22, 1970. Originally conceived by Senator Gaylord Nelson of Wisconsin, it was celebrated in Idaho no less enthusiastically than anywhere else across the country. Teach-ins were held in colleges and many high schools. Elementary school children made posters and listened to presentations scaled to their grade level. In Coeur d'Alene, a Forest Service official talked to students at Harding Elementary School about Smokey the Bear. In Idaho Falls, three hundred students at Skyline High School joined a bicycle brigade to dramatize the pollution dangers of automobiles. In Boise, radio station KGEM moved its transmitter to the city dump to draw attention to the problem of solid waste disposal. Schoolchildren almost everywhere did their bit by collecting litter. In a speech at Idaho State University, Frank Church called for "a major national commitment" to clean up the environment and "reverse this disastrous pattern of migration" into the cities by rejuvenating small town and rural America.[107] Pocatello City Councilman Perry Swisher pointed to the "failure to do something about tertiary [sewage] treatment, which is killing us."[108]

There were a few naysayers. Albert Carlson, president of Idaho Power, thought the ecology issue "generates more emotion than intelligent discussion."[109] Lou Kriston, editor of the Challis *Messenger,* warned, "attempting to curb pollution by curbing development and progress is no real answer... Let's not stop the construction of power plants, but improve them."[110]

But the passion for environmental concern was so great, it even swept up Samuelson. Idahoans, he wrote in an article published by the Priest River *Times,* "recognize more and more deeply that man must manage his activities so as to complement, rather than destroy, his natural environment."[111]

The environment had become "The One Big Issue," former Governor Smylie wrote in his column. He noted the "apparent failure" of politicians to understand the "depth of the public's new interest" in the topic. "The old order is changing" in Idaho. "We are much more jealous about what people do or permit to be done to the good earth around us." He believed that 1970 "marks some sort of great divide in the consideration of environmental issues." He pointed to the controversy over the White Clouds as "probably the bell-ringer."[112]

ENDNOTES

1. For the national reactions to *Silent Spring* see Frank Graham Jr., *Since Silent Spring* (Boston: Houghton-Mifflin, 1970).
2. "Pesticide Furor," editorial in Boise *Statesman* (December 14, 1962): p. 6.
3. "Secret Weapon Against Bugs," editorial in Twin Falls *Times-News* (July 2, 1945): p. 4.
4. "The Pesticides Problem," editorial in Boise *Statesman* (May 17, 1963): p. 4.
5. "The Cautious Spray in Targhee," editorial in Idaho Falls *Post-Register* (June 24, 1963): p. 4.
6. "Forest Service Discloses Insect Control and Research Plans," Challis *Messenger* (May 21, 1964): p. 10.
7. Salmon *Recorder-Herald* (June 4, 1954): p. 4.
8. "Forest Spray Plans Given Chamber OK," Salmon *Recorder-Herald* (June 11, 1964): p. 1.
9. "Saving the Timber," editorial in Boise *Statesman* (June 10, 1964): p. 4.
10. "500 Protest DDT Spray on Forests," Boise *Statesman* (November 12, 1964): p. 15.
11. "Disturbing Factor," editorial in Twin Falls *Times-News* (June 23, 1964): p. 4.
12. "Idaho Forester Sees Spraying as 'Necessity,'" Salmon *Recorder-Herald* (July 9, 1964): pp. 1, 5.
13. "Fear of Pesticides," editorial in Salmon *Recorder-Herald* (August 20, 1964): p. 4.
14. "No Silent Spring?" editorial in Twin Falls *Times-News* (June 10, 1965): p. 4.
15. "More Evidence in Case Against DDT," editorial in Lewiston *Morning Tribune* (January 6, 1969): p. 4.
16. "Idaho Should Ban Use of DDT," editorial in Boise *Statesman* (July 15, 1969): p. 4.
17. "City Can Do without DDT," editorial in Boise *Statesman* (January 22, 1970): p. 4.
18. "The Smoke Nuisance," editorial in Boise *Capital News* (November 20, 1923): p. 4.
19. "Smoke Nuisance," editorial in Boise *Statesman* (February 18, 1938): p. 4.
20. "Announces Plans for $12-Million Paper Pulp Mill," Lewiston *Morning Tribune* (June 21, 1949): p. 12.
21. "New PFI Chief Says Challenge Offered by Pulp-Paper Project," Lewiston *Morning Tribune* (October 7, 1949): p. 16.
22. "PFI Pulp and Paper Mill Starts Production," Lewiston *Morning Tribune* (December 29, 1950): p. 12.
23. "Council Hears Angry Protest over Pulp Smell," Lewiston *Morning Tribune* (January 3, 1951): p. 12.

24. "A Link to Our Future," editorial in Lewiston *Morning Tribune* (January 7, 1951): p. 4.
25. "Odor from Pulp Mill Will Stay if PFI Is to Continue, Davis Says," Lewiston *Morning Tribune* (January 23, 1951): p. 12.
26. "Group Hits Pulp Mill Nuisance in Opening Abatement Campaign," Lewiston *Morning Tribune* (February 1, 1951): p. 16.
27. "PFI Doing All It Can to Minimize Odor of Pulp, Paper Chemist Says," Lewiston *Morning Tribune* (February 10, 1951): p. 10.
28. "Anti-Pulp Smell Group Organizes as Valley People's Association," Lewiston *Morning Tribune* (March 9, 1951): p. 10.
29. "Jury Hears Description of PFI Methods of Producing Pulp Paper," Lewiston *Morning Tribune* (June 15, 1955): p. 16.
30. "Jury Denies Motion to Dismiss Arnold Damage Suit Against PFI," Lewiston *Morning Tribune* (June 16, 1955): pp. 1, 10.
31. "Little Chance Is Reported for Bill on Air Pollution," Boise *Statesman* (March 1, 1957): p. 16.
32. "PFI Says It Would Like State Air Pollution Law," Lewiston *Morning Tribune* (January 24, 1959): pp. 1, 3.
33. John Corlett, "Air Pollution Bill Voted by Senate," Boise *Statesman* (February 3, 1959): p. 5.
34. "Solons Promise They Will Push Pollution Bill," Lewiston *Morning Tribune* (January 25, 1959): p. 12.
35. "Air Pollution Bills Said Unnecessary," Boise *Statesman* (February 14, 1959): p. 16.
36. Sam Day, "Health Board Now Has the Authority to Control Air Pollution—Carver," Lewiston *Morning Tribune* (February 14, 1959): pp. 12, 8.
37. SHD, "A Display of the Art of Compromise," editorial in Lewiston *Morning Tribune* (February 26, 1959): p. 4.
38. "Unanimous Vote Given Air Pollution," Boise *Statesman* (February 27, 1959): p. 7.
39. "Proof Asked on Pollution," Lewiston *Morning Tribune* (May 19, 1961): p. 14.
40. "State Asked to Order PFI to Cut Fumes or Shut Plant," Lewiston *Morning Tribune* (December 12, 1959): pp. 12, 5; "State Air Pollution Commission Runs into Smoggy Controversy," Pocatello *Idaho State Journal* (December 12, 1959): p. 22.
41. "Public Needs Pollution Facts, Not Fiction, Says Chief," Lewiston *Morning Tribune* (June 8, 1961): p. 6.
42. Larry Bacon, "Air Pollution Commission? It Sounds Good on Paper," Pocatello *Idaho State Journal* (January 23, 1967): p. 3.
43. "Health Officers to Prepare Plan for City Air Pollution Study," Lewiston *Morning Tribune* (June 7, 1961): p. 6.
44. Sam Day, "Valley Air Polluted: PFI Pulp Mill Named Main Source," Lewiston *Morning Tribune* (July 10, 1963): pp. 14, 10.
45. Sylvia Herrell, "Industry Pollution Cooperation Beats Regulation, Smylie Says," Lewiston *Morning Tribune* (July 12, 1963): p. 16.
46. "U.S. Air Pollution Report on Lewiston-Clarkston Incenses State Commission," Boise *Statesman* (December 18, 1963): p. 24.
47. "Whether Air Pollution Here Is a Health Hazard Is Moot Question—Dr. Carver," Lewiston *Morning Tribune* (December 17, 1963): p. 9.
48. B.H., "A Public Approach to Air Pollution," Lewiston *Morning Tribune* (December 4, 1965): p. 4.
49. "Recommendation Issued for Pollution Abatement," Lewiston *Morning Tribune* (March 3, 1967): pp. 20, 12.
50. "Delegates from Caribou County Plead with Lawmakers for Clean Air Assist," Boise *Statesman* (February 17, 1967): p. 12.
51. "Soda Springs Delegation Tells Effects of Air Pollution in Area," Pocatello *Idaho State Journal* (February 17, 1967): p. 2.
52. "Measure for Air Pollution Control Passes House after Debate, 48-16," Boise *Statesman* (March 2, 1967): p. 10.
53. "Board Receives Complaint about Snake River Pollution," Lewiston *Morning Tribune* (May 5, 1967): pp. 24, 19.
54. "Idaho Still Has Water Pollution," editorial in Idaho Falls *Post-Register* (September 18, 1967): p. 4.

55. "Any Teeth?" editorial in Twin Falls *Times-News* (November 20, 1961): p. 4.
56. "Unless Demanded," editorial in Twin Falls *Times-News* (January 26, 1962): p. 4.
57. "Waste Disposal—Necessary but Complex," editorial in Idaho Falls *Post-Register* (November 5, 1962): p. 4.
58. "Board Told Pollution Control Will Improve with Technology," Lewiston *Morning Tribune* (May 15, 1965): p. 14, 9.
59. "Board Favors Tougher Stand," Coeur d'Alene *Press* (August 25, 1965): p. 1.
60. "A Crash Program to Fight Pollution?" editorial in Lewiston *Morning Tribune* (October 18, 1965): p. 4.
61. "Six-Year Water Pollution Program Opens in Idaho," Idaho Falls *Post-Register* (October 11, 1967): p. 22.
62. "C-C Directors Oppose Dredging of St. Joe," Coeur d'Alene *Press* (January 18, 1968): p. 1.
63. "Rivers Should Be Protected," editorial in Boise *Statesman* (January 29, 1968): p. 4.
64. "Stronger Dredge Law Needed," editorial in Boise *Statesman* (February 3, 1968): p. 4.
65. "Idaho Should Change Mine Law," Idaho Falls *Post-Register* (February 6, 1968): p. 4.
66. "Samuelson and GOP Senators Irk Chase," Coeur d'Alene *Press* (February 12, 1968): p. 12.
67. "The Dredge Temper," editorial in Idaho Falls *Post-Register* (February 18, 1968): p. 4.
68. "One of Two Conclusions Is Valid," editorial in St. Maries *Gazette-Record* (February 22, 1968): p. 12.
69. "Federation Members Seek Controls on Gem Dredging," Boise *Statesman* (April 4, 1968): p. C6.
70. "Governor's Conference Endorses Dredging," Pocatello *Idaho State Journal* (November 4, 1968): p. B1.
71. "Stand for Dredge Mining," editorial in Boise *Statesman* (November 6, 1968): p. 4.
72. "Another Chance at Dredge Control," editorial in Lewiston *Morning Tribune* (January 20, 1969): p. 4.
73. "Debate Pitched at Dredge Mining Hearing," Idaho Falls *Post-Register* (February 14, 1969): p. 1.
74. Bill Hall, "Tourism Doesn't Ravage Rivers," editorial in Lewiston *Morning Tribune* (February 23, 1969): p. 4.
75. "Senate Chairman Says Compromise Likely on Dredge Mining Legislation," Pocatello *Idaho State Journal* (February 17, 1969): p. B6.
76. "Board Should Have Acted Sooner," editorial in Boise *Statesman* (July 29, 1970): p. 4.
77. Don W. Samuelson, *His Hand on My Shoulder: A Life Story of Hunting, Fishing, Love and Politics* (Sandpoint, Id.: ParBest and Dickens, 1993).
78. "Bill Passed to Restrict Dredging," Boise *Statesman* (February 14, 1970): p. 10.
79. "State GOP Backs Wild River Dredging," editorial in Boise *Statesman* (February 15, 1970): p. 4.
80. "Conservationists Win on Dredging," editorial in Boise *Statesman* (March 6, 1970): p. 4.
81. "Problems of Atomic Waste Explained to Sewage Men," Boise *Statesman* (October 15, 1956): p. 14.
82. "Idaho Site's Pesky Chore: Dumping the Reactor 'Ash,'" Idaho Falls *Post-Register* (May 11, 1958): p. 8.
83. J. Schifferdecker, "A-Waste Storage in Idaho Revealed," Boise *Statesman* (September 11, 1969): pp. 1, 2.
84. "Officials Say Eastern Idaho Nuclear Waste Is No Threat," Lewiston *Morning Tribune* (September 12, 1969): p. 2.
85. "Atom Waste Disposal Leaves Questions," Boise *Statesman* (September 15, 1969): p. 4.
86. O.A. (Gus) Kelker, "Erkins Demands 'Unbiased' Probe of AEC Dumping Plan," Twin Falls *Times-News* (September 21, 1969): pp. 1, 2.
87. "Let's Move Now," editorial in Twin Falls *Times-News* (September 30, 1969): p. 4.
88. "Scientists See Environment Fouled by A-Waste Disposal," Lewiston *Morning Tribune* (March 15, 1970): p. 1.
89. "Mobile Graveyard," editorial in Idaho Falls *Post-Register* (March 22, 1970): p. 4.
90. "An Aluminum Plant on the Snake?" editorial in Lewiston *Morning Tribune* (April 25, 1967): p. 4.

91. "Water Pollution and Idaho," editorial in Idaho Falls *Post-Register* (July 1, 1968): p. 4.
92. David Zarkin, "Burning of Wastes Adds to Pollution of Air by Affecting Temperature, Cleanliness," Boise *Statesman* (October 11, 1968): p. B9.
93. "Smylie Asks 'Total' Effort in Conservation Matters," Boise *Evening Statesman* (May 2, 1966): p. 27.
94. "Idaho Pollution," editorial in Idaho Falls *Post-Register* (October 13, 1968): p. 4.
95. "A Challenge for Every Community," editorial in Boise *Statesman* (April 1, 1969): p. 4.
96. "Church Gives Challenge on 'New Conservation,'" Coeur d'Alene *Press* (April 23, 1969): p. 1.
97. "Make It 'Pay as You Pollute,'" editorial in St. Maries *Gazette-Record* (January 22, 1970): p. 12.
98. Scott W. Reed, "Idaho Conservationist Contends Cost of Growth Sometimes Outweighs Benefits," Boise *Statesman* (January 25, 1970): pp. 1, 6.
99. "McClure Urges Environmental Concern," Boise *Statesman* (February 13, 1970): p. 8.
100. "Says Pollution Control May Become Profitable," Wallace *Miner* (November 20, 1969): p. 1.
101. "Simplot Shows the Way," editorial in Pocatello *Idaho State Journal* (February 11, 1970): p. 4.
102. "Industry's Anti-Pollution Obligation," editorial in Boise *Statesman* (April 14, 1970): p. 4.
103. "Robson Eyes Action for River Cleanup," Boise *Statesman* (August 1, 1969): p. C7.
104. "An Environmental Bill of Rights," editorial in Boise *Statesman* (October 3, 1969): p. 4.
105. "Idaho Environmental Council Sees 'Ecological Disaster' Ahead for Man," Pocatello *Idaho State Journal* (December 18, 1969): p. 3.
106. "Fortunate, Not Immune," editorial in Sandpoint *News-Bulletin* (March 5, 1970): p. 4.
107. "Church Calls for Population Dispersal into Rural Areas," Pocatello *Idaho State Journal* (April 23, 1970): pp. A1, B6.
108. "ISU Earth Day Airs Pollution," Idaho Falls *Post-Register* (April 23, 1970): p. 19.
109. Ralph Comstock III, "Idaho Power Chief Says Ecology Issue Stirs Up Emotion," Boise *Statesman* (March 7, 1970): p. 7.
110. Lou Kristan, "It's My Opinion," Challis *Messenger* (April 23, 1970): p. 2.
111. Governor Don Samuelson, "Environmental Problems Attract Attention of Idaho Legislature as Well as Citizens," Priest River *Times* (March 19, 1970): p. 5.
112. Robert E. Smylie, "The One Big Issue," Lewiston *Morning Tribune* (April 19, 1970): p. 5.

XII

The White Clouds Shoot-out

NOW WE RETURN TO THE FIGHT over the White Clouds. Like many shoot-outs in the Old West, it was easier to see who lost—to count the killed and wounded—than to say who won. This was no "High Noon," with the lonely but courageous marshal facing down a clutch of bad guys, while timid townsmen hid and waited to see who prevailed. It was more like a political "Gunfight at the OK Corral," where it was far from obvious how to distinguish the good guys from the villains.

Certainly, Don Samuelson lost the gubernatorial election, and Cecil Andrus was inaugurated as his successor in January 1971. But even with an innovative agenda for bettering the environment, Andrus's first State of the State Address was somewhat of a disappointing surprise. Although he pledged to continue opposing any White Clouds development and to work for environmental improvement, the list of what he wanted the legislature to do was anything but ambitious: continue matching funds for sewer treatment plants, limit out-of-state hunters, and increase funding for air and water pollution control agencies. There were only two new proposals, which lacked specifics, such as in the call for stream protection legislation, or was hedged by caution, as when asking for a law controlling surface mining, but with the caveat, "we surely don't want to place any unnecessary problems in the path of our mining industry."[1]

This was far different from what one might expect from the man who argued in 1966 that a vote for Samuelson was "a vote for his sterile, 19th century negative philosophy."[2] Nor was Andrus's initial program all that different from the kind of thinking one could find in the heart of Samuelson territory—"anything that threatens our environment," asserted an editorial in Samuelson's hometown paper in November 1970, "from within or without also threatens our economic well-being and, therefore, is intolerable."[3]

What, then, was the White Clouds fight all about? In the narrowest sense, it was a question of scenic preservation, but neither side showed any interest in limiting it to that level of argument. Rather, both sides saw the White

Clouds as a test case of how public lands ought to be managed. On one hand, preservationists were convinced that any mining would end with a ravaged landscape like that seen on the Yankee Fork. "Miners don't like the word, desecrated, but," in the opinion of the Idaho Falls *Post-Register*, "it's agonizingly appropriate."[4]

When Governor Samuelson first made public his support of the American Smelting and Refining Company's plan for the White Clouds at a public meeting in Boise, May 9, 1969, Ernest Day angrily retorted by resigning his chairmanship of the State Parks Board. "I don't see any sense of being part of a team which doesn't have enough regard for our resources to better differentiate between uses." Day was convinced that a road to the ASARCO claim would "open the entire White Clouds to irresponsible mineral exploration."[5] Day proceeded to wage passionate war against the proposal. "Besides being a crime against nature," he told the Boise Rotarians, "it is a bum business deal,"[6] a catchphrase which the Greater Sawtooth Preservation Council picked up and echoed around the state.

After hiking into the area in July 1969, Senator Frank Church assured a press conference in Boise that "a road to the heart of the White Clouds must destroy everything that is precious and unique about them."[7] Like most preservationists, he denied any possibility of restoration. "Those lush meadowlands that are mined will never be the same again," he declared.[8]

Mining opponents sometimes got carried away with their arguments. Bill Hall claimed Idahoans had become "environmental hermits and economic isolationists."[9] Mrs. Walter Dolan of St. Maries wrote to the *Morning Tribune* editor, calling for "no mining, no where."[10] Without going to such extremes, many preservationists believed that the threat to the White Clouds typified a danger to much of Idaho. "The same thing," according to a *Statesman* editorial, "could happen to any other scenic area in the state—the Seven Devils, the Bighorn Crags, the Selway country."[11] The least that should be done, according to a resolution passed by the Boise Jaycees, was to hold the area "inviolate" for at least twenty years.[12]

Preservationists insisted on co-opting "conservation," refusing to believe that anyone supporting mining in the White Clouds had any right to use the term to describe themselves. The *Morning Tribune* summarized the fight as "The Sportsmen vs. the Spoilers," concluding that "when it comes to a showdown [Samuelson] will fall in line with the exploiters."[13] The Idaho Falls *Post-Register* agreed that the governor "has shown a sorry lack of vision when it comes to conservation."[14] In an open letter to the governor, nature-writer Ted Trueblood of Nampa insisted that tourism would be a far better economic use of the White Clouds than mining: "mining is liquidation. You clean up and get out—and the scar lasts forever."[15] According to Gerald Jayne, then secretary of the Hells Canyon Preservation Council, Samuelson "understands neither what conservation is all about, nor the democratic processes involved with hearing public sentiment on conservation issues."[16]

Opponents of the preservationists countered by defending Samuelson's claim to be the real conservationist. Editorials were frequently reprinted by other papers during this controversy, but none circulated more widely than a piece titled, "He Loves Scenic Idaho." Written by Pete Hackworth for the Caldwell *News-Tribune* and Nampa *Free Press*, it was picked up and reprinted by the Challis *Messenger*, Priest River *Times*, Sandpoint *News-Bulletin*, Wallace *Miner*, and Twin Falls *Times-News* (and possibly others). Hackworth cited Samuelson's long record as a wildlifer to prove "he would be the last man to knowingly act to [Idaho's] detriment." Furthermore, "we want to make it crystal clear…that we are sincere and vocal proponents of conservation, of retaining wilderness areas of Idaho, of preserving our heritage of nature."[17]

As Samuelson saw it, the question was how to balance economic development with "preserving our heritage of nature." "I hold no narrow-minded, single-track opinion that all areas of Idaho should either be locked up on the one hand or fully developed on the other," he insisted in a mid-May 1969 statement, which was repeatedly circulated around the state in the months to come. "Each situation must be judged on its own merits."

As for ASARCO's White Clouds proposal, "they are not going to tear down mountains. They are only going to dig a hole."[18] And, he never tired of repeating, Custer County would receive a gigantic enhancement to its economy. In a county with 94 percent of its land in federal ownership, the tax base was extremely narrow. According to James Ellsworth, who represented the county in the Idaho Senate, it received only very small amounts from federal agencies—in 1967-68 $5,473 from the Forest Service, $280 from the BLM, and $12,958 in "lieu payments" for education. In breathtaking contrast, ASARCO would pay $720,000 a year in property taxes after investing $40 million to put the mine in operation and providing 350 new jobs (in a county of only about three thousand people).[19]

Samuelson heatedly denied that this was akin to the loss of Shoshone Falls' natural grandeur. Only one of the area's fifty-four lakes would be disturbed, and even it eventually would be restored "in an enlarged and improved condition."[20] He readily conceded that "the overall grandeur and majesty of the region is spectacular," but the proposed mine's actual site "as a localized spot is not unusually attractive," containing only "sagebrush on one side and a few scraggly trees on the other."[21] In his estimation, the tradeoffs obviously favored multiple use and approving ASARCO's plan.

Preservationists angrily fumed over Samuelson's "sagebrush…and a few scraggly trees." The *Statesman* declared his argument pure hokum, ironically noting, "it is amazing how much the scenic quality of Idaho declines when a mining company wants to put in an open pit operation."[22] The *Morning Tribune* sarcastically replied, "That's Right, Governor, We Know" what multiple use is; it "means selling your soul-satisfying outdoors for a mess of potage, and we are quite familiar with it"—with dredging on the St. Joe River, industrial wastes dumped in the Snake, and proposals for more dams in Hells Canyon.[23] Earnest Day, speaking as a National Wildlife Federation regional director, proclaimed that "no amount of money can replace the beauty" of the area.[24]

Nevertheless, preservationists could not rest the case on their superior sensitivity to the White Clouds' beauties and expect to win the battle for public opinion. They had to admit to what the *Post-Register* called "The Custer Dilemma," the stark fiscal reality pointed up by Senator Ellsworth. The *Post-Register* concluded that preservation costs just *had* to be paid "in one way or another," and skeptically predicted that tourism revenues would have to be greatly increased.[25] Senator Church was not so sure. After a press conference in Pocatello, the editor of the Challis *Messenger* reported that Church

> was well aware of Custer County's needs and he sympathizes with everyone here but that we had always had mining and it had never done much for us; that tourism would be the big thing for us and, in the long-run, we would realize more from tourism than we ever would from mining without the devastation to this beautiful area.[26]

This sounded as if he had listened to the Greater Sawtooth Preservation Council, organized to lobby for the White Clouds' designation as a national park. Citing Yellowstone National Park's economic impact—$57 million a year for surrounding communities—John Merriam, the council's president and chairman of the Idaho State University economics department, claimed that "no other action could provide such phenomenal economic benefits for the state."[27]

Not everyone was impressed with Merriam's analysis. Possibly recalling how modestly the Craters of the Moon National Monument had increased tourist revenues, Al Minton, head of the state's Department of Commerce and Economic Development, urged the need for basic industry, such as mining, as well as tourism. Samuelson countered Church and Merriam's bullish estimates of tourism's economic benefits, warning a group in Coeur d'Alene:

> If we are going to allow the Sierra Club and Alpine Club people to lock up our lands for conservation purposes, then our trained college people must be content with making beds at $1.25 per hour.[28]

Besides, the Challis paper's editor observed, the two biggest tourist draws in Custer County—the old Yankee Fork dredge and the ghost town at Custer—had nothing to do with natural scenery. (The implications of this fact apparently confounded both sides in the White Clouds fight. In any case, the historical aspects were totally unexplored.)

For all the newsprint devoted to the issue, no consensus was reached by the fall of 1969. Typical of the public reaction was a poll taken in Boise by the Greater Sawtooth Preservation Council. The *Statesman* reported that the poll demonstrated opposition to mining in the White Clouds, but the results were far from conclusive.[29] The poll, based on phone calls to 125 people, found 49 percent with no opinion. Only by excluding that half of respondents could it be said that 67 percent opposed mining. It would be just about as plausible to conclude that the poll showed the public to be undecided on the issue.

Two problems faced anyone trying to make a judgment about ASARCO's proposal. The first had to do with the mining industry's credibility; it had a terrible reputation for causing environmental damage in the past. Even R.J. Bruning, one of mining's most articulate apologists, ruefully conceded (as noted in the Prologue) that people kept the car locked when they knew your granddad was a horse thief. Almost everyone agreed with the IWF's Art Manley when he announced, "it's high time the mining industry came of age and accepted a reasonable measure of control in the public interest."[30] O.T. Power, recently retired head of the FMC phosphate plant in Pocatello, had no problem with Manley's dictum. "If mining must destroy," Power wrote, and "if it cannot pay the price of practical reclamation for continued beneficial use, then it should not exist."[31] The question remained—could the industry be trusted?

ASARCO officials did everything they could to prove their environmental sensitivity. William Salisbury, the geologist in charge, claimed that his exploratory camp "demonstrates that metal exploration can be conducted without disturbing recreational values."[32] John Collins, the company's chief geologist, said he was eager to meet with conservationists to discuss "what we can do within reason to accommodate the desires of conservationists in planning the mine."[33] In September 1969, the company hired ecological consultants from Boulder, Colorado, to study the situation. Forest Service officials verified that the company was most cooperative to work with. Congressman Orval Hansen reported after a visit to the ASARCO site that he was "very impressed with their approach."[34]

It is doubtful that ASARCO persuaded many people to change their minds. Those inclined to trust the company, like Governor Samuelson, accepted ASARCO's reassurances. He cited the phosphate industry's land-reclamation work in southeastern Idaho as an example of what could be done in the White Clouds: "they think they can improve on mother nature. This is working."[35]

This only provoked more scoffing from preservationists, who said, in effect, you still could not trust the old horse thief. ASARCO, like an eager suitor, promised everything, according to the *Morning Tribune*. The Lewiston paper cited the company's controversial smelter in Tacoma, Washington, to prove that "profit clearly is ASARCO's motive, if it becomes a matter of profit or conservation."[36] The Idaho Environmental Council, insisting the governor was hoodwinked by mining interests, called the site "Samuelson's Folly," and maintained that it would leave "a gigantic mess."[37] Earnest Day told the Boise Lions Club the mine "can't be anything but a scar and eyesore for generations to come," a site the *Statesman* magnified into being "at least half" of the whole White Clouds area.[38]

The second problem facing those trying to make a decision about the White Clouds' future was the credibility of Don Samuelson himself. Where the mining industry strove to overcome an unpopular past, Samuelson presumed that his long and honorable record as a wildlifer would incline people to trust him in the midst of controversy. His record was excellent; as the Sandpoint paper put it in an article announcing his 1966 governorship candidacy: "Don has long been active in conservation endeavors related to farming, mining, water, timber, wildlife and recreation."[39]

Yet, positions he took as governor sometimes seemed to go against that record. As seen in Chapter XI, he antagonized many conservationists in the anti-dredging movement. In addition, his speaking style "irritate[d] a lot of newsmen," to quote Robert Hammes of the St. Maries *Gazette-Record*. "His delivery of a set speech is awkward and unimpressive. His unrehearsed remarks are rambling, convoluted and often ungrammatical."[40] It seemed to be a style of "Political Suicide in Public," as Jack Carter termed it in the *Morning Tribune*.[41] Although Carter, Hammes, and others admitted that this didn't seem to offend ordinary voters, who apparently took Samuelson's verbal bumbling as proof that he was sincere and honestly doing the best he could, it alienated many of the more educated, who also tended to be influential opinion makers. Stan Burns of Boise, a long-time friend of Frank Church, wrote an open letter to the governor attacking his support of ASARCO as proof of his "ignorance of the basic values of life here in your adopted state."[42]

Samuelson shrugged off such criticisms, possibly because they seemed to come from the same kind of people who four years earlier had confidently predicted he would never get elected governor in the first place. "Never in the past three decades," hooted the Sandpoint *News-Bulletin* in 1966, "have so many political experts of Idaho daily newspapers been so wrong,"[43] a conclusion that Lewiston's Bill Hall (one of the most outspoken of those experts) admitted was true. Therefore, when those same experts insisted that he failed to understand conservation issues, Samuelson showed no inclination to take heed. He struck the Blackfoot *News* editor as a "man uncomplicated by any doubts of what is right or wrong."[44]

Andrus touched on the heart of the matter when he recalled that Samuelson was "especially tone deaf" to the new environmental conservation movement.[45] "Big Don" was still confidently ensconced in an unabashedly utilitarian conservation world as described in Chapter V. If mustangs got in the way of stockmen, then the mustangs had to go. The same kind of thinking (as noted in Chapter VI) had no trouble with the Air Force using the desert near Mountain Home as a bombing range. Similarly, Samuelson was fond of saying, "the No. 1 natural resource in Idaho is the taxpayer."[46] Tone-deaf as he was, he could not hear how this jarred on those environmentalists who believed that humanity could no longer see itself as the center of things; that the world needed to protect the mustangs, even if they served no economic purpose; that the desert had its own integrity, which could be violated by aerial bombing.

Samuelson and preservationists appeared to be in a standoff at the end of 1969. A statewide poll reported by the Coeur d'Alene *Press* in early December found 45 percent approving the job done by Samuelson. Asked how they would vote for governor, 29 percent favored the Democrats, 27 percent the Republicans, but 44 percent remained undecided.

Cecil Andrus did not fully enter the fray until February 1970. The Pocatello paper had quoted him in November as emphatically opposed to Samuelson's stand on the White Clouds, but at that time he remained noncommittal about his interest in campaigning for the governorship. By February, however, he began to make his move. Not only did he sponsor the bill banning dredging along designated wild rivers, but also he introduced legislation to regulate surface mining. Andrus announced that "we're going to have to make provisions for the protection of scenery and resources," pointing to the White Clouds as proof that the Samuelson administration was "willing to sell our birthright."[47]

His bill immediately gained the attention of both sides in the White Clouds battle. Apparently fearing its implications, which would require proof of revegetation plans as well as methods for minimizing environmental impacts, the Senate's Republican leadership tried to bury it in committee. Andrus responded by stating his belief that "eastern establishment miners" were lobbying against the bill, "attempting to use our state" for their own selfish purposes.[48] When the bill finally gained a public hearing, those testifying in favor included the Idaho Wildlife Federation, the Greater Sawtooth Preservation Council, the Idaho League of Women Voters, and Ernest Day. Representatives of the phosphate industry protested that it "must be protected from unreasonable requirements."[49]

In responding to the phosphate companies' complaints, Andrus demonstrated that he could strive for a "middle way." Working to keep the preservationists' support, he reiterated that his primary concern was the danger to the White Clouds. However, unlike the uncompromising stance of people like Gerry Jayne and Ernest Day, Andrus confessed that he had been unaware of his legislation's impact on the phosphate industry and immediately offered amendments to exclude it from the bill's purview. The *Statesman* grumbled that Andrus and Diane Bilyeu of Pocatello, the bill's co-sponsor, had not done enough homework, but the much more significant fact was Andrus's willingness to compromise. Struggling to keep the legislation alive, Andrus went so far as to express "great respect" for ASARCO and noted that "other companies are in the White Clouds doing far more damage than ASARCO." "We need this bill," he argued, "to put roadblocks in the way of people who want to destroy an area."[50]

Although Andrus failed to gain Senate approval of his bill, he succeeded in establishing himself as a man to be reckoned with regarding Idaho environmental issues. He "believes that the environment is the overriding concern of the Idaho electorate this year," according to R.J. Bruning, who interviewed Andrus when he visited Wallace in May 1970. "Andrus says resources should be used for their greatest good," and for that reason he favored banning all mining in the White Clouds.[51]

By the spring of 1970, Andrus recognized that the White Clouds had become a crucial touchstone. How one talked about them revealed how one thought about the environment. Samuelson echoed popular rhetoric about environmental concerns, but when it came time to talk about mining in the White Clouds, he lapsed back into references to the taxpayer as the "number one resource." In sharp contrast, Andrus told reporters in late June, "we are custodians of the area for future generations."[52] Reacting to accusations that a national park in the White Clouds would be "locking up" the area, Andrus replied that mining would "lock out the public for recreation."[53]

Far more than a matter of scenic preservation, the White Clouds came to symbolize how public policy should affect the environment. At one extreme, "multiple use" was seen as the way to prevent Idaho from becoming a tourist colony. Railing against the preservationist position, Aden Hyde, state legislator and editor of the *East Idaho Farmer*, warned, "if somehow, we don't put a stop to all that, opportunity will be a word lost from the Idaho vocabulary."[54] At the other extreme was Bill Hall's denunciation (quoted in the Prologue) that "Multiple Use Is Fishing for Carp."

Samuelson found no fault with the position taken by the Interim Legislative Committee after it visited the ASARCO camp in July 1970. Albion Representative Vard Chatburn blandly observed, "I'm sure there's room in Idaho for everyone…I don't think they'll have any trouble with revegetating the area. There isn't much vegetation there now."[55] Andrus dismissed Chatburn and his committee's report as a predictable whitewash. Consequently, Andrus looked like the preferred alternative when the Idaho Falls *Post-Register* reacted to Chatburn's comments: "the officials haven't got the message yet, it is our opinion, but the real issue [in] this campaign of 1970 is liveability."[56]

Never mind that only a small handful of hikers visited the White Clouds each year or that most Idahoans had no clear idea of what they even looked like. The real issue was how one assessed overall environmental integrity, and the White Clouds revealed a fundamental difference between the Hydes, Chatburns, and Samuelsons on one side, and the Halls and Andruses on the other. One side talked about resource development, the other about environmental stewardship and liveability.

The implications of that split are easier to see in retrospect than they were at the time. For the Forest Service, it meant an almost irresolvable double bind. With its traditional commitment to resource development—dating back to the beginning of the century when Major Fenn promised that no one would be left out—the agency faced a rocky relationship with environmentalists, who were convinced that at least the grosser forms of resource exploitation had to end. On the other hand, as Samuelson's attacks made clear, the Forest Service had trouble maintaining peace with conservatives, who thought the NFS conceded too much to environmentalists.

Nor was it immediately clear that the split meant Andrus would be the standard-bearer for environmentalists. Some, including Earnest Day of Boise and Scott Reed of Coeur d'Alene, campaigned for Dick Smith, who challenged Samuelson in the Republican primary by urging a twenty-year moratorium on all mining in the White Clouds. In the Democratic primary, Andrus had a hard fight to beat Vernon Ravenscroft, who tended to take a position more congenial to resource development. Although Andrus prevailed in the August 5 primary, he polled only 29,046 votes, compared to 47,431 for Samuelson and 33,256 for Smith. Furthermore, while Andrus carried eight of the nine counties with populations over 10,000, Ravenscroft won twenty-seven of Idaho's forty-four counties.

The tide decisively turned in the next two months. By October 1, 1970, a poll showed 55 percent favored some form of protection for the White Clouds, while those in favor of mining declined to 35 percent. The Idaho Environmental Council declared its support for Andrus and, with the Greater Sawtooth Preservation Council, bought full-page ads proclaiming, "Andrus Can Save White Clouds."[57]

The changing mood could be seen in an editorial exchange. The Payette *Independent-Enterprise* sought "A Middle Ground between Extremes," concluding with a motto, "rigid controls, yes, but lockup, no!"[58] "Environmentalists Don't Seek Lock-Up," the Boise *Statesman* heatedly responded. It dismissed as pure myth the notion that people concerned about the environment wanted to put a freeze on economic growth. "An expanding economy and environmental protection can go hand in hand."[59]

By the end of October, Andrus received endorsements not only from newspapers across the state, but also from national publications. Clare Conley, a Nampa native and now editor of *Field and Stream*, declared in favor of Andrus. Allowing mining in the White Clouds, in Conley's opinion, would be "only the first step" for Samuelson, ending in "a virtual lockout of sportsmen and other people who use the outdoors as a part of their lives without damaging it."[60]

This was not, of course, a single-issue campaign. When the *Statesman* formally endorsed Andrus, it listed six reasons, with environmental protection being second to his support for education, particularly for kindergartens, and concluded with support for his "positive approach." Nevertheless, the newspaper contrasted Andrus with Samuelson, who still "insists that any minerals" in the White Clouds "must be mined."[61]

Andrus won the November election. When the Associated Press quoted the governor-elect in December, he reiterated his commitment to maintaining Idaho's "quality of life," by pursuing "adequate funding of education and protection of the environment."[62]

Cecil Andrus succeeded in raising environmental concerns to a prominent place in Idaho politics by melding them with a "middle ground"—appealing to those small-town, conservative Idahoans like the Payette newspaper editor, as well as to the more urban and liberal minded, such as the *Statesman*'s editorial board. Andrus eventually served four terms as Idaho governor, as well as U.S. Secretary of the Interior in the Carter administration. This was due to his political acumen, and, by the same token, environmentalists in Idaho had to show their political savvy in the years to come, too.

"The View from a Snowy Peak" that the *Morning Tribune* took during the 1970 election, revealed a new political scene, one in which anyone forgetting the lessons of the White Clouds might face a fate similar to Samuelson's. Conservation may have tipped the election in 1970, but environmentalists could not rest on their laurels. (Though the national park designation never took hold, the White Clouds were protected under Forest Service auspices as part of the Sawtooth National Recreation Area.) Other environmental battles would continue just as surely as the approach of the next election. Invigorating as the view from the mountaintop was, environmentalists could not avoid returning to mundane valleys where it would be many years before they had another issue as clarifying as the fight to save the White Clouds.

ENDNOTES

1. "Andrus Extols Unity, Responsibility, Priorities in State of State Address," Boise *Statesman* (January 12, 1971): p. 10.
2. "Andrus Says Vote for Independent Is Vote for Samuelson," St. Maries *Gazette-Record* (October 6, 1966): p. 1.
3. "Growth Can Kill, Too," editorial in Sandpoint *News-Bulletin* (November 26, 1970): p. 4.
4. "Miners and Idaho's Castle Peak," editorial in Idaho Falls *Post-Register* (September 15, 1968): p. 4.
5. "Parks Board Chief Resigns at Hearing," Boise *Statesman* (May 10, 1969): p. 1.
6. "Boisean Hits Mine Potential of White Clouds," Boise *Statesman* (September 12, 1969): p. 12.
7. John Corlett, "Church Suggest Tramway as Alternate to Road for Mining in White Clouds," Boise *Statesman* (July 23, 1969): p. 14.

8. "Church Says Mining Fever Hurts Chances for Peak," Pocatello *Idaho State Journal* (July 25, 1969): p. 2.
9. B.H., "The White Clouds—Rich or Happy?" editorial in Lewiston *Morning Tribune* (July 4, 1969): p. 4.
10. Lewiston *Morning Tribune* (July 18, 1969): p. 4.
11. "Another Threat to White Clouds," editorial in Boise *Statesman* (November 15, 1969): p. 4.
12. "Jaycees of Boise Urge Moratorium on Mining," Boise *Statesman* (April 26, 1969): p. 16.
13. B.H., "The Sportsmen vs. the Spoilers," editorial in Lewiston *Morning Tribune* (May 11, 1969): p. 4.
14. "The White Clouds," editorial in Idaho Falls *Post-Register* (May 18, 1969): p. 4.
15. *Statesman* (June 2, 1969): p. A5.
16. "Mining Stand of Governor Draws Fire," Pocatello *Idaho State Journal* (August 3, 1969): p. 1.
17. "Editorial Defends Samuelson's Stand," Priest River *Times* (June 12, 1969): p. 1.
18. "Samuelson Reiterates Advocacy of Mining Development in White Clouds," Boise *Statesman* (May 15, 1969): p. A8.
19. "Two Legislators Back Mine Plan," Idaho Falls *Post-Register* (June 12, 1969): pp. 1, 13.
20. Richard Charnock, "Samuelson Defends Position on White Clouds Controversy," Boise *Statesman* (May 14, 1969, Afternoon Edition): p. 1.
21. "Samuelson Scores Forest Service 'Hoax' in White Clouds Dispute," Twin Falls *Times-News* (August 6, 1969): p. 10.
22. "His Real Problem Is Overquoting," editorial in Boise *Statesman* (August 8, 1969): p. 4; "Sage-brush…and Scraggly Trees," editorial in Boise *Statesman* (August 3, 1969): p. 4.
23. B.H., "That's Right, Governor, We Know," editorial in Lewiston *Morning Tribune* (September 19, 1969): p. 4.
24. "Boise Wildlife Aide Raps ASARCO Mine Plans in Idaho," Boise *Statesman* (August 15, 1969): p. D1.
25. "The Custer Dilemma," editorial in Idaho Falls *Post-Register* (June 29, 1969): p. 4.
26. "Sen. Church Gives Views on White Cloud Issue at Press Conference," Challis *Messenger* (July 31, 1969): pp. 1, 8,
27. "White Clouds National Park Said Answer," Pocatello *Idaho State Journal* (July 18, 1969): p. 2.
28. "Samuelson Reiterates Mine Stand," Boise *Statesman* (September 17, 1969): p. D1.
29. "Boise Poll Shows Opposition to White Clouds Mine," Boise *Statesman* (September 25, 1969): p. C9.
30. "Manley Critical of Remarks by Magnuson," Coeur d'Alene *Press* (June 21, 1969): p. 1.
31. O.T. Power, "Don't Overdo Tourism," Boise *Statesman* (June 4, 1969): p. 4.
32. "Mine Firm Drills for Molybdenite," Salmon *Recorder-Herald* (September 19, 1969): pp. 1, 5.
33. "Mine Geologist Tells Offer to Assure Restoration in White Clouds Area," Boise *Statesman* (August 14, 1969): p. D1.
34. Fred Dodds, "Hansen Designing Mining Law Change," Twin Falls *Times-News* (August 29, 1969): pp. 1, 2.
35. "Governor Cites Mining's Land Reclamation Work," Idaho Falls *Post-Register* (October 7, 1969): p. 2.
36. B.H., "Tell Us Again, Governor," editorial reprinted in Pocatello *Idaho State Journal* (October 9, 1969): p. 4.
37. "Council Says Governor Deceived in Mine Issue," Boise *Statesman* (October 7, 1969): p. 24.
38. "Boisean Claims Open Pit Will Scar White Clouds," Boise *Statesman* (October 25, 1969): p. 10; "Governor Clarifies His Stand," editorial in Boise *Statesman* (September 21, 1969): p. 4.
39. "Don Samuelson Enters Bid for Governorship," Sandpoint *News-Bulletin* (January 6, 1966): p. 1.
40. "Lots of People Helping Samuelson," editorial in St. Maries *Gazette-Record* (November 20, 1969): p. 14.
41. Jack Carter, "The Samuelson Style: Political Suicide in Public," Lewiston *Morning Tribune* (November 10, 1969): pp. 4, 5.
42. Boise *Statesman* (May 11, 1969): p. 5.
43. "Idaho Political Seers Lose Face," Sandpoint *News-Bulletin* (November 10, 1966): p. 2.
44. "Uncomplicated," editorial in Blackfoot *News*, reprinted in Twin Falls *Times-News* (June 2, 1969): p. 4.

45. Cecil Andrus and Joel Connelly, *Cecil Andrus: Politics Western Style* (Seattle: Sasquatch, 1998): p. 18.
46. "Governor Tells Stand on White Cloud Mine," Idaho Falls *Post-Register* (May 14, 1969): p. 1.
47. Paul M. Quinn, "Bills Propose to Control Idaho Pit, Strip Mining, Require Restoring Site," Boise *Statesman* (February 4, 1970): p. D1.
48. "Mining Bill Remains in Limbo," Coeur d'Alene *Press* (February 18, 1970): p. 5.
49. John Corlett, "Industry Spokesmen, Conservationist Rap Bill to Regulate Surface Mining, Water Pollution," Boise *Statesman* (February 20, 1970): p. 19.
50. "Senators Kill Bill to Regulate Surface Mining Effects in Idaho," Boise *Statesman* (February 26, 1970): 9.
51. R.J. Bruning, "Stream of Thought," Boise *Statesman* (May 24, 1970): p. 4.
52. "Andrus is Tagged 'Moderate' Candidate," Arco *Advertiser* (June 23, 1970): p. 1.
53. "Andrus Denounces Plan to Mine White Clouds," Boise *Statesman* (June 23, 1970): p. 10.
54. Aden Hyde, "Mine Laws, Parks Would Destroy Opportunity," reprinted from *East Idaho Farmer* in Boise *Statesman* (April 23, 1970): p. 4.
55. "Mining Road in White Cloud Area Favored," Idaho Falls *Post-Register* (July 21, 1970): p. 1.
56. "White Clouds: The Superficial View," editorial in Idaho Falls *Post-Register* (July 22, 1970): p. 4.
57. Boise *Statesman* (November 1, 1970): p. D20.
58. Payette *Independent-Enterprise* (October 8, 1970): p. 2.
59. Boise *Statesman* (October 17, 1970): p. 4.
60. "Outdoor Magazine Backs Cecil Andrus," Twin Falls *Times-News* (October 23, 1970): p. 20.
61. "Andrus for Governor," editorial in Boise *Statesman* (October 25, 1970): p. 4.
62. Earle L. Jester, "Andrus Holds to Aim of Protecting Idaho Ecology," Boise *Statesman* (December 20, 1970): p. B4.

A Note on Sources

T HE INFORMATION USED in writing *To the White Clouds* was derived primarily from newspapers published throughout Idaho from 1900 to 1970. In an ideal scholarly world, I would have relied mostly on "primary sources," that is, collections of unpublished materials housed in archives and research collections at various libraries and repositories around the state. But Idaho's situation is far from anything that a historical scholar might define as ideal; the state's research collections are spotty for almost any topic involving Idaho's conservation history. For my purposes, the locating files for the research collections were almost entirely empty. There is the striking exception of the Frank Church Papers, admirably housed and arranged in the Special Collections Room at Boise State University's Albertsons Library. Also valuable, but to a lesser extent, were the Len B. Jordan Papers, likewise at BSU. The Cecil Andrus Papers (at BSU) contain little prior to his January 1971 inauguration as governor. One could make a long list of collections that *do not* exist: R.H. Rutledge's papers, a Frontier Club collection, an Idaho Wildlife Federation archive, and so on.

The State Archives *do* exist, but it has been frugally funded—often little archival work has been completed beyond the basic boxing, labeling, and storing of large quantities of papers. The Idaho governors' collections generally do not have detailed inventories, so one could easily get engulfed by the papers of James H. Hawley (1911–13), H.C. Baldridge (1927–31), or Don Samuelson (1967–71) and not be heard from again for months. Similarly, it appears a substantial amount of Major Frank Fenn's papers are mixed in with the many boxes of his son's (Lloyd) collection. But it would take more time than what most historians would think well-invested and wise to ferret out just what, in fact, is there.

In marked contrast, the Idaho State Historical Society has assembled a remarkably comprehensive microfilm collection of Idaho newspapers. Admittedly it is not complete—there are lost issues, and sometimes even missing years, for some papers in the earlier periods—but the collection includes every issue yet known to be in existence. The collection provides a unique window into the day-to-day lives of people in every section of Idaho, past and present. Despite a particular editorialist's blind spots and obsessions that might limit one newspaper's reliability, I usually found that I could achieve balance by referencing views from other contemporary newspaper editors. Regardless of perennial complaints by readers that their local paper did not reflect local opinion, newspapers are, in fact, tolerably reliable thermometers of local passions and concerns. Editors may have ignored topics that we latter-day scholars are interested in, but it surely is true that few consistently ignored topics that the readers wanted covered.

By patiently working through newspaper back files, one can gain a reliable understanding of what concerned Idahoans over the years. But which back files? Time limitations prevent a researcher from going through them all; and obviously, the smaller a sample, the less reliable the results. My answer to this was to cover the major papers in each of the state's main geographical areas—the Lewiston *Morning Tribune*, the Twin Falls *Times-News*, and so on—and then select what I thought to be an adequate number of newspaper articles from nearby smaller towns for balance. For *To the White Clouds*, I reviewed every extant issue of newspapers published in the following towns and cities between 1900 and 1970 (arranged here geographically)—Sandpoint, Priest River, Coeur d'Alene, St. Maries, Lewiston, Kamiah, Kooskia, Grangeville, McCall, Cascade, Boise, Twin Falls, Hailey, Challis, Salmon, Arco, Idaho Falls, and Pocatello. In addition, for certain specific topics, a variety of other newspapers were checked. Regarding the Frontier Club, for example, I examined the Jerome *Northside News*, the Shoshone *Lincoln County Journal*, and several other Magic Valley weeklies for the years that the club seemed to be active.

I will let the reader decide whether I succeeded in properly selecting my sources, but I am convinced that overall I have delved as deeply as anyone into the topics covered in this book. I have reported my findings as fairly and honestly as I know how.

Sources

Archives

Albertsons Library, Boise State University—
Frank Church Papers
Len B. Jordan Papers
Robert Limbert Papers
Ted Trueblood Papers

Idaho State Historical Society—
Governor H.C. Baldridge Papers
Homer Fenn Papers
Governor Don Samuelson Papers

Government Documents

Biennial Reports of the Fish and Game Warden, 1901, 1913, 1921, 1925. Copies are available at the
  Idaho State Library, 325 W. State, Boise.
"Briefed Report" of the first Statewide Recreation Conference (1936), issued by the Idaho State Plan-
  ning Board. Idaho State Library copy.
"Dredge Hearing—Permit—Finch File," Idaho Department of Lands, 954 W. Jefferson St., Boise.
"General Laws of the State of Idaho," 1901–70. Published for each session of the Idaho legislature and
  commonly referred to as "Session Laws."
"Idaho Fish and Game Commission Minutes," Idaho Fish and Game Department, 600 S. Walnut
  St., Boise.
"A Preliminary Report on the Parks, Parkways, and Recreational Areas of Idaho, Prepared by the Idaho
  State Forestry Department" (January 1939). Idaho State Library.

Primary Newspapers

Arco—
Advertiser

Boise—
Capital News
Evening Statesman
Idaho Statesman
Intermountain Observer

Cascade—
News

Challis—
Messenger
Silver Messenger

Coeur d'Alene—
Independent
Journal
Press

Grangeville—
Globe
Idaho County Free Press
News
Standard-News

Hailey—
Times
Times-News-Miner
Wood River News-Miner
Wood River Journal

Idaho Falls—
Post
Post-Register
Register
Times
Times-Register

Kamiah—
Clearwater Progress
Progress

Kooskia—
Mountaineer

Lewiston—
Morning Tribune
Teller

McCall—
Payette Lakes Star
Star-News

Pocatello—
Idaho State Journal
Post
Tribune

Priest River—
Times

St. Maries—
Courier
Gazette
Gazette-Record
Record

Salmon—
Herald
Recorder-Herald

Sandpoint—
Bulletin
Daily Bee
News-Bulletin
Northern Idaho News
Panidan
Pend d'Oreille Review

Twin Falls—
News
Times
Times-News

Wallace—
Miner

Articles and Essays

Boag, Peter. "Mountain, Plain, Desert, River: The Snake River Region as a Western Crossroads," in David M. Wrabel and Michael C. Steiner (eds.), *Many Wests: Place, Culture, and Regional Identity*. Lawrence: University of Kansas Press, 1997.

Casper, Kathleen. "With the Wild Horse Hunters." *Popular Mechanics* XLVI (July 1926): 76–80.

Cook, R.G. "Pioneer Portraits: Weldon Brinton Heyburn." *Idaho Yesterdays* X (Spring 1966): 22, 26.

_____. "Senator Heyburn's War Against the Forest Service." *Idaho Yesterdays* XIV (Winter 1970/1): 12–15.

Cox, Thomas R. "Weldon Heyburn, Lake Chatcolet, and the Evolving Concept of Public Parks." *Idaho Yesterdays* XXIV (Summer 1980): 2–15.

Cronin, William. "The Trouble with Wilderness: Or, Getting Back to the Wrong Nature," in Char Miller and Hal Rothman (eds.), *Out of the Woods: Essays in Environmental History*. Pittsburgh: University of Pittsburgh Press, 1997.

Davidson, Jenny Emery. "Power Switches on the Middle Snake River: The Divergent Histories of Two Hydroelectric Projects." *Idaho Yesterdays* XLIV (Summer 2000): 22–32.

Ewert, Sara Elizabeth Dant. "Peak Park Politics: The Struggle over the Sawtooths, from Borah to Church." *Pacific Northwest Quarterly* XCI (Summer 2000): 138–49.

Fisher, Vardis. "An Essay for Men." *Esquire* (September 1936): 35, 137ff.

Gustafson, Philip. "Everybody Flies in Idaho." *Saturday Evening Post* (October 22, 1955): 32–33, 89.

Hays, Samuel P. "From Conservation to Environment: Environmental Politics in the United States since World War II," in Char Miller and Hal Rothman (eds.), *Out of the Woods: Essays in Environmental History*. Pittsburgh: University of Pittsburgh Press, 1997.

Hornocker, Maurice G. "Stalking the Mountain Lion—to Save Him." *National Geographic* CXXXVI (November 1969): 638–54.

"The Issue: U.S. or Private Dams." *Life* (November 9, 1953): 27–31.

Jackson, Donald. "Whose Wilderness." *Life* (January 9, 1970): 109–10, 112.

Limbert, R.W. "Among the 'Craters of the Moon.'" *National Geographic* XLV (March 1924): 303–28.

"Mountain Heart of Idaho." *Sunset* (September 1947): 12–15.

Muir, Jean. "Wild Horse Roundup." *Saturday Evening Post* (September 28, 1946): 24–25ff.

Neuberger, Richard L. "Hell's Canyon, the Biggest of All." *Harpers Magazine* (April 1939): 527–35.

"Primitive or Wilderness—Which Shall It Be?" *Rudder Flutter* (November 1958): 2–3.

Rhodes-Jones, Carolyn. "An Evolving View of the Landscape: Trappers, Tourists, and the Great Shoshone Falls." *Idaho Yesterdays* XXIII (Summer 1979): 19–27.

Rowley, William D. "Bureaucracy and Science: The Role of Sustained Yield in Managing Range Resources in the National Forests." *Idaho Yesterdays* XXVII (Summer 1984): 30–36.

"The Selway-Bitterroot Wilderness." *Living Wilderness* 74 (Autumn-Winter 1960–61): 45–61.

Shenon, Philip, and John C. Read. "Down Idaho's River of No Return." *National Geographic* LXX (July 1936): 94–136.

Skow, John. "Farewell to Hells Canyon." *Saturday Evening Post* (July 1, 1967): 76–83.

Sparr, Stephen H. "The Value of Wilderness to Science," in Francois Leydet (ed.), *Tomorrow's Wilderness*. San Francisco: Sierra Club, 1963.

Stacy, Susan M. "The Naval Proving Ground." *Idaho Yesterdays* XLIII (Fall 1999): 25–32.

Tatro, W.C. "The Idaho State Sportsmen's Association—Its Objects and Aims." *Idaho Fish and Game* (June 1914): 4–5.

"Three Great Western Wildernesses: What Must Be Done to Save Them?" *Living Wilderness* 1 (September 1935): 9–10.

Waite, Robert G. "Zane Grey and Thunder Mountain." *Idaho Yesterdays* XXXIX (Winter 1996): 18–23.

Wells, Merle, and Larry Jones. "Salmon River Navigation." *Idaho Yesterdays* XLI (Spring 1997): 24–30.

Books, Dissertations, and Published Reports

Allen, Thomas B. *Guardian of the Wild: The Story of the National Wildlife Federation, 1936–1986.* Bloomington: Indiana University Press, 1987.

Allin, Craig W. *The Politics of Wilderness Preservation.* Westport, Conn.: Greenwood, 1982.

Andrews, Richard N.L. *Managing the Environment, Managing Ourselves: A History of American Environmental Policy.* New Haven, Conn.: Yale University Press, 1999.

Andrus, Cecil, and Joel Connelly. *Cecil Andrus: Politics Western Style.* Seattle: Sasquatch, 1998.

Arrington, Leonard J. *History of Idaho*, 2 vols. Moscow: University of Idaho Press and Idaho State Historical Society, 1994.

Ashby, Leroy, and Rod Gramer. *Fighting the Odds: The Life of Senator Frank Church.* Pullman: Washington State University Press, 1994.

Ashworth, William. *Hells Canyon: The Deepest Gorge on Earth.* New York: Hawthorne, 1977.

Bailey, Robert G. *Hell's Canyon.* Lewiston, Idaho: R.G. Bailey, 1943.

————. *River of No Return.* Lewiston, Idaho: Bailey-Blake, 1935.

Baldwin, Donald N. *The Quiet Revolution: Grass Roots of Today's Wilderness Preservation Movement.* Boulder, Colo.: Pruett, 1972.

Bowen, Gordon S. *Grandjean: Man of the Forests.* Boise: privately printed, 1987.

Carhart, Arthur H. *The National Forests.* New York: Alfred A. Knopf, 1959.

Carson, Rachel. *Silent Spring.* Boston: Houghton Mifflin, 1962.

Chase, Alston. *In a Dark Wood: The Fight over Forests and the Rising Tyranny of Ecology.* Boston: Houghton Mifflin, 1995.

Clymer, Frances B., and Charles R. Preston. *Unbroken Spirit: The Wild Horse in the American Landscape.* Cody, Wyo.: Buffalo Bill Historical Center, 1999.

Cohen, Michael P. *The History of the Sierra Club, 1892–1970.* San Francisco: Sierra Club, 1988.

Conservators of Hope: The Horace M. Albright Conservation Lectures. Moscow: University of Idaho Press, 1988.

Cox, Thomas R. *The Park Builders: A History of State Parks in the Pacific Northwest.* Seattle: University of Washington Press, 1988.

Dahlgren, Dorothy, and Simone Carbonneau Kincaid. *In all the West, No Place Like This: A Pictorial History of the Coeur d'Alene Region.* Coeur d'Alene: Museum of North Idaho, 1991.

DiSilvestro, Roger L. *The Endangered Kingdom: The Struggle to Save America's Wildlife.* New York: John Wiley, 1989.

Dodd, Douglas W. "Preserving Multiple-Use Management: The U.S. Forest Service, the National Park Service, and the Struggle for Idaho's Sawtooth Mountain Country, 1911–1972." Ann Arbor, Mich.: UMI Dissertation Services, 2002.

Dunlap, Thomas R. *Saving America's Wildlife.* Princeton, N.J.: Princeton University Press, 1988.

Easterbrook, Gregg. *A Moment on the Earth: The Coming Age of Environmental Optimism.* New York: Viking, 1995.

Etulain, Richard W. *Re-Imagining the Modern American West: A Century of Fiction, History, and Art.* Tucson: University of Arizona Press, 1996.

Ewert, Sara Elizabeth Dant. "The Conversion of Senator Frank Church: Evolution of an Environmentalist." Ph.D. dissertation, Washington State University, 2000.

Fiege, Mark T. "A World in the Making: The Social and Ecological Construction of Idaho's Irrigated Landscape." Ph.D. dissertation, University of Utah, 1994.

Frome, Michael. *The Forest Service.* New York: Praeger, 1971.

Gabrielson, Ira N. *Wildlife Refuges.* New York: Macmillan, 1943.

Gannett, Henry. *19th Annual Report of the U.S. Geological Survey to the Secretary of the Interior, pt. 5: The Forest Reserves.* Washington, D.C.: Government Printing Office, 1899.

Gilligan, James P. "The Development of Policy and Administration of Forest Service Primitive and Wilderness Areas in the Western United States." Ph.D. dissertation, University of Michigan, 1953.

Goodwin, Victor O., and John A. Hussey. *Sawtooth Mountain Area Study, Idaho: History.* N.p.: U.S. Forest Service and National Park Service, 1965.

Graf, William L. *Wilderness Preservation and the Sagebrush Rebellion.* Savage, Md.: Rowman and Littlefield, 1990.

Graham, Frank, Jr. *Since Silent Spring.* Boston: Houghton-Mifflin, 1970.

Grey, Zane. *Thunder Mountain.* New York: P.F. Collier, 1935.

Harbury, Martin. *The Last of the Wild Horses.* Garden City, N.Y.: Doubleday, 1984.

Hawley, James H. *History of Idaho: The Gem of the Mountains,* 3 vols. Chicago: S.J. Clarke, 1920.

Hays, Samuel P. *Beauty, Health, and Permanence: Environmental Politics in the United States, 1955–1985.* New York: Cambridge University Press, 1987.

Hendee, John C., George H. Stankey, and Robert C. Lucas. *Wilderness Management,* 2nd ed. Rev. Golden, Colo.: North American Press, 1990.

Hirt, Paul W. *A Conspiracy of Optimism: Management of the National Forests since World War II.* Lincoln: University of Nebraska Press, 1994.

Kingsbury, H.J. *Bucking the Tide.* Seattle: privately printed, 1949.

Langston, Nancy. *Forest Dreams, Forest Nightmares: The Paradox of Old Growth in the Inland West.* Seattle: University of Washington Press, 1995.

Leopold, Aldo. *A Sand County Almanac, and Sketches Here and There.* New York: Oxford University Press, 1949.

Loftus, Bill. *Idaho State Parks Guidebook.* Lewiston, Idaho: Tribune, 1989.

Louter, David. *Craters of the Moon National Monument: Historic Context Statements.* Seattle: National Park Service, 1995.

McKenna, Marian C. *Borah.* Ann Arbor: University of Michigan Press, 1961.

McPhee, John A. *Encounters with the Archdruid.* New York: Farrar, Straus and Giroux, 1971.

Malone, Michael P. *C. Ben Ross and the New Deal in Idaho.* Seattle: University of Washington Press, 1970.

Morgan, Clay, and Steve Mitchell (eds.). *Idaho Unbound: A Scrapbook and Guide.* Ketchum, Idaho: West Bound, 1995.

Nash, Roderick. *Wilderness and the American Mind.* New Haven, Conn.: Yale University Press, 1982 [1967].

Palmer, Tim. *The Wild and Scenic Rivers of America.* Washington, D.C.: Island Press, 1993.

Parsell, Neal. *Major Fenn's Country.* Kooskia, Idaho: Upper Clearwater-Lochsa-Selway Chamber of Commerce, n.d.

Perry, Bill. *Our Threatened Wildlife: An Ecological Study.* New York: Coward-McCann, 1969.

Petersen, Keith. *River of Life, Channel of Death: Fish and Dams on the Lower Snake.* Lewiston, Idaho: Confluence Press, 1995.

Peterson, F. Ross. *Idaho: A Bicentennial History.* New York: W.W. Norton, 1976.

Richardson, Elmo. *Dams, Parks and Politics: Resource Development and Preservation in the Truman-Eisenhower Era.* Lexington: University of Kentucky Press, 1973.

Roberts, Paul H. *Hoof Prints on Forest Ranges: The Early Years of National Forest Range Administration.* San Antonio: Naylor, 1963.

Roth, Dennis M. *The Wilderness Movement and the National Forests: 1964–1980.* Washington, D.C.: U.S. Forest Service, 1984.

Runte, Alfred. *Public Lands, Public Heritage: The National Forest Idea.* Niwot, Colo.: Roberts Rinehart, 1991.

Ryden, Hope. *Mustangs: A Return to the Wild.* New York: Viking, 1972.

Samuelson, Don W. *His Hand on My Shoulder: A Life Story of Hunting, Fishing, Love and Politics.* Sandpoint, Idaho: ParBest and Dickens, 1993.

Schwantes, Carlos A. *In Mountain Shadows: A History of Idaho*. Lincoln: University of Nebraska Press, 1991.

_____. *So Incredibly Idaho! Seven Landscapes that Define the Gem State*. Moscow: University of Idaho Press, 1996.

Shabecoff, Philip. *A Fierce Green Fire: The American Environmental Movement*. New York: Hill and Wang, 1993.

Smith, Elizabeth M. *History of the Boise National Forest, 1905–1976*. Boise: Idaho State Historical Society, 1983.

Smylie, Robert E. *Governor Smylie Remembers*. Moscow: University of Idaho Press, 1998.

Stacy, Susan M. (ed.) *Conversations: A Companion Book to Idaho Public Television's "Proceeding On Through a Beautiful Country," A History of Idaho*. Boise: Idaho Educational Public Broadcasting Foundation, 1990.

Steen, Harold K. *The U.S. Forest Service: A History*. Seattle: University of Washington Press, 1976.

Swain, Donald C. *Federal Conservation Policy, 1921–1933*. Berkeley and Los Angeles: University of California Press, 1963.

Trefethen, James B. *An American Crusade for Wildlife*. Alexandria, Va.: Boone and Crockett Club, 1975.

U.S. Forest Service. *A National Plan for American Forestry*. Washington, D.C.: Government Printing Office, 1933.

University of California, Wildland Research Center. *Wilderness and Recreation—A Report on Resources, Values, and Problems*. Washington, D.C.: ORRRC Study Report 3, 1962.

Wells, Merle W. *Gold Camps and Silver Cities: Nineteenth Century Mining in Central and Southern Idaho*, 2nd ed. Moscow, Idaho: Bureau of Mines and Geology, 1983.

Woodward, Tim. *Tiger on the Road: The Life of Vardis Fisher*. Caldwell, Idaho: Caxton, 1989.

Worster, Donald. *The Wealth of Nature: Environmental History and the Ecological Imagination*. New York: Oxford University Press, 1993.

Wyman, Walker D. *The Wild Horse of the West*. Lincoln: University of Nebraska Press, 1945.

Index